D-DAY

THE FIRST 24 HOURS

D-DAY

THE FIRST 24 HOURS

WILL FOWLER

This edition published in 2004 by Silverdale Books
an imprint of Bookmart Ltd
Registered Number 2372865
Trading as Bookmart Ltd
Blaby Road
Wigston
Leicester LE18 4SE

British Library Cataloguing in Publication Data:
A catalogue record for this book is available
from the British Library

Copyright © 2003 Amber Books Ltd

ISBN: 1-84509-060-8

Editorial and design by
Amber Books Ltd
Bradley's Close
74–77 White Lion Street
London N1 9PF
www.amberbooks.co.uk

Project Editor: Charles Catton
Designer: Jerry Williams
Picture Research: Lisa Wren/Natasha Jones

Picture credits
Amber Books: 71, 86, 99(b), 106, 131, 158(b); TRH Pictures: 2, 6–7 (US National Archives), 8, 9, 11, 13 (both), 14, 16, 18, 23, 24 (US National Archives), 25, 28 (RAF Museum), 30–31 (IWM), 32, 34 (IWM), 35, 37, 38, 39, 41, 42, 44–45 (US National Archives), 46–47, 48, 49 (IWM), 50 (US National Archives), 51, 53, 55, 57 (US National Archives), 59 (DOD), 60, 65, 66, 68 (US National Archives), 70(IWM), 76–77 (IWM), 79, 80, 81, 82, 84 (US National Archives), 85, 87(US National Archives), 88 (US National Archives), 92–93, 94–95 (IWM), 97, 99(t), 100, 102, 104 (IWM), 107 (US Army), 120, 121, 123, 124, 128–129 (DOD), 132 (IWM), 133, 135 (IWM), 140 (USCoast Guard), 142 (IWM), 145, 158(t), 161 (IWM), 164 (IWM), 168 (IWM), 169, 174 (IWM), 175 (IWM), 177, 178–179 (US National Archives), 181 (US Army), 185, 186 (IWM); US National Archives: 10, 26, 27, 54, 62, 75, 78, 91; John Csaszar: 111, 114–115, 127, 138, 187; Photos12.com: (Coll-DITE-USIS), 72–73, 116, 117, 144, 183; (KEYSTONE Pressedienst) 156-7; POPPERFOTO: 64, 119, 122, 136, 163, 165, 176, 180; Süddeutscher Verlag: 112, 141; Topham Picturepoint: 96, 103, 166–167, 172

Map credits
Peter Harper: 20–21, 22, 43, 58, 63, 98, 110, 118, 126, 130, 134, 162, 171, 182
Patrick Mulrey: 67, 159

Printed in Italy by Eurolitho S.p.A., Cesano Boscone (MI)

CONTENTS

1. The Road to Operation Overlord   6

2. Intelligence and Resistance   30

3. Logistics and Technology   46

4. Special Operations   76

5. H-Hour   94

6. Utah Beach   114

7. Omaha Beach   128

8. Gold Beach   146

9. Juno Beach   156

10. Sword Beach   166

11. The Price   78

D-Day Order of Battle   188

Index   190

CHAPTER ONE

THE ROAD TO OPERATION OVERLORD

The Americans pressed for an invasion of Northern Europe as early as 1942, but it would take two more years for the plans and training to reach fruition. US, British, Canadian troops and men and women from the occupied countries of Europe were now massed on a crowded island, as the Allied air forces pounded communications and defences in preparation for the invasion. Now these soldiers awaited the order to go.

BY THE SPRING OF 1944, the Western Allies and the Soviet Union knew that the war in Europe was moving, at times slowly, towards the defeat of Nazi Germany and her partners. However, they had not always enjoyed this confidence.

In September 1939, under its leader Adolf Hitler, Nazi Germany attacked Poland, and France and Britain declared war. Poland fell in a month. To secure her northern flank, Germany then invaded Denmark in April 1940 and had a tough and costly fight for Norway. In June that year, the defeat of France followed after a six-week 'blitzkrieg' ('lightning war') campaign. France was divided into a Nazi-occupied north and west and a southern 'neutral' pro-Nazi Vichy zone. In April 1941, Germany and her allies overran Yugoslavia in 11 days. Greece fell after a tough fight, and by the end of May, German

Left: Men and equipment are off-loaded from a US landing craft on a beach in Devon during a training exercise. The beaches of Devon were chosen for their similarity to the beaches of Normandy, with their long, sloping sands running gently into the sea.

Above: German gunners back fill sand and soil against the concrete gun pit of a 15cm (5.9in) K 18 gun in a coastal artillery position. On the right they are putting turf in place to landscape the pit, which is camouflaged from the air by a netting frame suspended over the gun.

paratroopers had seized the island of Crete. The Soviet Union was still bound by a 1939 non-aggression treaty it had signed with Nazi Germany, while the United States, though sympathetic to Britain, was reluctant to become embroiled in a European conflict. In the spring of 1941, Britain stood alone.

So at the beginning of Operation Barbarossa, the name of the German attack on the USSR in June 1941, and the Japanese air assault on the US fleet at Pearl Harbor in December 1941, the Axis partners of Germany, Japan and Italy enjoyed considerable military successes. In December 1941 however, the German forces were halted outside Moscow, but the following spring, four armies thrust deep into the Caucasus and reached the Volga at Stalingrad. By the winter of 1942, the German Sixth Army was embroiled in fighting at Stalingrad, while hundreds of miles to the south, at El Alamein, in the deserts of Egypt, Rommel's *Afrika Korps* had been fought to a stop by the British Eighth Army. Late 1942 was the high water mark of Nazi Germany's territorial expansion.

The British counter attack at El Alamein in October 1942 and the Soviet victory at Stalingrad in early 1943 marked the 'end of

the beginning'. Germany and her allies were now being pushed onto the defensive. North Africa was cleared of Axis forces by May 1943. British and US forces invaded Sicily in July 1943 and at about the same time, German tank forces were defeated in a massive armoured battle at Kursk in the Soviet Union.

In late 1943, the British and United Forces launched a three-pronged assault on mainland Italy and Hitler's fascist ally, Benito Mussolini, was forced out of power as Italy surrendered and re-entered the war on the side of the Allies. Fighting northwards through Italy, a country which Churchill had called 'the soft underbelly of Europe', was incredibly tough, as the Germans used natural and manmade obstacles to delay the Allied advance.

By 1944, the Allies were bogged down in front of Monte Cassino and only just holding the beachhead at Anzio. On

FORTRESS EUROPE

Immediately after the fall of France in 1940, the German forces occupied French naval installations and with them, the local defences. Later, after Britain had failed to sue for peace, field defences had been dug along the French coast and barbed wire entanglements and minefields had been positioned blocking beaches that might be used by amphibious raiders. They were not the concrete bunkers that were constructed in 1942–44, but many were zigzag slit trenches that would be dug by soldiers with their own resources and defence stores after capturing enemy territory.

In 1941, the *Organisation Todt* (OT) (see box below) had concentrated on building reinforced concrete U-boat pens, Luftwaffe airfields and bases and coastal gun positions in the Pas de Calais. The four batteries in the Pas de Calais covered the narrows of the Channel and could subject Dover, Ramsgate and Folkestone on the British mainland to periodic shell fire. The biggest guns, the three 40.6cm (16in) weapons in the Lindemann battery at Sangatte, could shell all three towns. 'Hellfire Corner', as this area of England was known, remained under threat until the late summer of 1944. Some of the guns had originally been emplaced to give supporting fire for Fall Seelöwe (Operation Sea Lion), the proposed invasion of Britain in 1940.

Thirteen coastal artillery batteries were eventually constructed along the French coast, as well as one each in Belgium, the Netherlands and Norway, three in Germany and three in Denmark.

the Eastern Front, the Germans were fighting a slow withdrawal to the borders of Poland, delaying the Soviet advance with local counter-attacks. On March 28, in grim echoes of Stalingrad, the First Panzer Army, commanded by General Hans-Valentin Hube, was trapped in the Ukraine by the combined armies of Gens Zhukov and Konev. Two days later, helped by attacks by two *Waffen-SS* divisions, they broke out and reached safety by 7 April.

In Britain, the US and British land, sea and air forces waited for orders to open a 'Second Front', and the invasion of occupied northern Europe would begin. Like any military operation, the day was designated D-Day, and the hour of attack, H-Hour. Though many of the naval and air forces had already been in action in the Mediterranean and over Europe, for many of the soldiers D-Day would be the lethal validation of three or more years of training.

COMFORTABLE POSTING

For the German Army, garrison duty in France – and particularly Paris – was a comfortable posting and was used to allow units exhausted by combat on the Eastern Front time to recover. Relations were often reasonable between the Germans soldiers and ordinary Frenchmen and women. For 21-year-old Gefreite Klaus Herrig, a wireless operator with the *Kriegsmarine* Signal Corps based in Le Havre, 'Our relationship with the French was more correct than friendly. We used to go to the local café for a beer, but there were no strong personal connections. Our discipline was good and the German troops, in general, behaved themselves.'

Monsieur Cassigneuel, a farmer near St Aubin, concurred. 'Our Germans were fine. We had no problems at all. We had horses on the farm and they had horses too. Many of the Germans were farmers and we were all the same age, we did the same kind of work, and we talked a lot about the way things were done. They told us about German methods and we told them about the way we did things in France. We swapped information. It was quite good really!'

Below: German officers inspect a concrete bunker built on the seafront of a northern French town. The embrasure for the machine gun or light artillery piece inside is angled to give covering fire across the beaches. Barbed wire blocks the seawall.

However, not everyone was happy, and Resistance groups were formed, sponsored and assisted by Britain and the United States, to collect intelligence on, for example, the design and layout of the coastal defences and to sabotage the Nazi war effort in occupied Europe.

BUILDING PLANS

Between June and September 1942, no major construction work was undertaken on defences, but in 1942 the situation began to change. On 23 March, Hitler issued 'Führer Directive 40' that anticipated both limited and large scale enemy incursions along the western coast of Europe. The British raid at St Nazaire in 1942 and the disastrous attack at Dieppe later that year gave added impetus to construction work on defences that were named by Hitler *Atlantikwall* (the Atlantic Wall). In the planned construction programme, 15,000 bunkers and emplacements of Types 'A' and 'B' – like the massive structures built on the *Westwall* on Germany's western border – were to be built. These coastal defences, featured in propaganda films and photographs, eventually stretched 2685km (1668 miles) from the Spanish border to the North Cape in Norway. They combined coastal artillery to engage shipping, infantry and artillery

This vast operation is undoubtedly the most complicated and difficult that has ever taken place. It involves tides, wind, waves, visibility, both from the air and the sea standpoint, and the combined employment of land, air and sea forces in the highest degree of intimacy and in contact with conditions which could not and cannot be fully foreseen.

Prime Minister Winston Churchill,
Statement to the House of Commons, 6 June 1944

positions, protected by minefields, flame-throwers and barbed wire that could destroy any troops and vehicles that managed to make a landing. Some 17.6 million cubic tonnes (17.3 million cubic tons) of concrete and steel reinforcing bars went into these defences and vast armies of slave labourers lived and worked in appalling conditions to construct them. The Germans were very skilled at boring tunnels, and hospitals, command posts, magazines and shelters were dug deep into rock. At the peak of the construction programme, 260,000 men were employed, of whom only ten percent were German.

Left: An armoured machine gun and observation post on the Atlantic Wall. Some of the defences had been taken from the French Maginot Line and the obstacles built by the Belgians and Dutch in the late 1930s. Many were very effective.

Above: A Soviet Krokodil *cartoon shows Hitler caught in the pincers of three years of the war in the East. If the Germans could defeat an Allied landing in Europe they were confident that they could hold the Red Army's advance and perhaps negotiate a peace.*

Bunkers were all gas proof, with double doors and a manually operated filtration system. As well as an entrance, normally an armoured door protected by a machine gun port, there was also an escape shaft if the door was damaged. Behind the front-line positions, the Germans built the Type 621 and Type 622 troop shelters in which men could take cover during heavy bombardments and emerge to deliver counter-attacks or man the weapons in bunkers.

A small, distinctive design that German engineers borrowed from the Italians was the *Tobruk*. This was a two- or three-man concrete bunker with a short flight of steps to an ammunition store and shelter with a circular access. It came in three forms. The simplest, the *Ringstand*, was open-topped with a circular rail for mounting a machine gun. The 5cm (1.97in) mortar position had a concrete pillar on which the mortar was mounted with the ammunition store offset down steps. The *Panzerstellung* mounted a tank turret, normally from a French light tank like the Renault FT-17 or R35, that had been captured in 1940.

The Atlantic Wall also included barbed wire, mines, ditches, concrete 'Dragon's Teeth' concrete cubes, steel tetrahedrons, vertical steel girders and 'Czech Hedgehog' anti-tank obstacles. In the light of experience at Dieppe, where Churchill tanks had been unable to cross the low sea wall to exit the beach, the OT engineers designed *Panzermauer* – huge reinforced concrete walls 3m (9.8ft) high and 2m (6.5ft) thick that had anti-tank gun emplacements built into them. In some cases, existing defences from wars in the 19th century were effectively incorporated with observation posts added to the top of castles or field gun bunkers built into the walls.

Many of the coastal defence guns were French, Czech or Soviet weapons. The formidable Belgian 'Element C' or 'Belgian gate' steel girder anti-tank obstacles were positioned as anti-invasion obstacles on open beaches. These obstacles, which could be rolled into position and bolted together, were known as *Rollböcke*.

CAMOUFLAGE AND CONCEALMENT

The concrete on bunkers and gun positions was given a textured surface by ensuring the shuttering was not smooth and reinforcing rods were left exposed to allow camouflage netting to be hung. Further landscaping was provided by soil banked up around the positions. Stone cladding helped positions to be blended into cliffs or among buildings. Some bunkers that had been constructed on the sea front of a coastal town were painted with false windows and doors to resemble a bungalow or villa.

So massive were the bunkers and battery positions of the Atlantic Wall that today many of them remain intact on the cliffs and foreshores of northern Europe.

OSTARBEITER

Eastern Workers, Polish or Russian slave workers in the occupied territories in World War II, were identified by an armband with the letter 'O' on it. *Ostarbeiter* were employed in dangerous or exhausting work, including the construction of defences like the Atlantic Wall. They had poor rations and those who attempted to escape were often hanged publicly as a deterrent to others.

The construction of the Atlantic Wall was not undertaken exclusively by German soldiers, Organisation Todt staff and slave labourers. The local population throughout Europe found work that ranged from simple manual labour to complex construction projects undertaken for the Germans by contractors.

After the Liberation of France, a brutal purge took place of men and women who had collaborated, or had been thought to have collaborated, with the Germans. In June 1946, Jean Paulham the French writer and intellectual wrote:

'The purge has been hard on writers. The engineers, entrepreneurs and builders who constructed the Atlantic Wall live peacefully among us. They are building new walls. They are building the walls of the new prisons where we lock up the journalists who made the mistake of writing that the Atlantic Wall had been well built.'

ORGANIZATION TODT (OT)

OT was the German state construction organization established in 1938 and named after its director, Fritz Todt. OT built military facilities in Germany and occupied Europe. Much of the work was of a very high standard, and motorways, air raid shelters and fortifications remain as mute tributes to German engineers and their enslaved labour force. Major OT projects included the *Reichsautobahn* motorways, the *Westwall* fortifications on Germany's border with France and later the *Atlantikwall*, the coastal fortifications that stretched from the North Cape of Norway to the Bay of Biscay. To carry out this work, OT employed prisoners of war, concentration camp inmates and foreign civilian workers who had been kidnapped by German forces. It was brutal and dangerous work as military positions were constructed in coastal cliffs or deep underground. Construction work was also undertaken by local labour hired by the Germans and paid well for their work. Ironically, in the Channel Islands, some of the Nazi defences were built by British men who appreciated this good pay.

As the war dragged on, OT was pressed into bomb damage repair work and later the construction of underground factories. Todt, and later Albert Speer, had huge powers that allowed them to bypass bureaucracy and so OT became one of the most efficient organisations within the Third Reich. Critics of the organisation recalled meetings nicknamed the 'Concrete Exchange' in which the Navy, Army and Air Force would bid for the services of OT. OT was attracted to the major projects, much loved in Nazi Germany, in which huge quantities of concrete could be used in as short a time as possible and a craze for record figures developed.

Along the coast, the positions were either *Widerstandsnesten* (WN) (Resistance Positions) or *Stützpunkte (*Support Points). In an after-action analysis, the Canadian Army described a *Widerstandnester.* It was built around one or two casemates with anti-tank guns covering the shore. Mortars provided indirect fire and *Tobruks* armed with machine guns, tank turrets or light anti-tank guns gave direct fire. Anti-tank ditches and minefields with barbed wire surrounded the position.

The commanding officer of the sector held by the 716th Division likened the 40 to 50 *Widerstandsnesten* to a string of pearls strung along the coast. Critically, though

Below: The crew position the camouflage net over a captured French 105 mle 1913 Schneider gun that has been sited to cover a possible landing site on the French coast. The gun could fire a 15.74kg (34.7lb) shell out to 12,000m (13,130 yards).

Above: A 7.5cm (2.95in) Feldkanone 38 in an open pit. Faced by the threat of Allied bombers, the Germans began to emplace their artillery in massive concrete casemates. Though this restricted their firing arcs, it offered far greater protection for the piece itself.

ERWIN ROMMEL

In 1940, the 49-year-old commander of the 7th Panzer Division, Erwin Rommel, was a career soldier who had served with distinction in World War I, winning the highest decoration for gallantry, the *Pour le Mérite*, in 1917. On the basis of his experience in World War I, he published *Infanterie greift an* (Infantry Attacks) and this book drew him to Hitler's attention. In Poland in 1939, Rommel commanded Hitler's personal bodyguard battalion. In France in 1940, he commanded the 7th Panzer Division which won the nickname *Gespensterdivision* (Ghost Division) because of its rapid advance. Rommel went on to command the *Deutsches Afrika Korps* (DAK) in North Africa from 6 February 1941 to 9 March 1943 during which time he outfought the British and Imperial forces on numerous occasions. After a brief period in Italy, he took command of an Army Group in northern France from January 1944. He worked tirelessly to prepare the defences of the Atlantic Wall and urged commanders to improve defences with field works and obstacles. On 5 June, because the weather was so bad, he left France for Ulm in southern Germany to celebrate his wife's birthday, confident that a landing would not take place. When he was alerted to the landings he immediately returned and was back at his headquarters at La Roche Guyon at 16:00 hours on 6 June.

In the evening, his 36-year-old Adjutant, Captain Helmut Lang, remembered the Field Marshal's anger that the Panzer Lehr and 12th Waffen-SS Panzer Division were not under his command. If they had been, they would have been closer to the coast and in position to deliver an immediate counter-attack. Conscious of the chaos in the German chain of command, Rommel said, 'If I was commander of the Allied forces right now I could finish the war off in fourteen days... If Montgomery only knew the mess we are in, he'd have no worries tonight.'

With Field Marshal von Rundstedt, he urged Hitler on two occasions to make peace after the Allies had gained a firm foothold ashore. Rommel was badly wounded by Allied fighter ground-attack aircraft on 17 July and was convalescing in Germany at the time of the July Plot. Though not a conspirator, Rommel was disenchanted with Hitler and the plotters had considered him as a potential Chief of State. Under torture, a conspirator blurted out his name and Hitler sent Generals Burgdorf and Meisel to Rommel's home with poison. They offered him the choice of suicide or a public trial which would involve his wife and son. He chose suicide. He died on 14 October 1944 and was buried with full military honours.

Field Marshal von Rundstedt, the commander-in-chief in the West, had proposed that a second line of defences or *Zweite Stellung* should be constructed further inland, very little work had been done, so the Atlantic Wall lacked both depth and strength.

In the Seventh Army sector in Normandy, the priorities for defences were (on orders from the *Oberkommando der Wehrmacht* (OKW), German High Command) the Channel Islands, Cherbourg, the east coast of the Cotentin Peninsula and Orne estuary and north of Caen, the coast between the Orne and the Vire and finally the west coast of the Cotentin peninsula south of Cap de la Hague.

From 12 December 1943, when Field Marshal Erwin Rommel took command of Army Group B, a new urgency was injected into defensive work along the coast and, by

Left: A formal portrait of Field Marshal Erwin Rommel, who enjoyed considerable celebrity in Germany for the success of the Afrika Korps *in the Western Desert. Hitler now entrusted Rommel with the defence of the northern French coast.*

D-Day, work in the first three areas was almost complete. Rommel had discovered that the Atlantic Wall was a wall in name only and propaganda films and photographs suggested that it was much stronger than it really was. The Anglo-Canadian raid in Dieppe in August 1942 had been played up by German propaganda to suggest that the Atlantic Wall was a credible defence and magazines like *Signal* had diagrams of defences that were at best imaginative.

Though ports were well defended with concrete bunkers, some built on breakwaters covering the approaches from the sea, and the Pas de Calais was also well covered, other stretches of the coast were still vulnerable. In the Normandy area in January 1944 the LXXXIV Corps received three engineer battalions, two for fortress construction and one for mine laying. In addition, 2850 men from the former French Labour Service were employed on building secondary defences behind the front-line coastal positions. Finally, men of the *Ost* battalions – formed from former Russian prisoners of war – were brought in to help in construction work.

Right: Field Marshal Gerd von Rundstedt (left), with Paul Hausser of the Waffen-SS, *at a parade in Paris following the defeat of France in 1940. In 1944 von Rundstedt commanded Army Group West that included troops in France.*

figured to cover beaches and were screened from the sea by massive concrete walls. On long exposed beaches, notably what would become Omaha beach, infantry and artillery positions were dug on bluffs and headlands or built into dunes to deliver interlocking fire along the length of the flat sand.

The arrangement that split responsibility for defence between the Army and the Navy might seem rather complex. The logic was that the men of the *Kriegsmarine* could accurately identify Allied and German warships, whereas Army gunners might in error, inflict casualties through 'friendly fire'. Naval fire control centres were effectively 'battleships on land' consisting of a tower with several floors containing range finders and communications equipment linked by radio and land line to the batteries. Where the terrain permitted, the floors were built into the sides of cliffs.

By June 1944, there were 700 distinct designs of bunker, command post or shelter in the Atlantic Wall. A typical battery layout consisted of the fire control post (*Leitstand*) in either the Navy design M120, M162 or M262 or the Army 636 or 636a.

The covered gun emplacements (*Schartenstand*) were either the Army 656, 652, 671 or 679 or the Navy M170, M176, M270 or M2762 designs.

Army standard crew accommodation was either type 501, 502, 621 or 622, while the Navy had one, the M151.

Ammunition was stored by the Army in types 134, 607 or 641 while the Navy used the M145 or FL246. Within the the battery perimeter were offices, latrines, the cook house, water tanks and a First Aid post, all built from timber, bricks or concrete panels. For close-in defence, the Army used the type 611, 612, 667, 677 or 680 bunkers with interlocking fields of fire.

On the outer fringes were slit trenches and *Tobruks* and beyond that, minefields and belts of barbed wire. The wire

KARL RUDOLF GERD VON RUNDSTEDT

One of the most experienced and high-ranking officers in the German Army, Gerd von Rundstedt was born in Aschersleben on 12 December 1875. He served as a General Staff officer in World War I, fighting in France and Turkey. He rose rapidly in the *Reichswehr*, but was retired as a Colonel General after criticising the action against Czechoslovakia in 1938. He was reinstated in time for the Polish campaign of 1939 where he commanded Army Group South and France and the Low Countries in 1940 where he commanded Army Group A. He was promoted to Field Marshal after the fall of France on 19 July 1940. In the USSR in 1941, he commanded Army Group South as it pushed into the Ukraine. Hitler sacked him on 12 December 1941 for a tactical withdrawal near Rostov, but on 1 March 1942, he was appointed as Commander in Chief of Army Group West in France. Here he was responsible for the preparation against the expected Anglo-American invasion. Hitler sacked him on 2 July 1944 following the failure to stop the D-Day landings. Finally, von Rundstedt was brought out of retirement to command the Ardennes Offensive of December 1944. He knew about the July Bomb Plot but did not participate and after its failure he presided over the Court of Honour that dismissed the conspirators from the Army. After the war, von Rundstedt served a sentence for transmitting the Commando Order of 18 October 1942, which called for the immediate execution of any commandos captured by German troops. He was released on 5 May 1949 because of serious illness and died at Hanover on 24 February 1953.

Above: Allied air attacks on coastal positions were carefully orchestrated so that they would not give any indication of where the D-Day landings would fall. For every one attack on Normandy there were two on coastal positions elsewhere. This picture may show the port of Cherbourg.

and minefields were sited to funnel attackers towards machine guns and direct fire weapons or placed in defiles along which men or vehicles would be forced to advance.

Among the weapons covering these 'killing grounds' was the fearsome *Abwehrflammenwerfer* (Defence Flame-thrower), a static flamethrower containing 30l (7.7gal) of fuel. It was dug in so that only the nozzle projected and was fired electrically by remote control. This produced a flame that lasted for only one second but was 4.5m (5yd) wide and 2.7m (3yd) high with a range of 27.4m (30yd).

Rommel had ordered that 'millions of mines' should be delivered to the coast. Allied air attacks on road and rail links prevented their delivery. However, this meant that these mines were available to the Germans during the grim fighting on the borders of the Reich in late 1944 and early 1945.

By October 1943, about two million mines had been laid and by May 1944 this had risen to six million. However, a report by a Seventh Army staff officer Colonel Oehmichen revealed that 750,000 anti-tank 'T-Mines' had been laid in the Seventh Army sector by May 1944. Of these, 6000 had been laid forward of the beaches on obstacles, a figure of 440 mines per kilometre (0.6 miles) of front. In fact, after-action analysis by the Allies revealed that only 30 mines had been laid per kilometre of beach obstacles breached on D-Day.

The same study revealed that in the Fifteenth Army sector, which included the Pas de Calais, the Germans had emplaced 22 anti-tank weapons for every one to ten kilometres (0.6 to 6 miles) of front, of which three were heavy weapons. To the west, the Seventh Army had only slightly more than 12 guns covering the same distance of which only one was heavy.

The arithmetic became even more unbalanced when force strengths were compared. The Fifteenth Army had 18 Infantry and two Panzer Divisions to cover a 550km (340 mile) coastal sector. The Seventh Army had only 14 Infantry and one Panzer Division to cover 1600km (990 miles).

Above: A captured German coastal position shows how guns in case-mates were sited to protect them from fire from the sea, which in this picture is to the right. The concrete apron covers the seaward side of the embrasure from direct fire.

In North Africa, Rommel had experienced the weight of Allied firepower both on land and from the air and he knew that the landings would have to be stopped in their tracks on the beaches. As had been demonstrated at Dieppe in August 1942, this would be the killing ground. He even sketched out his ideas showing obstacle belts on the shore with landing craft foundering on them or being sunk by coastal artillery.

'The enemy,' he explained, 'is at his weakest just after landing. The troops are unsure, and possibly even seasick. They are unfamiliar with the terrain. Heavy weapons are not yet available in sufficient quantity. This is the moment to strike at them and defeat them.'

BATTLE OF MANOEUVRE

Rommel's superior, Field Marshal von Rundstedt, envisaged a battle of manoeuvre in France in which superior German tanks and tactics would destroy the Allied armies after they had landed. Von Rundstedt had only served on the Eastern Front or in the early years of the war in the West and had no idea of the sheer weight of vehicles and ordnance that the Allies and particularly the Americans could bring to bear on a front. He had no conception of the awesome and accurate firepower of battleships or weight of high explosives that Allied bombers like

the Boeing B-17 or Avro Lancaster could deliver when used in tactical support.

After D-Day, some of the more heavily protected ports and the Channel Islands were left to 'starve' by the Allies. With limited offensive capability, but massive defences they did not constitute a threat to the Allies as they pushed eastwards towards Germany. In 1945, the French ports of Lorient, St Nazaire, La Palisse and La Rochelle were still in German hands, as were the Channel Islands.

The islands were the most heavily fortified part of the Atlantic Wall as Hitler was obsessed with this small bit of British territory that was in German hands. The defence plans called for 414 reinforced concrete structures for Guernsey, 234 for Jersey and 153 for Alderney. Tunnels and underground chambers provided 50,000 sq m (164,000 sq ft) of cover, while 20,000m (65,620ft) of anti-tank walls and field railways protected and served the islands. It was a tough objective, but at the height of operations in May 1943, 25,500 cubic metres (83,660 cu ft) of rock had been excavated and in September that year, 40,881

DOUGLAS SKYTRAIN/DAKOTA

Originally a commercial airliner known as the Douglas DC-3 and manufactured in Santa Monica, California, this aircraft was designated C-47 by the USAAF and called the Skytrain, while the RAF, who operated over 1200 of these planes, called it the Dakota. It was the aircraft from which all the major US and British airborne assaults were launched in World War II.

Fitted with folding bench seats as a troop transport it carried 28 fully armed soldiers, while with a reinforced floor and wider doors it was used to carry 2700kg (6000lb) cargoes, a representative load being two Jeeps, a 6pdr anti-tank gun, or 14 freight baskets. The Dakota had a wingspan of 29m (95ft), was 19.3m (64ft 5in) long and was powered by two 895kW (1200hp) Pratt and Whitney 'Twin Wasp' R-1830 engines. It had a top speed of 370km/h (230mph) and range of 2440km (1500 miles). Total production reached 10,123 and it was still in service during the Vietnam war more than 20 years later.

cubic metres (134,100 cu ft) of reinforced concrete had been produced. By the end of the war, the Channel islands had consumed over 613,000 cubic metres (2,011,000 cu ft) of concrete.

The islands had a total of 16 coast defence batteries as well as heavy and light flak positions. The most powerful guns were at the Mirus battery on Guernsey that consisted of four captured Russian 30.5cm (12in) guns located at Le Frie Baton on the west of the island. With radar locating, the guns could engage targets at ranges up to 32km (20 miles).

FIRST CONTACT

It was a *Luftwaffe* radar company in Guernsey operating *Freya* and *Wurzburg* systems that at 22:40 hours on 5 June picked up the first images of approaching aircraft, some of which appeared to be towing gliders. The information was passed up the line to Regimental Commander Colonel Oelze. When he was put through to the LXXXIV Corps in St Lô

demanding that an air alert should be called, an urbane General Staff officer rang back with the message:

'The Gentleman of the Staff wished their comrades on the island a good night; advising them to be on the look out for small ghosts only, and urging caution before sowing any more wild oats.'

By the end of June 1944, with US troops now in control of the Cotentin Peninsula and Cherbourg, the 15cm (5.9in) guns of *Batterie Blücher* on Alderney opened fire on US troops on the north-west corner of the peninsula. Since the flak protection was very dense over the island the Allies decided against bombing the battery, but deployed the battleship HMS *Rodney* which on 12 August fired 72 406mm (16in) shells at the battery. Though the German guns were

Below: US Army Truck half-ton 4x4 Amphibians, widely known as 'Amphijeeps', in a vehicle park in Britain. Huge numbers of men, weapons and equipment were crowded into parks and camps throughout southern England from 1943 onwards.

Above: A machine gun crew on the left of the picture fires live ammunition over the heads of US soldiers who advance up a beach in a 'battle inoculation' exercise, allowing them to adjust to live rounds being fired.

Left: In an idyllic scene in rural England, US soldiers prepare for an exercise. To GIs acquainted with Britain only by Hollywood's images, scenes like this seemed almost too true to believe.

We were quartered in the cricket pavilion on the sports field belonging to the Players tobacco factory in Nottingham. We used to play them at baseball on Saturdays and cricket on Sundays; we weren't very good at cricket and they weren't very good at baseball so it sort of evened itself out. It was a lot of fun.

Lieutenant Colonel Nathaniel Hoskot
507th Parachute Infantry, 101st Airborne Division

Small booklets were published and distributed to each American soldier, telling him how to 'get along' with the British… 'Pubs are a tremendous factor in Anglo-American relations. In my experience and among my own close friends, I know of countless cases of Englishmen establishing extremely cordial relations with our boys… The so-called British reserve breaks down completely inside a pub. A lot of friendships and a lot of real understanding is developed over a glass of beer. Of course by the same token, pubs are wonderful places for a fight… That is to be expected. Because after a man gets a few drinks under his belt, he forgets all the little lessons in Anglo-American relations he has learned in the booklet.'

Major Thor M Smith
SHAEF Staff

in open pits, the damage was minimal and only one gun had to be transported to Guernsey for repair.

The first GIs to come to Britain – the initials 'GI' stood for Government Issue, which appeared on vast amounts of US equipment – landed in Northern Ireland within a few months of the US entry into the war. Their presence was at this stage largely symbolic but they were the start of a friendly invasion of thousands of men and women whose presence would, for three years, be felt in every corner of the UK.

For the British who had already suffered nearly three years of war, the Americans were both a tonic and an irritant. They were generous, charming and gregarious, but their higher rates of pay and the superior cut and quality of their uniforms made them instantly attractive to even the coolest of British girls. The irritated British boyfriends and husbands, remarked that the Americans were 'overpaid, over sexed and over here'. The GIs retorted, 'You're underpaid, under sexed and under Ike', Ike being the affectionate nickname for the American General Dwight D Eisenhower now Supreme Commander of the Allied forces.

Even the Canadians had difficulties with the GIs. The Canadians were quick to point out that they had been in the war since 1939. One commented: 'It used to brass us off to see some Yank come into a pub flashing five-pound notes, and try to buy the one bottle of whiskey in the place plus a place in the dart game plus the barmaid plus everything. I'd say most of the fights occurred because the Yanks had too much money and didn't understand the climate of England in those days, and they often got their faces pounded in for it'.

The cultural clash was further complicated by the fact that the US Army was segregated. Black soldiers in the US Army were used largely for semi-skilled work and were regarded with some contempt by white GIs in combat units. When British girls socialized with black Americans there were fights between black and white GIs, which were

Left: Bombs fall from USAAF B-17 Flying Fortress bombers in a box formation over Germany. Despite their heavy defensive armament, they were vulnerable to the aggressive tactics of Luftwaffe fighter pilots who pressed home their attacks.

often broken up violently by the US Military Police. Timuel Black, a black GI in the Quartermaster Corps, commented: 'The ordinary British were absolutely amazed, looking at these two armies. I guess they hadn't thought about their two armies, too: the colonial and the regular. But they were chagrined by this racial situation, which they'd never seen.'

However, the majority of US servicemen integrated well with British society and some even married local girls, who returned to the United States after the war as 'GI brides'.

By 1944, there were half a million US servicemen in Britain and they were arriving at a rate of 150,000 a month in troop transports crossing the Atlantic. By the spring of 1944, their numbers, combined with those of the British and their allies had produced a total force of two million servicemen and women packed into camps, bases, airfields and ports. Among soldiers and civilians the joke circulated that Britain was only prevented from sinking under the weight of men, weapons and equipment by the tethered anti-aircraft barrage balloons that kept it afloat.

Until D-Day, US naval operations from Britain had consisted of anti-submarine patrols in support of the convoys crossing the Atlantic.

In January 1943, the United States Army Air Force (USAAF) 8th Air Force moved into Norfolk and Suffolk with its fighters and bombers and airfields were carved out of the flat agricultural land. At the time of D-Day, the 8th would be commanded by the experienced Lt Gen James Doolittle. It was later joined by the 9th' under Lt Gen Lewis Brereton, and 15th under Maj Gen Nathan Twining, in daylight raids against targets in Germany and occupied Europe. USAAF fighters were instrumental with the RAF in the defeat of the *Luftwaffe*, which meant that any invasion of Europe would be undertaken with complete air superiority.

FEAR OF FIGHTERS

As German casualties rose, their fighter pilots were accused by Hermann Göring of suffering from *Jägerschreck* (fear of fighters). By the end of May 1944, *Luftflotte III* had seen its force of 891 aircraft shrink to 497, of which 266 were fighters and 200 were bombers. The losses in experienced pilots and leaders was also critical, with eleven squadron commanders being killed in the spring of 1944.

In Normandy *SS-Sturmmann* Jochen Leykauff of the 12th *SS-Hitlerjugend* Division watched the skies and thought 'that the swarms of bombers daily droning their way overhead could unload their 'blessings' upon us, had us worried. Above all else, one kept an eye out for low level fighters. But then, certainly, our own fighters, would come – we thought'.

The British Army and the RAF were the beneficiaries of the prodigious US armaments industry that provided everything from the C-47 Dakota transport aircraft, to tanks like the ubiquitous M4 Sherman, down to the compact M1 carbine.

THE JEEP AT WAR

Below, on the roads of Britain, big American trucks were accompanied by the little 4x4 Jeep – which is hardly surprising since nearly 700,000 were built before the end of the war. The one-ton (1270kg) Jeep was manufactured by Ford and Willys though the prototype work had been done by Bantam, the car manufacturer. The early models went to the UK and USSR as part of the Lend-Lease aid. The origin of the name 'Jeep' may be from the initials 'GP' which stood for 'General Purpose'. It was powered by a Willys 441 or 442 'Go Devil' 2.2-litre 65hp (48kW) inlet-over-exhaust engine. Drive was through a three-speed gearbox with synchromesh on second and third gears, with a two-speed transfer box with six forward and two reverse gears. Brakes were hydraulic and top speed was about 100km/h (62mph) with a maximum range of 450km (280 miles), though this could be extended with extra fuel tanks.

Churchill said that the British were able to fight like a nation of 58 million instead of 48 million, thanks to US aid and equipment.

By the end of May 1944, almost everyone could sense that an invasion of Europe was coming. As US Army units moved south by truck and train to new camps and concentration areas, friendships which had developed in the intensity of war time Britain now had to be compressed into an exchange of scribbled letters, some of which would never receive answers.

However, without the men and equipment from the US, the British and Commonwealth forces, as well as units made up of men who had escaped from occupied Europe, would have been unable to land in sufficient strength in France to defeat the enemy. But with only days to go before D-Day, there was still a fear that even with huge amounts of men and equipment, the Allies might land, but be unable to break through the Atlantic Wall, or be trapped in a pocket against the coast.

CHAPTER TWO

INTELLIGENCE AND RESISTANCE

Before the first Allied soldiers had landed in France, the war was already being fought on land. The French Resistance gathered intelligence, sustained national morale and launched attacks against German forces. Allied intelligence officers from the American OSS and British SOE assisted in these operations and would later ensure drops of weapons and explosives to remote areas. Resistance came at a price, and many men and women were executed or transported to concentration camps by the Germans.

THE ALLIES ENJOYED a unique intelligence advantage over the Germans since they had constructed copies of the German electronic encryption machine known as Enigma and broken the codes used by the German Armed Forces.

Intercepted traffic included such routine messages as unit strengths, ration and ammunition requests. With this information, the Allies were able to build up a good picture of the German Army's order of battle on the other side of the Channel. They were also assisted by reports from the French Resistance and by USAAF and RAF reconnaissance missions which provided high- and low-level photographs of the obstacles and fortifications under construction. Low-level sorties, which were far more hazardous than the fast, high-altitude flights, produced photographs which were taken

Left: Following the Allied landings in June 1944, many men who had been uncommitted joined the Resistance, forming groups like this one in a French courtyard. They carry a mixture of British-supplied and captured German small arms.

from an oblique angle that allowed seamen and soldiers to analyse coastal features and routes off designated beaches. As part of the deception plans, for every mission flown over Normandy, two were flown over the Pas de Calais. Once the invasion was launched, air reconnaissance became intense – on the night of 6–7 June, the 10th Photo Reconnaissance Group alone handled 10,000 prints.

For the German forces in Europe in early 1944, there were two simple questions to which they needed answers: where would the Allies land, and when would this happen? The Allies were not only helped by the Ultra intercepts but by the Japanese embassy in Berlin, which sent regular detailed reports about the German work on coastal defences by radio to Tokyo. Their codes had been broken and Allied intelligence teams were able to build up a very detailed picture of the Atlantic Wall, in some cases down to the location of machine gun and mortar positions. The knowledge, learned via Ultra, that U-boats were now being kept in port in France in preparation for an Allied invasion, allowed the US to send bigger convoys across the Atlantic in 1944. Better still, the *Kriegsmarine* had transmitted details of the offshore minefields that had been laid in the Bay of the Seine. With this information, safe lanes could be identified for the invasion fleets to pass through.

So the armies on both sides of the Channel knew that 1944 would be a decisive year. In the middle of April, the Allies learned that the Germans were convinced that an attack would be launched in the next four weeks. However, the staff officers with the

Right: General Heinz Guderian in his half-track command post during the invasion of France in 1940. His half-track carries a variety of radios and an Enigma encryption machine, seen in the bottom left of the photograph. The Germans were convinced that Enigma was completely secure.

Kriegsmarine were adamant that the Allies would need five consecutive days of good weather. Moon, tides and weather, as well as the perceived strength of the Anglo-American armies in Britain, pointed to mid-April as the most likely date and to the relief of the German garrisons, this date came and passed without incident.

On 8 May, a decoded message from *Luftflotte III* caused Allied planners real worries when it identified from the pattern of Allied bombing that the likely area for landings would be the coast between Le Havre and Cherbourg. The German

ENIGMA

The Enigma was a highly sophisticated mechanical encryption system that superficially looked like a typewriter. The German engineer, Arthur Scherbius, developed it in 1923 from a design by a Dutchman HA Koch. The German Army and Navy saw its potential and bought it in 1929. They believed that it would make the transmission of radio messages faster and completely secure. In its simplest form, for every letter it sent there were hundreds of millions of possible solutions. However, the Germans forgot how few letters there are in the alphabet; that no letter could stand for itself; and that the machine had no number keys, so figures had to be spelled out. The Polish Army began reading some signals in 1932, the French intelligence services in 1938 and the British in February 1940. For the British, the secrecy of the project was at such a high level that they classified it as 'Ultra Secret' and so it became known as 'Ultra'. On 1 June 1944, the Anglo–American team at Bletchley Park began to use the world's first computer to break German codes. Developed at the Post Office Research Laboratory at Dollis Hill, it was code-named 'Colossus' because of its enormous size. It came into service just in time to speed up operations on D-Day.

Army, however, continued to believe that landings would be further north, near Dieppe or Calais.

The secret of where and when the landings would take place, was, of course, closely guarded. 'If the enemy obtains as much as 48 hours' warning of the location of the assault area, the chances of success are small,' warned Lt Gen Frederick Morgan, Chief of Staff to the Supreme Allied Commander (COSSAC) planning team. He concluded: 'Any longer warning spells certain defeat.'

All the maps and plans of the invasion beaches were marked 'Bigot'. This was a classification higher than Top Secret. Officers who had been cleared to work on the plans were given a special security clearance – 'Bigoted'. This curious code word was an anagram of the words 'To Gib' that had been stamped on the papers of officers destined for Gibraltar and the subsequent invasion of North Africa in November 1942.

However, even the strictest security precautions can have unexpected leaks. Sidney Dawe, a 54-year-old man who created crosswords for a British newspaper, *The Daily Telegraph*, started using clues for words that worried Bigot security

staff. They were all code names in Operation Overlord. On 2 May, the word 'Utah' appeared, two weeks later 'Omaha', then 'Mulberry' and when he offered 'Neptune' he was arrested and interrogated. He was no enemy agent, only an innocent school physics teacher who appeared to have stumbled on the words by chance.

Forty years later, it was revealed that the words had been picked up by one of his pupils, who, as an inquisitive small boy, had loitered around US camps and bases near Leatherhead. Amazingly, he had picked up the words, but unaware of their significance, offered them to his teacher as unusual words for the crossword.

As a further aid to security, civilian travel between Britain and Eire was halted and from April, a coastal belt 16km (10 miles) deep stretching from the Wash to Land's End and either side of the Firth of Forth was closed to all but authorized travellers.

ICI LONDRES

In Britain, soldiers rehearsed amphibious and air landing tactics exhaustively but had only a vague idea of where they would be landing.

With only a few reconnaissance aircraft, the Germans were forced to rely on intercepts of Allied radio traffic in southern Britain to provide intelligence. They learned a lot about real units, but also picked up false radio traffic. However, the most critical piece of intelligence came through the interrogation of captured French Resistance workers. The Germans knew that among the *messages personnels* broadcast to occupied France by BBC Radio-Londres were two parts of a poem by Verlain:

Les sanglots longs
des violons
de l'automne

It would be followed by the words,

Blessent mon coeur
d'une langeur
monotone.

The first alerted Resistance groups that the landings were imminent, and the second told them to begin operations that night, including attacks on road and rail communications. The Germans, notably the signals intelligence unit at Gen Salmuth's Fifteenth Army headquarters at Tourcoing, knew that the two-part message was significant. The message was hidden among many others including such cryptic sentences as 'Mathurin likes spinach', 'Acid makes litmus paper turn

Above: Cradling his Bren Light Machine Gun, a member of the French Resistance strikes a pose after D-Day. The robust reliable Bren LMG was an ideal weapon for the Resistance. Though it had a slow rate of fire, it was very forgiving of rough handling and dirt.

red' and 'My wife has sharp eyesight'. Some of these were secret instructions and others were invented and included to confuse the Germans.

At the Fifteenth Army headquarters, the signallers had logged the first message, broadcast on 1 June and repeated on the following three days. Then on 5 June, the second message went out on the BBC at 12:15, 21:20, 22:00 and 21:15 hours.

Most German officers thought that the messages were only a general call for attacks by rail workers in France. Field Marshal von Rundstedt simply did not believe that, in his words, 'General Eisenhower would announce the invasion over the BBC!' In Admiral Krancke's naval headquarters the signals were also logged, along with a note that nothing was likely to happen.

Despite attempts by the Free French in London to impose some sort of control on the French Resistance, and the Allies giving it the grand title 'FFI' (Free French Forces of the Interior), it was a loosely structured force. The groups of men and women who had taken to the countryside were popularly known as the 'Maquis' after the mountain scrub in Corsica where bandits hid from the law. Some of these were young men and women were also avoiding compulsory labour service in Germany. The Maquis would launch the ambushes on German convoys after the D-Day landings.

URBAN RESISTANCE

The Resistance, which was largely urban, had been in existence longer than the Maquis, and included the *Organization Civile et Militaire* (OCM), the *Organization de Resistance de l'Armee* (ORA), the *Communist Francs-Tireurs et Partisans* (FTP) and *Liberation Nord*. Resistance groups were in turn broadly split into two types, 'networks' (*réseaux*) and 'movements'. The former were secretive and usually small while movements were larger and thus less secure. The networks collected intelligence, conducted sabotage and organized escape routes, and were thus linked to the Allied intelligence organizations like Special Operations Executive (SOE), MI6 and the Office of Strategic Services (OSS) or the Free French BCRAM. Movements aimed to target the French people, to shake them out of the lethargy of defeat and occupation and eventually organize them for action. Their main weapon was the publication of clandestine newspapers.

In the Normandy area, it was estimated that there were 3000 insurgents ready to respond to the message broadcast by the BBC French Service. Resistance fighters were active in Cherbourg, St Lô, Caen and Le Havre. They had taken to the country in Calvados, south of Caen, and in the Department of Eure to the east. On D-Day, the men in the Calvados region blew up eight bridges, destroyed over 100 vehicles and cut innumerable railway lines including the Paris–Cherbourg line near Carentan, the St Lô–Coutances line, the Paris–Granville line near Saint Manvieu and the Caen–Bayeux and Caen–Vire lines. They also cut the trunk telephone link from Caen to Smolensk and the cables connecting the headquarters of the LXXXIV Corps in St Lô with the 91st Division in Valognes as well as the St Lô–Jersey link and Cherbourg–Brest connections. In the Eure Department, Marcel Baudot, the departmental chief, banded the various Resistance groups together, making them into a formidable force.

Right: American Army Air Force B-17s drop weapons containers over a rural drop zone in France in one of the post D-Day missions. Similar supply drops for the Resistance had been going on for several years. With their big bomb bays, bombers were ideal for this type of work.

Later, once it became clear that the Allies had secured a firm beachhead in Normandy and would eventually liberate France, many previously uncommitted Frenchmen and women joined the Resistance.

The attacks on D-Day by the 100,000 men and women of the Resistance across France were to include 1050 planned interruptions of the French railway network. This forced the Germans to rely on trucks, which could carry far less than trains and used up valuable petrol. By D-Day, 85 per cent of all railway traffic in France served the Germans and of that two-fifths served the *Wehrmacht* (Armed Forces). The attack on railway communications called for the destruction of 571 railway stations and junctions and 30 main lines in the hours before D-Day. These operations were code-named 'Green'.

The innocuously named 'Tortoise' operation involved cutting telephone communications as well as demolishing bridges and destroying roads. Disruption of the local and long-distance telephone lines forced the Germans to use their scarce radio communications, which also gave the Allies opportunities to gain intelligence by radio interception of the Germans' communications.

DELIVERING THE GOODS

While this was happening, RAF and USAAF aircraft flew into France to drop containers of arms, explosives and other equipment to Resistance groups in remote DZs.

On the Allied side of the Channel, the British and Americans used Ultra to plot the movement of German units in France, monitor reports on their strength and efficiency and eavesdrop on orders from Paris and Berlin. Most usefully, Ultra allowed the Allies to monitor how good their own security was; for example, did the Germans suspect that Normandy was to be the landing site, or were the deception plans still working? After the D-Day landings had taken place, Ultra intercepts confirmed that the Germans were still convinced that there were more Allied forces ready to launch an attack on the Pas de Calais coast.

Photographic information was overprinted on maps which would then be issued to soldiers in the first waves ashore.

At Oxford University, the Inter-Services Topographical Unit under Col Sam Bassett of the Royal Marines appealed to the British public over BBC Radio for holiday snaps and postcards of 'any part of the world'. These would show beaches, buildings and terrain at ground level. Within 24 hours of the broadcast, Bassett received a desperate call telling him the BBC had been inundated with photographs and postcards. Eventually, over ten million pictures were collected and 50 US servicewomen were flown over from the US to sort and classify them.

Finally, in the months before D-Day, X-Craft, 15.5m (51ft) long miniature submarines crewed by four or five men of the Royal Navy assigned to the Combined Operations Pilotage Parties (COPP), surveyed the beaches.

The COPP were the idea of 33-year-old Lieutenant Commander (later Captain) Nigel Clogstoun-Willmott. The Combined Operations headquarters, under Lord Louis Mountbatten, created a wartime establishment for the COPP with its headquarters at Hayling Island Yacht Club between Portsmouth and Chichester on the south coast of England.

The COPP were teams of about ten men, commanded by a Royal Navy Lieutenant Commander or Lieutenant, and manned by three Naval officers who were responsible for navigation, reconnaissance and administration, an Army captain who also covered reconnaissance, a sergeant bodyguard, three enlisted naval men to paddle canoes if needed and a mechanic. Clogstoun-Willmott kept the

PLASTIC EXPLOSIVES

PE 808 plastic explosives, a British invention perfected at the Royal Ordnance Factory at Bridgwater just before the war, was composed of cyclotrimethylene-tritramine, a powerful but sensitive explosive which the British called Research Department Explosive or RDX. Mixed as 91 per cent RDX and nine per cent plasticizing agent it was a stable, waterproof and shock-proof putty-like material which could be moulded into containers or directly onto a target. It was a superb weapon for the Resistance, ideal for attacks on railways and other vulnerable targets. It was a yellow-brown colour and came in 75 x 30mm (3 x 1.2in) 100g (4oz) waxed paper cartridges. PE 808 had a characteristic marzipan smell which if inhaled would give the user a splitting headache, known as a 'gely [gelignite] headache'.

As a demolition charge, it was set off using a Composition Explosive (CE) TNT primer and a No 27 Mk 1 detonator. The detonator was a 45mm (1.8in) long thin aluminium tube containing fulminate of mercury at the closed end. A safety fuse was inserted into the open end and pinched in place with special pliers called 'crimpers'. This fuse, safety fuse No 11, consisted of a black powder core surrounded by a waterproof fabric cover. It burned at 0.6m (2ft) per minute.

Above: A Free French broadcast on BBC Radio Londres. For many Frenchmen, just listening to the forbidden French language broadcasts from the BBC was an act of resistance. The radio was an invaluable way of sending secret messages as well as sustaining French morale.

numbers small so that a COPP could quickly fly anywhere as a group.

He also developed rubberized canvas suits for swimmers, who carried torches, waterproof watches and compasses as well as small arms and commando knives. The COPP teams were ordered to avoid combat, but were well-trained in close combat techniques and could be formidable opponents.

Soon after the ball-point pen had been invented, Clogstoun-Willmott arranged for them to be issued for making notes underwater. COPP teams learned how to get ashore using submarines, canoes and rudimentary dry suits. They measured currents, tidal stream, depths and gradients onshore using fishing lines and pegs and they also collected samples of sand and shingle from beaches to assess if vehicles could cross them without bogging in.

The Americans and British forces had used COPP teams in the landings in Sicily and Salerno in 1943. COPP were now accepted by the British planners.

On the morning of 6 June, two COPP midget submarines, *X-20* and *X-23*, would be in position to guide the British and Canadian landing craft in their run in to the beaches at Arromanches and Ouistreham. The X-Craft would signal the correct channels for landing craft with a combination of light, radio and sound.

The Americans were reluctant to use the COPP submarines because they feared that if they were discovered, the Germans would realize that an invasion was imminent.

As early as January 1944, COPP X-Craft were investigating a beach in the Bay of the Seine, at Saint-Laurent-sur-Mer that would later be part of Omaha beach. The submarines were towed part of the way across the Channel by a trawler and then moved under their own power close to the coast.

Right: Combined Operations Pilotage Party (COPP) canoeists in training in Britain. The canoe was an ideal way of moving stores and equipment to the shore of a beach without attracting attention – in the dark it was almost invisible against the sea.

Under water, they were capable of three knots and on the surface, eight.

PLANS, LIES AND PROPAGANDA

Planning by the British for the Second Front, as the landings in France were known, had begun as early as September 1941, when the US was not yet in the war, and when, on the Eastern Front, the Russians were in full retreat. When the US entered the war they pressed for an immediate assault on the French coast, but the British Prime Minister, Winston Churchill, was adamant that the campaign against Nazi Germany should be slower and more systematic. Despite American opposition, his views prevailed.

In April 1943, when Gen Morgan was appointed Chief of Staff to the Supreme Allied Commander, with headquarters at Norfolk House, St James's Square, London, his brief was to turn ideas for an invasion of northern Europe into a concrete plan.

At a weekend conference in Largs, Scotland, the COSSAC staff selected Normandy. Morgan had favoured Normandy because it would give the Allies the advantage of surprise. Among the other factors his staff considered was that the Allied air forces could provide effective cover over the battlefield, and that the Germans could not quickly reinforce their troops in the area. The beach head could therefore be isolated.

The coast of Normandy, from near La Madeleine in the west to Ouistreham in the east, was selected because it had open beaches, though the river Orne and the Caen Canal in the east might restrict movement if the major bridges were destroyed. The coast was within range of fighter and bomber cover, and the Allied ship-borne invasion force assembled in the ports of southern England could be marshalled safely in the Channel before entering the Bay of the Seine and the Normandy beaches.

Morgan remains one of the unsung heroes of D-Day who warned his team: 'the term planning staff has come to have a sinister meaning. It implies the production of nothing but paper. What we must contrive to do is to produce not only paper but action.' The original plan envisaged a first-wave landing by only three divisions. On appointment as commander of 21st Army Group, Montgomery pressed for changes. Morgan and Montgomery argued, and in his memoirs, the irascible Field Marshal wrote: 'Morgan considered Eisenhower was God; since I had discarded many of his plans he placed me at the other end of the celestial ladder.' However, Eisenhower wrote that Morgan was the man who 'made D-Day possible'.

The new plan now called for landings by two US and two British Corps. The Corps were, landing from west to east, the US VII Corps under Lt Gen 'Lightning Joe' Collins (Utah beach), the US V Corps under Lt Gen Leonard 'Gee' Gerow (Omaha beach, near St Laurent), the British XXX Corps under Lt Gen GC Bucknall (Gold beach, near Arromanches), with Canadian troops of the British I Corps under Lt General JT Crocker (Juno beach, near Courseulles) and the rest of I Corps (Sword beach near Ouistreham).

The airborne forces – the United States 82nd Division under Maj Gen Mathew Ridgeway and 101st Division under Maj Gen Maxwell D Taylor would land in the west. The British 6th Division under Maj Gen RN Gale would land in the east. These operations would begin before dawn to secure the flanks and the western exits through flooded areas behind the US beachheads.

In the space of 24 hours, 175,000 men, 1500 tanks, 10,000 other vehicles and 3000 artillery pieces would be carried across the Channel in a vast fleet and landed on these beaches in an operation code-named 'Neptune'.

The landings would be at half tide because this would mean that anti-shipping obstacles were exposed and there was less danger of landing craft being damaged or sunk, and it would also give the Allies more space to deploy their forces on the beaches. The Germans had made the logical assumption that any landings would be at high tide, since this would spare men and vehicles the exposed dash across the open beaches.

At the 'Trident' conference in Washington in May 1943, the date for D-Day was set for May 1944. It was Churchill who insisted that the landings in France be given an operational name befitting their size and importance and proposed the name 'Overlord'. At the 'Eureka' conference in Teheran, in November 1943, the Allies made a firm commitment to the operation. A month later, at the Sextant conference in Cairo in December 1943, Gen Dwight D Eisenhower was selected as Commander in Chief.

CHURCHILLIAN RHETORIC

In a typically grand gesture, Churchill had broadcast that occupied Europe could expect liberation 'before the fall of autumn leaves'. When autumn 1943 had come and gone, his comment was a gift to German propagandists. Leaflets cut to look like leaves were scattered with the slogan 'I have fallen, O Churchill! Where are you? Where are your soldiers?'

The leaves appeared again in March 1944 with a cartoon of Churchill as a soldier on one side and on the other a parody of a French popular tune of the period.

J'y va-t-y, j'y va-t-y pas?
Si j'y va pas, Staline quoi donc qui me dira?
Si j'y va quoi que ce'st qu'Hitler y me fera?
Tant pis, j'y va pas!

Do I go or don't I go?
If I don't what will Stalin say?

Below: General Dwight Eisenhower chats to a GI in Britain. He had an easy way with soldiers, even if he often asked the same simple questions like 'Where are you from?' and 'What did you do in the 'States?' Eisenhower was the protegé of the US Chief of Staff, George Marshall.

If I do what will Hitler do to me?
OK, so I don't go!

On 1 April the Germans produced another leaf leaflet. On one side it read 'St Liberation' and on the reverse 'April Fool!'

In the spring of 1944, in a piece of inspired irony, a parody of an Allied leaflet was produced. It read 'Down with requisitioning. Peasants of France, stop giving to the Germans. All requisitions are for the Germans. We must keep everything from now on. Because the next landing will bring us the Allies which we have to feed. There will be the British, the Americans, the Canadians, the Australians, the Hindus, the Africans, the Russians etc. They are ten times more than the Germans. Consequently, they will need ten times more food. And we won't let them requisition us. They will be our Allies so we will give them everything for nothing, this will be our contribution to freedom.'

For consumption at home, Dr Joseph Goebbels, the Minister for Propaganda, used two tools. The first was the new *Vergeltungwaffe* (Vengeance weapons) that would soon be directed against Britain. Launch sites for these new rockets, known as V-1s, were under construction in northern France and the campaign would begin on 13 June. It was thought that these attacks would persuade the British and American governments to reduce the weight of bombing attacks by the USAAF and RAF against Germany.

Another tool was to whip up the fear of Bolshevism and the Allied plans to turn Germany into a non-industrial pastoral country, suggested by the British Peer Sir Robert Vansittart and later by the secretary to the US Treasury, Henry Morgenthau. Goebbels made much of these 'Jewish' plans to inspire German soldiers to fight and German civilians to endure the Allied bombing. His motto was 'Strength through Fear'. Many Germans were led to believe that if a Dieppe-style defeat could be inflicted on the Anglo-American armies in the West, the Allies would be reluctant to attempt another landing. This would then free Germany to concentrate on fighting the USSR in the East and hopefully force it to negotiate a peace.

The Germans could direct propaganda at the French civilian population and at Allied forces waiting across the Channel, but they were drawing a large amount of Allied propaganda in return. In the overall deception and psychological warfare campaign being waged against German forces, the Allies used 'black', 'white' and 'grey' propaganda.

'Black' propaganda was untrue, or from a concealed source. The most dramatic example of this were the radio broadcasts organized by the pre-war journalist, Sefton Delmer. Using powerful BBC transmitters, by D-Day he had combined two 'black' stations into one called *Soldatensender Calais angeschlossen der Deutsche Kurzwellensender Atlantik* (The soldier's Calais broadcast in association with the German Atlantic short-wave broadcasting station). It combined excellent music with news and comment and purported to be broadcast by disgruntled German troops in France.

'GREY' AND 'WHITE' PROPAGANDA

The second 'grey' (or 'dirty white') technique was a daily newspaper *Nachrichten für die Truppe* (News for the Troops). The USAAF dropped 250,000 to 750,000 every night over targets designated by the 21st Army Group.

Both of these operations aimed to concentrate the minds of the German serviceman on the deficiencies of the 'enemy within', the Nazi Party officials who were safe, away from the front, or commanders who were prepared to sacrifice their soldiers.

The BBC was the source of 'white' propaganda, along with 3.24 billion leaflets dropped by the USAAF and RAF that presented the news or information without giving it a slant or 'spin'.

As training progressed in the UK, Allied and German planners ignored propaganda, looked at the hard facts and tried to decide when would be the most suitable dates for a landing. The 5, 6 and 7 June looked most promising, when tide conditions and moon phase would mean that the Channel would be at half-tide at dawn, and the moon would rise late at night. The ideal conditions would be a wind over the beaches that was not more than a 'moderate breeze' of 10 to 15 knots (28 to 33km/h (17 to 21mph)). There had to be no heavy swell. Forward visibility needed to be 5 to 8km (3 to 5 miles) and for air support to be effective, low cloud needed to be well broken with its base 300m (1000ft) above the surface. However, there would be a difference of half an hour in the time of half-tide on the US beaches in the west and British ones in the east.

Like all military operations, the Allied soldiers knew that even if the plan was good and they achieved surprise and delivered overwhelming fire power, once they were in contact with the enemy, the battle would become a violent and unpredictable one and would be costly, even for the victor.

Though the coast from Dunkerque to Le Touquet was so close that in places it could be seen from mainland Britain, it had been dismissed by the COSSAC team as too obvious and too heavily defended.

The Allied planners turned this to their advantage, with an elaborate deception plan code-named 'Bodyguard' which included an operation named 'Fortitude South', which they

Above: A simple three dimensional rubber map is shown to senior British officers and civil servants. Planners went to considerable pains to ensure that soldiers and ships' crews were familiarized with the shores they would be approaching and over which they would fight.

used to try to convince the Germans that landings would take place around Calais. Dummy and real landing craft and vehicles were positioned to look like an invasion force and false radio signals were broadcast from Kent by mobile transmitters, to simulate large military formations.

The most impressive part of the deception scheme was the creation of the 1st US Army Group or FUSAG, commanded by Gen George S Patton. This had been set up in genuine headquarters in October 1943 with the role of assuming command of US armies in France following D-Day. Later, the role passed to 12th US Army Group but FUSAG was kept alive and notionally located on the east coast between the Thames and the Wash. From here, it could threaten the Pas de Calais. Considerable effort went into this

fiction under the code-name 'Quicksilver'. To give added credibility to FUSAG, Patton was seen in the area and written about in the press. These reports and photographs would be picked up in neutral countries like Spain and Portugal and forwarded to Germany.

Through 'Fortitude South', the Germans would be convinced that even after they had taken place, the Normandy landings were just a trick and that the main attack would still come at Calais. Indeed, after 6 June, Hitler refused to release the armoured formations in the area to move south to Normandy. Part of the reason for this was that through Quicksilver, the Allies had also managed to convince the Germans that they had more forces in Britain that could therefore be committed to other operations. If this was true, they could afford to launch a feint against Normandy, before attempting the main attack on the Pas de Calais.

It was so effective that on D-Day, the sober analysts of Foreign Armies West Headquarters, the German army intelligence team that covered the Anglo-American armies, produced an appendix to their report (No 1288) that read: 'According to a believable *Abwehr* [German intelligence service] report of 2 June, the forces in southern England are divided into two army groups, the 21st British Army Group and the 1st US Army Group… Not a single unit of the 1st US Army Group, which comprises around 25 large formations north and south of the Thames, has so far been committed. The same is true of the ten to 12 combat formations stationed in central England and Scotland.

This suggests that the enemy is planning a further large-scale operation in the Channel area, which one would expect to be aimed at the coastal sector in the Pas de Calais area…'

Below: The distinctive 'ski ramp' outlines of a V1 launching site are clear in this aerial photograph. As these rudimentary cruise missiles began to fall on southern England, the destruction or capture of the launch sites became a priority for the RAF and Allied land forces.

Another deception plan called 'Fortitude North' convinced the Germans that there was a threat to southern Norway. Thus German men, weapons and resources were consequently squandered in both Pas de Calais and Norway. 'Fortitude North' was given conviction by fake signals and intelligence about 'Skye Force', made up of a notional Fourth Army. Signals about arctic training and cold weather operations were used to enhance this illusion. The British 3rd Infantry Division conducted some of its training in Scotland with exercises like 'Burger 1' and 'Burger 2' launched from Black Isle across the Moray Firth to Burghead Bay. All this helped to sustain the idea that Norway was a potential objective. Other deception plans included 'Zeppelin', a fictional invasion of the Balkans from Italy.

TECHNOLOGICAL TRICKERY
On the night of 5-6 June, technology joined the D-Day deception plans when Allied bombers began dropping 'chaff'

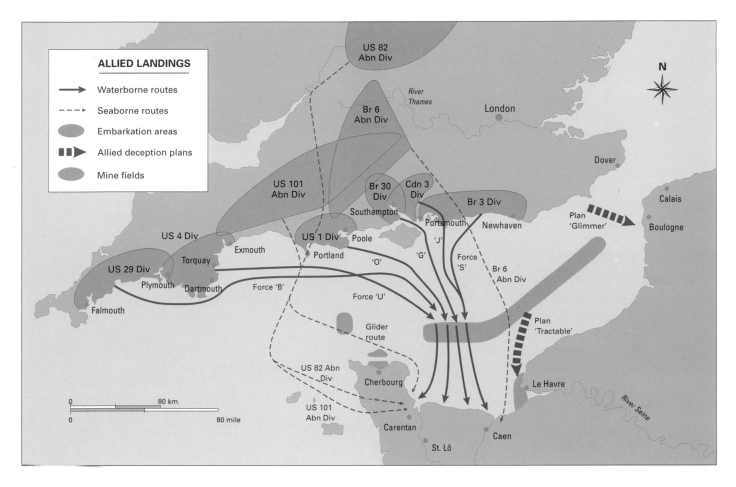

Above: The complex airborne and amphibious landings that made up Operation Overlord could be wrecked by bad weather, confusion in the darkness and enemy action. The Germans were determined to stop the landing, but believed that it would be in the Pas de Calais area.

or 'window', strips of metal foil that reflected radar signals that looked like large numbers of aircraft on radar screens.

In Operation Taxable eight Avro Lancaster bombers of No 617 Squadron RAF flew in two waves with 3km (2 miles) between each aircraft and 13km (8 miles) between each wave. By releasing chaff every five seconds, they produced an image of an 'invasion fleet' approaching Le Havre 25 x 22km (16 x 14 miles) in area. The pilots flew an orbiting flight pattern and so created the impression that the fleet was advancing towards the coast at 14km/h (7 knots).

To add to the confusion, aircraft of No 218 Squadron RAF flew Operation Glimmer, a similar electronic spoof directed towards Boulogne. In both operations, aircraft also flew jamming missions that were designed to give the impression that they were attempting to conceal the approaching fleets.

Uniquely, the Allies were able to monitor the effectiveness of these deception plans (and the secrecy of Operation Overlord), not only because of Ultra but through another secret asset. German agents, who from 1940 onwards had been parachuted into Britain or landed by E-boats or U-boats, had been quickly captured and 'turned', supplying the *Abwehr* with doctored information. 'Turning' was a brutally simple operation. The spy was given two choices: work for the Allies, or be tried on camera and hanged. Only a tiny number of men chose death. The reports of these spies further helped to confirm that the real threat was either across the narrowest part of the Channel or against Norway.

A Spanish double-agent, Juan Pujol Garcia, code-named 'Garbo' by the British because he was an excellent actor, appeared to be a very reliable source of intelligence for the Germans. They knew him as 'Arabel'. He had a brilliant case officer, Tomàs Harris, who with Pujol, invented a ring of 14 sub-agents and 11 well-placed informers. The Germans were so impressed by Arabel's work that in June 1944 they informed him by radio that he had been awarded the Iron Cross for his services to the Third Reich. Six months later, the British awarded him the MBE.

On 15 May 1944, the plans for D-Day had been finalized and Gen Eisenhower gave a full-scale briefing to King George

VI, Prime Minister Winston Churchill and his senior British and American commanders at St Paul's School in London.

Rear Admiral Morton L Deyo of the US Navy recalled that the Supreme Commander's smile and confidence was worth an extra 20 divisions. 'That day it was worth more. He spoke for ten minutes. Before the warmth of his quiet confidence, the mists of doubt dissolved. Not often has one man been called upon to accept so great a burden of responsibility. But here was one at peace with his soul.'

The soldiers who would land on D-Day had a different perspective on briefings and speeches. Private Mason of the 2nd Battalion East Yorks remembered when 'Eisenhower came and gave us the once over. He was a bright and breezy person but loaded with bull'.

At the briefing at St Paul's School, Montgomery emphasized that 'armoured columns must penetrate deep inland, and quickly, on D-Day; this will upset the enemy's plans and tend to hold him off while we build up strength'.

What worried him was the speed at which the Germans could bring reinforcements to Normandy. He estimated that though the Allied landings would face about five divisions, by the end of the next day this could have risen to ten. In a week, 18 Allied divisions could be confronted by 24 German ones, ready to deliver a counter-attack.

'The enemy,' he said, 'will do his level best to Dunkirk us.' The Allies, however, had the unique resource of air and sea power and of the former, Montgomery said: 'Air must hold the ring and must hinder and make very difficult the movement of enemy reserves by train or road towards the lodgement area.'

He was to be proved correct in this assessment by Lt Gen Friedrich Dihm, the Special Assistant to Rommel. Interrogated after the war by the US Army, he said: 'Except for this air supremacy, it would have been possible, in my opinion, to prevent a successful invasion during the first days after the initial assault. These were the most critical days for the Allies. Later, the constant and increasing reinforcement of the Allies could be less and less equalized by the arrival of German reinforcements, hindered by the destruction of important traffic routes.'

After 6 June, this dominance was exemplified by one *Kampfgruppen,* (battle group), based in Brittany, that took ten days to reach Normandy, moving on roads bombed and blasted by the USAAF and RAF, and attacked by the Resistance.

Right: A grim faced General George Patton inspects a neatly turned out parade of GIs. Patton was known as a stickler for military etiquette. His presence in south east England was given considerable publicity as part of the Allied deception plan indicating a landing on the Pas de Calais.

CHAPTER THREE

LOGISTICS AND TECHNOLOGY

The vast resources of the United States as well as the ingenuity and experience of British engineers and soldiers combined to produce some original and formidable weapons for D-Day. Modern versions of specialist equipment like the AVRE are still being developed today, while the remains of the Mulberry harbours off the Normandy coast are testimony to Allied ingenuity. Rommel cited the military proverb 'sweat saves blood', but the Allies could counter with 'brains save sweat'.

As Allied planners looked at the challenges of D-Day – the initial landings and the subsequent fighting, they considered how existing military equipment and technology could solve their problems and whether new weapons and systems needed to be developed.

Before any troops had gone ashore, the beaches and German defences would be saturated with heavy naval gunfire, but one innovation would be rocket firing landing ships. These would deliver salvos of 1000 12.7cm (5in) 0.9kg (2lb) rockets fired in three salvos or 'ripples', which, though less accurate than naval gunfire, would have a massive blast effect from their high explosive warheads. To one American soldier, these craft looked 'like a direct steal from *Popular Science* or *Amazing Stories*'.

Left: US soldiers dash ashore from a landing craft in a training area in southern England. One man appears to be carrying a Bangalore Torpedo to breach wire obstacles. The watchtower in the background is probably for the directing staff to supervise live firing.

Above: Early trials for Duplex Drive (DD) tanks with a modified Valentine in Staines reservoir in England. The DD system would be fitted to M4 Shermans and prove very effective as well as a considerable surprise to the Germans, who saw tanks emerge from the sea on D-Day.

As the landing craft started their run in to the shore, they would launch 'DD', or Duplex Drive Sherman tanks, though some crews asserted that the initials DD actually stood for 'Donald Duck'. Invented by the Austrian émigré and armoured vehicle designer, Nicolas Straussler, DD was a tank with high waterproof canvas and rubber skirts, and a drive off the main engine to two propellers that could 'swim' ashore at a steady four knots (7km/h/4.5mph). On the beach, the crew would drop the skirts that had given the tank its buoyancy and would be able to engage enemy bunkers and defences with its 75mm (2.95in) gun.

British experience at Dieppe in 1942 had shown the need for specialized tanks and armoured vehicles to breach defences and clear obstacles. The tanks were dubbed 'Funnies' and the Churchill tank operated by the 79th Armoured Division was basis for most of these new vehicles. It was ideal for this role since it had a roomy interior, thick armour and a regular shape that could take external mounts for equipment.

The most famous was the Churchill Crocodile flamethrower that could engage enemy targets at 80–120m (260ft–390ft) with 80 one-second bursts of flame. New flamethrower fuel had been developed that was thicker and more viscous and consequently stuck to its target. It was carried in a six tonne trailer linked by a flexible hose to a flame gun in the hull machine gun position. When the fuel had been expended the trailer could be jettisoned and the

Churchill became a conventional gun tank. In Normandy, the weapon and its crew were regarded with such fear and loathing by the Germans that captured Crocodile crews were often executed.

The Armoured Vehicle Royal Engineers (AVRE) was armed with a 7.92mm (0.31in) Besa machine gun but its principal weapon was a huge 290mm (11.4in) gun firing a 20kg (44lb) demolition charge up to 80m (260ft). The AVRE could also carry fascines, huge bundles of brushwood to fill in anti-tank ditches. In north-west Europe, the AVRE and the Crocodile became a formidable pair, the former capable of blowing apart heavy German fortifications while the latter 'flamed out' the wreckage. It was often sufficient for a Crocodile to project unignited fuel into a wrecked bunker to induce the survivors to surrender.

The Churchill was also used as an Armoured Recovery Vehicle (ARV).

Another tank, known as a Bobbin, carried a 100m (110yd) long roll of reinforced matting on a huge drum on the front of the hull that could be unrolled on soft wet sand or loose shingle to give other vehicles a surface that would provide traction.

ARKs (Armoured Ramp Carriers, sometimes known as ARCs), equipped with folding bridges, could span demolished bridges or cross anti-tank ditches. 'Crabs' were mine-clearing Sherman tanks with a revolving drum at the front which was fitted with weighted chains. These flailed their way through minefields at 2.5km/h (1mph), safely exploding the mines in their path. They retained the turret and gun of a conventional tank and could be used in this role if necessary. The Crab concept, conceived by a South African officer, had already proved its worth at El Alamein, breaching Axis minefields.

The BARV (Beach Armoured Recovery Vehicle) was a turretless tank with winches or small bulldozer blades for towing or pushing stranded vehicles off the beach.

The Funnies were the brainchild of Maj Gen Sir Percy Hobart, known as 'Hobo' behind his back. An officer who had already made a name for himself as an armoured

Below: A British Royal Engineer overhauls the spigot mortar on a Churchill Armoured Vehicle Royal Engineers or AVRE. The big demolition round likened to a 'flying dustbin' can be seen on the right. The AVRE would prove formidable throughout the liberation of Europe.

Our friends from the East[ern Front] cannot imagine what they're in for here. It's not a matter of fanatical hordes to be driven forward in masses against our line, with no regard for casualties and little recourse to tactical craft; here we are facing an enemy who applies all his native intelligence to the use of his many technical resources, who spares no expenditure of material and whose every operation goes its course as though it had been the subject of repeated rehearsal. Dash and doggedness no longer make a soldier...

Field Marshal Erwin Rommel

innovator in the 1930s, he was made responsible for developing the specialized tanks when the Chief of the General Staff, Gen Sir Alan Brooke gave him command of the 79th Armoured Division.

Lt Ian Hammerton of the 79th Armoured Division remembered that after Hobart had briefed his command on their new role, he left behind 'a sad and disillusioned collection of men. No sweeping across fields of France at cavalry speed in our Cruiser tanks – just sweeping mines. But surely, came the thought, after we have cleared a few mines, we will be able to be let loose and tally-ho after the foe? Surely, after all our training...'

In fact on D-Day on Sword beach, Captain A Low saw one of his mine-clearing tank crews use their spinning flail to pulverize a particularly active German gun position.

In strict secrecy, the British had conducted experiments with these specialized tanks against dummy enemy positions built on remote ranges. They had worked in these test conditions,

but not all had been tested in combat – D-Day would be their debut.

The American amphibious 6x6 DUKW truck had already been in action in the Mediterranean theatre. Its ability to 'swim' out to offshore transports and freighters and move up to 2.5 tonnes of stores or equipment to dumps and positions inland, would make it a vital logistic vehicle in the early stages of the landings. The vehicle had the added advantage of being able to drive ashore if bad weather threatened, rather than riding out a storm at sea. The DUKW, universally known as the 'Duck', had a crew of two and was capable of 80km/h (50mph) on land and 9km/h (6mph) in water. It had a range of 120km (75 miles) on land.

Off Omaha beach on D-Day, 22-year-old Staff Sergeant William Lewis of the 116th Infantry Regiment watched DUKWs founder in the rough sea. 'The DUKWs, not very seaworthy, would ride up a swell and instead of coming back down it would go into it, and go under. They just shipped water, turned over sideways and sunk.'

Conventional wheeled and tracked vehicles were equipped for deep wading with exhaust and air inlet extensions, as well as waterproofing grease on the engine.

Among the men who landed with US Forces on D-Day were airfield construction troops of the IX Engineering Command and by 21:45 hours they had constructed an emergency airstrip near Omaha beach. To build the strip,

Right: A Churchill tank crosses a seawall in England using an ARK – Armoured Ramp Carrier bridge layer. To the Germans the use by the British of 'Funnies' – specialized tanks for gap crossing, mine clearance or bridge laying – seemed almost profligate, but they undoubtedly saved lives.

Above: Loaded with stores, DUKWs manoeuvre around a cargo ship. The ability of these amphibious trucks to collect stores from ships and carry them ashore to logistics dumps without having to unload them made for speed and a faster build-up of men and equipment in France.

they used the specially developed Pierced Steel Planks (PSP) that were each light enough for two men to carry, and slotted together like pieces of a jigsaw puzzle. PSP was strong enough to withstand the impact of landings and takeoffs by fully laden fighter-bombers, and with its pattern of punched holes it gave both traction to aircraft wheels and sufficient drainage in summer storms.

British Commando and airborne soldiers were equipped with specially designed folding bicycles and motorbikes on which they could carry their weapons and specialized equipment including explosives and radios. Many of the invading German soldiers had bicycled into France in 1940 and now, like a lethal cycle tour, the British would be back on the Continent to return the compliment.

TRAINING

For many of the servicemen and women involved in Operation Overlord there was no special training – they continued to hone the skills they had first learned in basic and technical training. However, for units that were to be the lead formations on D-Day, there was an added emphasis on practising beach landings. Some Allied units, like the

Our training was rough, we never had nothing easy. We would get up and run four miles in twenty minutes and this was before breakfast. We would have to run two or three mile obstacles... No-one realized how horrible our training was. We would take two or three 30-mile (48km) hikes a week... The fog was so low and thick that if you stood... straight up you could probably see no more than four or five feet (1.2 or 1.5m)... I was born in Charlottesville, Virginia, and I was never in the northern part of the country... where the cold is. The higher you went on the moors the deeper the swamp got. It would be covered with blocks of ice at times and it was miserably cold.

Private Felix Branham
16th Infantry Regiment, US 29th Infantry Division

MEDIA AT WAR

Before D-Day, journalists from the British, Canadian and American print and radio media were trained for their role in the invasion. Some 558 were accredited to the Allies. The BBC alone had 48 who were well-trained as soldiers, though unarmed, and they were the men who brought the first eyewitness accounts of the landings. Among the journalists who covered D-Day and the fighting in north-western Europe were Alan Moorehead, Ed Murrow, Drew Middleton, Richard Dimbleby and Ross Munro. For the *Daily Telegraph*, a youthful Cornelius Ryan covered the landings from the nose of a Marauder bomber. In 1962, he published *The Longest Day*, one of the first eyewitness accounts of D-Day from both the German and Allied perspectives. Richard Dimbleby, who would become a respected anchorman for BBC Television after the war, was also in a bomber above the beaches. Searching for German troops, they saw close to the front line 'a solitary peasant harrowing his field, up and down behind the horses, looking nowhere but before him and at the soil.' The most dramatic pictures of the landings at Omaha were taken by the veteran photographer Robert Capa and rushed back to London where in the excitement, the dark room assistant drying the negatives caused the emulsion to melt and destroyed all but a handful. All journalists and photographers accepted that their work might be censored if it contained 'information that might be useful to the enemy'. For men and women who transgressed, there was the threat of prosecution and imprisonment, though denying journalists access to the front, and so to the stories, was far more effective.

US 1st Infantry Division ('The Big Red One') had already fought in North Africa, Sicily and Italy and could draw on their combat experience.

Across the Channel, the Germans practised alerts, with men being called out of their accommodation to man their defence positions. In 1942 and even in 1943, training was more relaxed, though coastal positions could be raided by British Commandos which gave some of these alerts a certain urgency. Coastal defence forces learned how to identify different types of ships and anti-aircraft crews were kept busy by constant Allied air raids. When men were not training, they were used to lay mines and build new obstacles on the beaches. The naval forces on both sides of the Channel were already busy with patrols, mine clearance, small scale attacks and reconnaissance.

Naval gun crews knew that they would be providing the fire support for the landings and trained to work quickly and efficiently. Allied fighter aircraft were already roaming across the skies of northern France, attacking the few *Luftwaffe* aircraft they encountered or strafing railway locomotives, trucks and coastal shipping. Bombers attacked larger targets. For the navies and air forces there was no obvious transition from training to operations.

For some British individuals and units, Overlord was the return to a continent from which they had been ejected in the humiliating evacuation at Dunkirk in 1940. Since then, they had been training in Britain.

The civilian population was moved out of farms and villages in Norfolk, Dorset and Wiltshire, and their homes became training areas for house-to-house fighting. Exercises called 'battle field inoculation', using live ammunition and explosives, gave soldiers a feel for combat. Mechanized exercises were conducted across the British countryside on a huge scale and one tank troop commander knew that D-Day was coming when his regiment was told that in training they need no longer use farm gates to access fields – they could drive through hedges, fences and walls.

From February 1944, the British Isles were 'sealed' with no contact between them and neutrals like Eire, Spain, Sweden and Portugal. Men became fitter and tougher through extra physical training and carried out long route marches loaded with full bergens containing personal kit, weapon, ammunition, entrenching tool and any other items of military equipment.

However, everyone knew that though they might be fit and well trained, when the fighting began in France there would be a strong element of luck in their survival in battle, and everyone wanted to be lucky.

With just over a week to go before D-Day, troops had been briefed and at last been told their destination, and they also knew that they were the fittest they would ever be, and were very well trained. Now they were confined to secure camps. In the preceding months and years they had

Right: Watched by their rather apprehensive comrades, British soldiers leap across a communications trench during training. They are understandably nervous since all have fitted the big sword bayonets to their 7.7mm (.303in) SMLE rifles.

practised basic military, technical and trade skills and amphibious operations.

The British, American and Canadian Divisions were divided into assault, back-up and follow-up forces. The assault forces, who would be in the first wave, were concentrated along the south coast with the follow-up in South Wales and East Anglia. In the west, the US VII Corps' 4th Division assault force was concentrated around Torquay and Dartmouth. The US V Corps' 29th Division was in Dorset around Poole and Weymouth. The British XXX Corps' 50th Division was in Hampshire around Winchester and Southampton while to the east, the 3rd Canadian Division was located around Portsmouth. The sea-side resort of

Our training was hard but purposeful, we were being whipped into a real fighting unit. Our officers and NCOs did their job well, we were really good and we knew it. I had taken over a Bren gun...I reckoned I was the best there was, my reflexes were quick, my work rate was high and I was very fleet of foot. There was a certain rapport between all ranks which is difficult to describe. No one dared let our Platoon Commander down, or they were never allowed to forget it, we were behind (him) to a man.

Private Albert King
1st Battalion Worcestershire Regiment, British 43rd Infantry Division

Below: Shrouded in dust and smoke, GIs race for the trees close to a beach on a training area in England. Though there were fatalities during these exercises, there was none of the terror and destruction that was to come on Omaha beach.

Shoreham was the embarkation port for the British I Corps' 3rd Division. To the north, inland, the US 82nd and 101st Airborne Divisions and British 6th Airborne Divisions were in positions near airfields.

Above: An Allied capital ship, HMS Holmes, *seen bombarding German coastal positions on 6 June 1944. The phenomenal firepower of the cruisers and battleships off the D-Day beaches made a significant contribution to the breakout on the day, especially on Omaha.*

The back-up formations were the British VIII Corps near Reading, the XII Corps near Canterbury and the Canadian II Corps, west of Dover. Most of the follow-up force were grouped in areas that had their own ports from which they would sail. The US V Corps' 1st Division were grouped around Fowey in Cornwall, the 29th Division around Swansea in South Wales, the US VII Corps' 90th Division around Cardiff and the 9th Division in Somerset. To the east, the British XXX Corps' 7th Armoured Division and 49th Division were grouped in East Anglia to the west of Felixstowe, while to the south, the British I Corps' 51st Division was in Essex.

For the air crew and ships companies, however, the war was already under way as they patrolled close to, or raided, the German-occupied French coast. Here the Germans improved their defences and hoped that if the Allies landed, it would not be in their sector, because they knew that when it happened it would be a bloody business.

SEAPOWER

Across the Channel, the German Naval Group Command West was under Admiral Theodore Krancke, an experienced officer, who in 1940 had captained the pocket battleship KMS *Admiral Scheer* on operations that sank 17 merchant ships in the Atlantic and Indian Oceans. His command now included three destroyers available in 8 Flotilla, four torpedo boats in 4 and 5 Flotilla and 44 *Schnellboote* (S-Boats or Fast Boats) spread along the coast between Ostend, Boulogne and Cherbourg. The U-Boats that had been the scourge of the Allied Atlantic shipping were still a serious threat with 49 based in Brest, Lorient, St Nazaire and La Palice. Some 35 put to sea before 24:00 hours on 6 June.

For defence, the Kriegsmarine had 18 minesweepers in the western Channel and Bay of Biscay, 53 motor minesweepers in ports from Dunkirk to Le Havre and 22 smaller minesweepers along the coast. Among the auxiliary craft available were patrol boats, minelaying barges and flak ships.

> I heard one torpedo come sliding down the side of the hull, but it didn't explode. Then the next one caught the stern end and tore off about 30ft (9m)... It was like there was a big door back there, but we didn't sink. I managed to get up on top. The tracer bullets were as thick as hair on a dog's back.
>
> *Sergeant Ewell B Lunsford*
> *4th Medical Battalion, US 4th Infantry Division*

The German motor torpedo boats designated *S-Boote* were known by their crews as *Eilboot* (Boat in a hurry) or *E-Boot*, from which came the British designation, E-boat for enemy boat.

The greatest test for the *S-Boote* was the Allied invasion of Normandy. There were five flotillas of *S-Boote* based along the coast opposite southern England in 1944 under command of Captain Rudolf Petersen, based in Schweningen, Germany.

The flotillas were the 8th *Schnellboote Flotilla* at Ijmuiden, Holland, the 2nd at Ostend, Belgium, the 4th at Boulogne, France and the 5th and 9th at Cherbourg, France. The 9th was commanded by the aristocrat Lt Comdr Götz Baron von Mirbach. The total strength of these flotillas was 31 battle-ready, and six conditionally battle-ready, craft.

Before D-Day, the *S-Boote* had caused the invasion fleet serious losses. On 26 April 1944, the US Army 4th Infantry Division undertook an exercise code-named 'Tiger'. Landing craft were in a 5km (3 mile) convoy transporting troops and vehicles across Lyme Bay in Dorset to the sandy beaches at the Slapton Sands Assault Training Area, Devon. It was a rehearsal for their landings at Utah beach in Normandy. During the night of 27–28 April, convoy T4, consisting of eight US Navy Landing Ship Tanks (LST) with an inadequate Royal Navy escort was attacked by nine *S-Boote* from the 5th and 9th *Schnellboote Flotilla* based in Cherbourg. The Germans sank LSTs 507 and 531 and severely damaged LST 289, which limped into Dartmouth harbour. The Germans returned safely having suffered no losses, but 441 US soldiers and 197 sailors perished in the attack – more than were to die at Utah beach on D-Day and the loss of the tank landing craft imposed constraints on Allied planners.

James Murdoch, an officer aboard LST 507 reported 'all of the Army vehicles were loaded with gasoline, and it was the gasoline which caught fire first. As it spread on the deck and poured into the fuel oil which was seeping out of the side of the ship, it caused fire on the water around the ship.' The intense flames led one German officer to assume that he had hit a tanker.

For the successful action, Capt Rudolf Petersen was awarded Oakleaves for his Knight's Cross. The attack on the 'Tiger' convoy was not made public until after D-Day, since it would have provided the Germans with an indication that the invasion of Europe was coming. This secrecy resulted in a myth of a 'cover up' over Tiger. For Allied intelligence officers, there was a real fear that the German raiders might have been able to take prisoners, since among

the officers in the craft were ten who had special knowledge of Overlord. Eventually, the bodies of these ten men were recovered. It was a grim business for the crew of HMS *Obedient* who were faced by 'hundreds of bodies of American servicemen in full battle gear floating in the sea. Many had their limbs and even their heads blown off… Of all those we took on board, there were only nine survivors.' Recovered bodies that were pronounced dead were pushed back into the sea, as there was no space on board to return them to the mainland. Julian Perkins, an officer in the Royal Navy, remembered that 'small American landing craft with their ramps down were literally scooping up bodies. It was a ghastly sight.'

On the night of 6 June, when the first airborne landings were reported, the *S-Boote* put to sea at 03:00 hours but made no contacts. Between 6 June and 13 June, the *Kriegsmarine* losses in ship-to-ship action were four patrol boats, two destroyers, two minesweepers and one S-Boat. Mines and air attacks accounted for two minesweepers, five *S-Boote* and one flak ship. Six vessels were scuttled.

The *Kriegsmarine* torpedo boats and *S-Boote* sank two destroyers, the Norwegian *Svenner* and the USS *Nelson*, four landing ships, three landing craft, three freighters, one motor torpedo boat and one tug.

At the other end of the scale from the small groups of raiding German *S-Boote* a huge Allied force was being assembled in ports around southern England. The most powerful elements were the Allied battleships that were described as 304mm (12in) or 381mm (15in) according to their main armament, but this does not give a true impression of their

ADMIRAL SIR BERTRAM RAMSAY

Born in 1883, Ramsay served on destroyers in World War I and by 1935 was Chief of Staff to the Atlantic Fleet. When he reached 55, he retired as a Vice Admiral. Ramsay was recalled to service in 1939 and was Flag Officer Dover responsible for Operation Dynamo – the evacuation of Dunkirk in 1940 – for which he was knighted. As Deputy Naval Commander Expeditionary Force he was responsible for the landings in Algeria in 1942 and Sicily in 1943. In 1944, he was appointed Naval Commander-in-Chief for Operation Neptune, the naval phase of D-Day which would be the largest amphibious undertaking in history. Urbane and very professional, 'Bert' Ramsay was killed in an air crash in January 1945.

Above: Inter-Allied cooperation as officers of the USAAF, US Navy, RAF and British Army discuss potential targets. The Allies had already landed in Sicily and Italy in 1943, and learned valuable lessons about the coordination of naval and aerial bombardment assets.

firepower. The relatively elderly USS *Texas*, built in 1912, had ten 355mm (14in) guns in five turrets, with an additional 16 127mm (5in) guns. The battleships HMS *Warspite*, a veteran of the Battle of Jutland in World War I, and HMS *Ramilies* each had eight 381mm (15in) guns.

Firing from a relatively stable platform these ships could deliver enough firepower to pulverize an area twice the size of a football pitch in seconds at ranges of up to 29km (18 miles). Experience in World War I and the landings in Italy had shown that the weight of fire in a broadside could sometimes change the course of a land battle in minutes. Rommel would say of naval gunfire: 'the effect is so immense that no operation of any kind is possible in the area commanded by this rapid-fire artillery, either by infantry or tanks.'

On D-Day, the USS *Texas* would between 05:50 and 12:00 hours conduct five shoots. Critically, at Omaha, it would help clear the Vierville exit and support troops near Longueville and Formigny. In the following two days it would engage so many targets that on 9 June it had to return to England to replenish its magazines. The *Texas* would soldier on to provide naval gunfire support for landings in the Pacific in 1945.

Monitors, like HMS *Erebus* and HMS *Roberts*, were unique warships with a draft of about 3.3m (11ft). Designed purely for shore bombardment, they normally mounted one turret with two 381mm (15in) guns and could move closer to the shore to fire more accurately.

Off the D-Day beaches on 6 June, the Allied naval forces were divided into the Western Naval Task Force, TF 123, under Rear Admiral AG Kirk USN aboard the USS *Augusta* who covered the US beaches, and the Eastern Naval Task Force under Rear Admiral Sir Phillip Vian on the anti-aircraft cruiser HMS *Scylla*, who covered the British and Canadian beaches.

Vian was a veteran of World War I with a distinguished career in World War II and had commanded one of the British sectors for the invasion of Sicily and an escort carrier group off Salerno. When he was assigned command of the

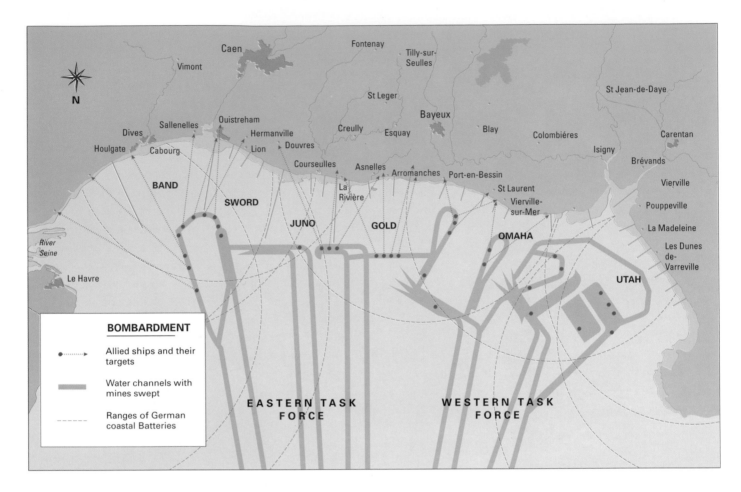

Above: The complex approaches for landing craft and bombardment ships showing how they approached the beaches and the batteries they were tasked with engaging. The duels between the German coastal batteries and warships are a forgotten epic of D-Day.

Right: An M4 Sherman on the beach in training. Care had to be taken to ensure that tanks were proofed against seawater if they were landing over the beach. On the day itself there was a considerable swell, and many vehicles were swamped before they were even through the surf.

Eastern Naval Task Force he worked the ships' crews hard in a series of realistic exercises. On D-Day, the high speed and manoeuvrability of his flagship allowed him to control his entire sector and though assigned no bombardment tasks *Scylla* opened fire at shore targets at 05:31 hours and at 07:29 hours.

There were five bombarding forces off Normandy. Force 'A', under Rear Admiral M Deyo USN aboard the USS *Tuscaloosa*, was covering Utah beach. Bombarding Force 'C', under Rear Admiral C. Bryant USN aboard the USS *Texas*, was assigned to Omaha beach. Force 'K', commanded by Capt EWL Longley-Cook RN aboard the cruiser HMS *Argonaut*, covered Gold beach. Force 'E' under Rear Admiral FH Dalrymple-Hamilton RN aboard the cruiser HMS *Belfast*, was assigned to Juno. Finally, Force 'D', under Rear Admiral WR Patterson RN aboard the cruiser HMS *Mauritious* covered Sword beach.

At Utah beach, the Americans of the 4th Infantry Division had the 356mm (14in) battleship USS *Nevada*, the 381mm (15in) monitor HMS *Erebus*, and the cruisers USS *Tuscaloosa*, USS *Quincy*, HMS *Hawkins*, HMS *Enterprise* and HMS *Black Prince* as well as the Dutch gunboat HNMS *Soemba* on call, with eight destroyers in support.

At Omaha, the 1st Infantry Division had the 355mm (14in) battleship USS *Texas* and 304mm (12in) USS *Arkansas* with the cruisers HMS *Glasgow*, and FFS *Montcalm* and *Georges* of the Free French Navy on call. In addition there were eleven destroyers in the bombardment force.

The effectiveness of the US naval fire support became so highly valued by the US Army in Normandy and the Cotentin Peninsula that Admiral Kirk had to warn Gen Bradley that too much firing was wearing out the rifling on the guns that would soon be supporting landings in southern France.

In the British plan, the supporting fire of the warships would last 20 minutes longer than that allocated by the Americans, since the British were acutely aware of the German armour threat from the east and would be landing half an hour later than the Americans. At Gold beach the British were to have four cruisers on call, HMS *Orion*, *Ajax*, *Argonaut* and *Emerald* as well as the Dutch gunboat HNMS *Flores* and 13 destroyers including the Polish vessel ORP *Krakowiak*.

At Juno beach, the bombarding force supporting the Canadians consisted of the cruisers HMS *Belfast* and *Diadem* and eleven destroyers including the Free French FFS *Combattante*. Sword beach, on the other hand, had the 381mm (15in) battleships HMS *Warspite* and HMS *Ramillies*, the 15in monitor HMS *Roberts*, the cruisers HMS *Mauritius*, *Arethusa*, *Frobisher*, *Danal* and the Polish ORP *Dragon*. Among the 13 destroyers was the Norwegian HNMS *Svenner*.

Destroyers would provide a screen to protect the battle-ships and transports from attack by E-boats and U-boats.

Besides the 1213 warships that would be in action at D-Day, there were to be 4126 landing ships and landing craft, 736 ancillary vessels and 864 merchant ships. The landing craft ranged from the conventional troop- and vehicle-carrying variants like Landing Craft Assault (LCA) and Landing Craft Tank (LCT) to more exotic types. These included the LCGL (Landing Craft Gun Large) armed with two 119mm (4.7in) naval guns and between two and seven 20mm (0.78in) Oerlikon guns or two 119mm (4.7in) guns and two 2pdrs (40mm/1.57in). There were 14 LCT(R) (the rocket-firing variant) armed with 1064 127mm (5in) rockets in the Western Task Force and 22 in the Eastern, and LCA (HR) (Hedgerow), which fired a variant of the Hedgehog anti-submarine bomb to blast a path through minefields. In the front of the force LCS (M) (Landing Craft Support (Medium)) carried Forward Observation Officers (FOOs), equipped with radios and powerful binoculars who would direct and correct fire onto enemy positions.

With the prospect of poor weather and the almost inevitable congestion caused by so many vessels of all sizes operating in relatively confined waters, the naval planners knew that there would be losses and casualties – even without the attentions of the enemy.

Above: A German anti-tank gun in action. For lack of weapons, the Germans began to use captured Soviet and French guns mounted on new wheeled or tracked carriages. Many were effective, but there was always a problem of ammunition supply for the rather exotic calibres.

Off Utah, Assault Force 'U', Task Force 125, consisting of 12 convoys was under Rear Admiral DP Moon USN aboard the USS *Bayfield*. Assault Force 'O', Task Force 124, was assigned to Omaha. It consisted of nine convoys commanded by Rear Admiral L Hall Jr USN aboard the USS *Ancon*. Assault Force 'G' off Gold beach consisted of 16 convoys under command of Commodore Pennant RN aboard HMS *Bulolo*. Off Juno beach, Assault Force 'J', commanded by Commodore GN Oliver RN aboard HMS *Hilary* was made up of ten convoys. Finally at Sword beach, Rear Admiral AG Talbot RN aboard HMS *Largs* (formerly the French liner *Charles Plumier*) was to ensure that 12 convoys delivered their men and equipment to the Normandy shore.

There were follow-up forces for the British and American beaches. TF 126 or Follow-Up Force 'B' under Commodore CD Edgar USN on USS *Maloy* would bring US troops, while Follow-Up Force 'L' under Rear Admiral WE Parry would cover the Gold, Sword and Juno beaches.

Long before any of these ships had crossed the Channel, at 04:00 hours on Sunday 4 June, Lt George Honour, a 25-year-old officer in the Royal Naval Volunteer Reserve (RNVR) was in position with the smallest craft in the invasion. It was the midget submarine *X-23*, part of the COPP and he had arrived off the French coast near the mouth of the River Orne.

RESCUE AT SEA

As a branch of the US Armed Forces, the US Coast Guard (USCG) manned 97 vessels on D-Day, excluding landing craft and USCG-manned attack troop transports. For the crossing and the landings, 60 fast 25m (83ft) wooden-hulled cutters of the USCG Rescue Flotilla sailed alongside the landing craft. Commanded by Lt Comdr Alexander V Stewart USCG Reserve, their mission was to rescue men either in the water or from sinking craft. Within minutes of H-Hour a USCG cutter had picked up the first of 450 men to be saved on D-Day. By the close of Overlord, the USCG had picked up 1437 fighting men and one female nurse.

'I had a quick look through the periscope and saw a cow on the beach and a fixed light on the pier. I didn't expect them to leave any lights on. You could see the flare path of Caen airport and planes landing.'

The periscope on an X-Craft was 'about as big as a man's thumb' and so almost impossible for the enemy to see with the unaided eye. Clogstoun-Willmott recalled that 'there was no feather of water [from the periscope] and just a little stick sticking up... so it probably didn't look like a periscope.'

Despite its size it gave a clear image. During a pre-D-Day reconnaissance mission near the Point du Hoc, Clogstoun-Willmott was able to watch a German soldier on a French trawler. 'I was able to see this fellow quite distinctly, with his collar up and his rifle slung over his shoulder. I could even see the shape of the curved pipe he was smoking, one of the German cherrywood pipes.'

Off the D-Day beaches, George Honour realized he was too far to the right and so moved along the coast. He took a fix from two churches. 'Once we had fixed our position bang on, there was nothing to do but wait.'

The X-Craft had a tiny galley with an electric cooker known jokingly as a 'gluepot' and the crew took it in turns to cook rations like bully beef and baked beans. The heads, or lavatory, was in the escape hatch, which opened up to the front and rear compartments. Clogstoun-Willmott remembered the heads as 'a disgusting device... in the wet and dry chamber, a little compartment about two foot wide which you flooded to get somebody out while you were under water.'

The submarines were battery powered with a diesel engine for re-charging. This took about two to three hours and the crew had to ensure that they were away from the coastline so that the noise did not alert the Germans. The main problem was condensation which meant that everything inside was damp.

The crew of five took watches with two sleeping in the bunks above the batteries and in the control room. Three men ensured that the submarine remained correctly stationed off the beach.

On 4 June as he lay about a mile off the coast, Honour watched German staff cars and trucks with soldiers coming down to the beach. 'They were having their Sunday make and mend, *spielen* or whatever they did in Germany.' Some were swimming and playing with a beach ball. 'That amused us because they obviously hadn't any idea we were there or what was soon to happen.'

The X-Craft waited on the seabed until between 24:00 and 02:00 hours on Monday morning and surfaced. It did not have a conning tower, almost no freeboard and a thin periscope, so even on the surface it was hard to detect. The crew erected the radio antenna and received a coded message that read 'Not coming on Monday'. This meant diving and spending another 24 hours underwater. In all *X-20* and *X-23* spent a total of 64 out of 72 hours submerged.

'So we just sat there' said Honour, explaining that the crew had maintenance tasks, but had ceased to watch the coast since 'we had seen everything we ought to see'.

The boat had its own oxygen supply, but after 48 hours 'it's almost as good as a strong Bass (beer), so you start to get a bit ga-ga. It's like being half canned, half-tight (drunk), being shut up like that on oxygen. We played poker dice, we all lost a fortune but that was about all you could do.'

On the afternoon of 5 June, in rough weather, minesweepers cleared ten channels called the 'Spout' through the eastern end of the German mine field, to the Normandy beaches. Force 'U' had 16 Royal Navy Fleet Minesweepers assigned to clear its path, while Force 'O' had 17 RN and 11 USN Fleet and 20 RN and 18 USN Motor Minesweepers. Off the British and Canadian beaches, Force 'G' had 16 RN Fleet and 10 RN Motor Minesweepers, Force 'J' had 16 RN Fleet and ten RN Motor Minesweepers and

TANK LANDING CRAFT

The first tank landing craft (LCT) developed by the British in 1940 were too small for all but short sea operations. Pressed by Churchill to produce a craft with greater capacity and better seagoing capabilities, the Admiralty converted three shallow draft-tankers under construction in the late 1930s for use on the Maracaibo River in Venezuela. The bows were cut away and a new section with a bow door hinged at the bottom was attached. A 21m (68ft) long double ramp allowed tanks or vehicles to be driven on or off. As HMS *Bachaquero*, *Misoa* and *Tasajera*, they were all used on D-Day. The main type of Landing Ship Tank used at D-Day was the LST(2) designed by John C Niedermair and mass-produced in the USA for the Royal Navy and US Navy. It was capable of carrying 20 Sherman tanks. Between D-Day and the end of September 1944, one Royal Navy ship, the LST *416*, made no less than 28 cross-Channel runs from England to Normandy, operating almost like a modern roll-on/roll-off ferry.

surfaced and prepared to marshal the amphibious force.

LAND FORCES

The Allied forces allocated to the first wave of landings consisted of the US 1st Infantry Division 'The Big Red One' at Omaha and the 4th Infantry Division at Utah. At Gold, it was the British 50th Infantry Division and 8th Armoured Brigade, at Juno the Canadian 3rd Infantry Division and Canadian 2nd Armoured Brigade, while at Sword it was the British 3rd Infantry Division with the 27th Armoured Brigade. The objective by the close of D-Day was to link up all the beach heads, with the exception of Utah, and to have penetrated up to 16km (10 miles) inland to liberate the towns of Caen and Bayeux. If this was achieved, the Allies could use the good east–west road link between the two towns.

Opposite them was the German Seventh Army commanded by Gen Friedrich Dollman who though elderly, was judged, generously, as a

Above: GIs patiently file back onto a landing craft ready to practise their landing once more. One of the reasons why the invasion was delayed until 1944 was that there was a shortage of suitable landing craft, particularly once the number of landing beaches rose to five.

Right: The German forces in France before D-Day. Armoured formations were concentrated around Calais, and it was the delay in releasing them to move south west that proved critical in the early days of the invasion of Normandy.

Force 'S' had 24 RN Fleet and 30 RN Motor Minesweepers. When the 3.2km (2 mile) wide channels had been cleared, motor launches marked the beginning and the channel was then demarcated with dan buoys made more conspicuous with flags or lights.

South east of the Isle of Wight, Area 'Z', a rendezvous area code-named 'Picadilly Circus' had been prepared and it was here that the shipping would initially converge before moving south through the 'Spout' to the designated invasion beaches. The fleet was on its way and from 05:15 hours on 6 June a massive bombardment by warships and bombers began to pulverize the German coastal defences.

At 06:30 hours, landing craft began to move towards the beaches. Off the British beaches, the two X-Craft

THE BEST BATTLE IMPLEMENT

The Rifle, Caliber .30, M1 'Garand' was designed by John Garand of the Springfield Arsenal in the late 1920s and adopted by the US Army in 1936. It was a robust semi-automatic gas operated rifle that weighed 4.3kg (9 lb), was 1107mm (43ins) long and had an eight-round box magazine. Sights were set out to 1100m (1200yd). Though it had the minor tactical drawback that the clip was ejected with a distinctive ping when the last round had been fired, Gen George S. Patton described the M1 Garand as 'the best battle implement ever devised'.

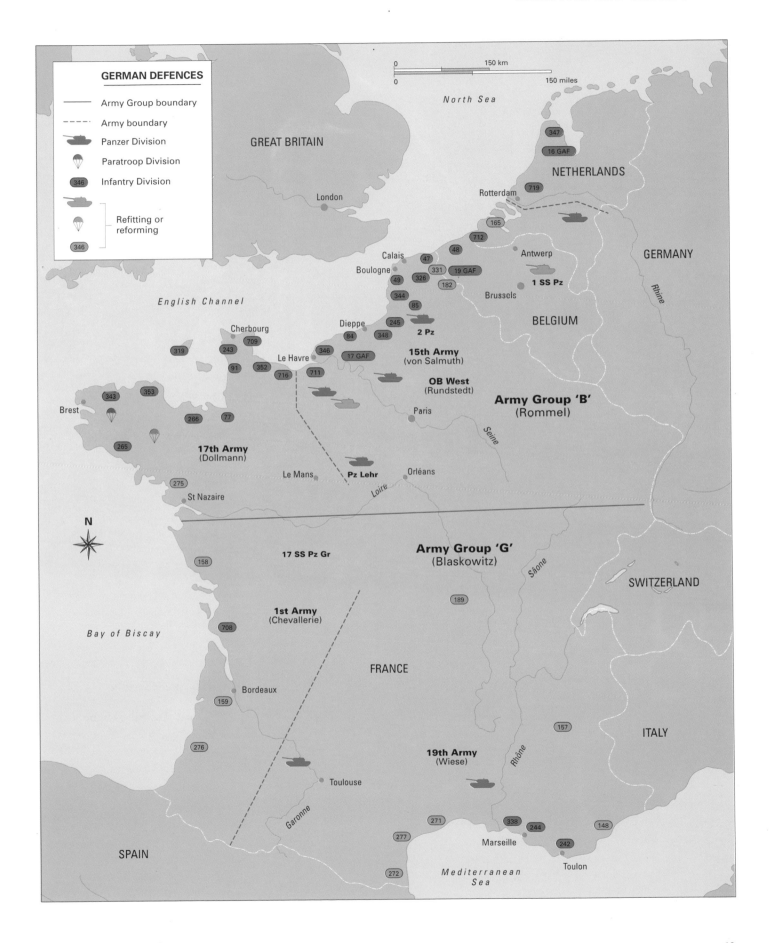

GERMAN DEFENCES

— Army Group boundary
-- Army boundary

Panzer Division

Paratroop Division

346   Infantry Division

⎱ Refitting or
⎰ reforming
346

GREAT BRITAIN

London

North Sea

0   150 km
0   150 miles

347
16 GAF

NETHERLANDS

Rotterdam   719

165

712

English Channel

48

Calais
47
Boulogne   331   19 GAF
49   326   182
344
85

Antwerp

Brussels

1 SS Pz

GERMANY

Rhine

BELGIUM

Cherbourg
709
319   243
91   352   716
343   353
266   77
265

Brest

Dieppe
84   348
346   17 GAF
245
711

2 Pz

15th Army
(von Salmuth)

OB West
(Rundstedt)

Le Havre

Paris

Seine

Army Group 'B'
(Rommel)

17th Army
(Dollmann)

Le Mans   **Pz Lehr**

Orléans

Loire

275

St Nazaire

N

158

17 SS Pz Gr

Army Group 'G'
(Blaskowitz)

Sâone

SWITZERLAND

1st Army
(Chevallerie)

189

708

Bay of Biscay

FRANCE

Bordeaux
159

157

ITALY

276

Garonne

Toulouse

19th Army
(Wiese)

Rhône

271
277

338   244

148

Marseille

242

SPAIN

272

Toulon

Mediterranean
Sea

competent officer by his colleagues, albeit one with no experience of war in the East. Ranged from west to east, the forces in the Normandy sector were the 243rd and 709th Divisions in the north of the Cotentin Peninsula around Cherbourg with the 91st Division in positions at its base near Carentan. On the coast between the rivers Vire and Orne were the 352nd and 716th Divisions with the 21st Panzer Division held in reserve around Caen.

Of all the German units defending the coast, the most significant was the 352nd Infantry Division. It was fresh, well-led and covered the Omaha beach head area. Its commander, Maj Gen Dietrich Kraiss had just put his troops through an anti-invasion exercise. A veteran of World War I, Kraiss had fought in Poland and France in World War II before taking command of the 169th Infantry Division in the invasion of the Soviet Union. It was during this campaign that he was awarded the Knight's Cross on 27 July 1942.

When, on 6 November 1943, he took command of the 352nd Infantry Division he brought extensive experience as well as energy to the task of preparing the formation to defend against an Allied attack. He emphasized training in close combat techniques against tanks, expansion of the coastal fortifications and ensured that young recruits were well-trained and fully integrated into the division.

On 6 June, he was at his Divisional headquarters near Littry where he urged an aggressive defence of the beaches. On D-Day, he at times directed the defence from a forward headquarters and from here visited regimental command posts and conferred with the commanders.

Following D-Day, the Americans thought that they had eliminated the 352nd Infantry Division, but Kraiss had in fact pulled it back to a new line 20km (12 miles) from the beaches. It held its new position until reinforcements were able to stiffen the line at St Lô. In fighting in August, Kraiss was severely wounded and died near St Lô. He was awarded posthumous Oak Leaves to his Knight's Cross.

The Germans had classified their units as capable of 'full attack', 'limited attack', 'full defence' and 'limited defence'. The 352nd was a 'full attack' formation. The area into which the US 82nd and 101st Airborne Divisions would be jumping, was occupied by the German 6th Parachute Regiment. This would be a battle between the elite airborne forces of two nations.

Left: A relaxed moment in a port in Britain as tracked vehicles are unloaded from a landing craft during loading trials. Though men and vehicles were packed onto landing craft, it was critical that they should be able to exit quickly as soon as the ramps went down in France.

Above: A German 37mm (1.45in) anti-aircraft gun in the ground role. Though the crew are dressed in camouflage smocks they are from the Heer or Army and not the Waffen-SS. Splinter pattern smocks had been introduced for the Army after experience on the Eastern Front.

However, in many areas the Germans had under-strength units filled with over-age men, while others were composed of former prisoners of war including Cossacks, Georgians, North-Caucasians, Turkomans, Armenians, Volga-Tatars, Azerbaijanis and Volga-Finns, mostly from areas of Central Asia in the Soviet Union. Though many of these men in these *Ost* (or East) Battalions could be expected to put up at best token resistance, particularly after heavy air and sea bombardment, their reinforced concrete bunkers would give them good protection and if they decided to fight, would make them hard to eliminate. The German propaganda ministry had made a virtue out of the necessity of using these former Soviet PoWs to bring German units up to strength.

They were portrayed in magazines like *Signal* as new allies in the fight against Bolshevism. German NCOs and officers in the battalions would help to ensure that the troops remained in position when the fighting started.

In the summer of 1943, several German battalions were sent from the Seventh Army to Russia and replaced by 21 Ost battalions. On D-Day more than a quarter of the Seventh Army's battalions were Ost formations. When they surrendered, their Asian appearance confused British and US troops who reported that they had captured 'Chinese' troops.

A photograph was even published showing Rommel inspecting a squad of Sikh soldiers, members of Infantry Regiment No 950. Captured in North Africa, they had fallen under the influence of Subhas Chandra Bose, the Indian nationalist leader who had established himself in Germany, and modelling himself on Hitler, adopted the title *Netaji* (Leader). Out of 15,000 Indian prisoners, 4000 had volunteered for service on the side of the Axis powers,

and by the end of the war had been absorbed into the *Waffen-SS*.

Interrogated after the war, Lt Gen Max Pemsel, Chief of Staff of the Seventh Army, recalled that the only full-strength division in the sector was the 319th Infantry Division on the Channel Islands. Though the Seventh Army pressed to have the garrison reduced and troops assigned to mainland France, Hitler was adamant that this tiny patch of British territory was to be held.

Just as units varied in quality, so too did equipment and weapons. Automatic weapons had increased rates of fire and sub-machine guns were widely available. In the M1 Garand, the Americans had a solid and reliable self-loading rifle – superior to the bolt action rifles carried by the British and many Germans.

The Germans had the 15cm (5.9in) *Nebelwerfer*, a highly effective multi-barrelled rocket launcher which the Allies had first encountered in Tunisia and because of the sound of the rockets in flight, the British had nicknamed them 'Moaning Minnies' and the Americans 'Screaming Meamies'. The *Nebelwefer* had a range of 6700m (4.2 miles) and a 10kg (22lb) warhead.

However the artillery in the Seventh Army's sector included many captured weapons that came from a total

Below: The sky fills with the black bursts of AA fire as a Luftwaffe bomber attempts an evening attack. Gunners were told on D-Day that every aircraft in the sky would be Allied and warned not to fire on them. Special invasion stripes were applied to aircraft to aid identification.

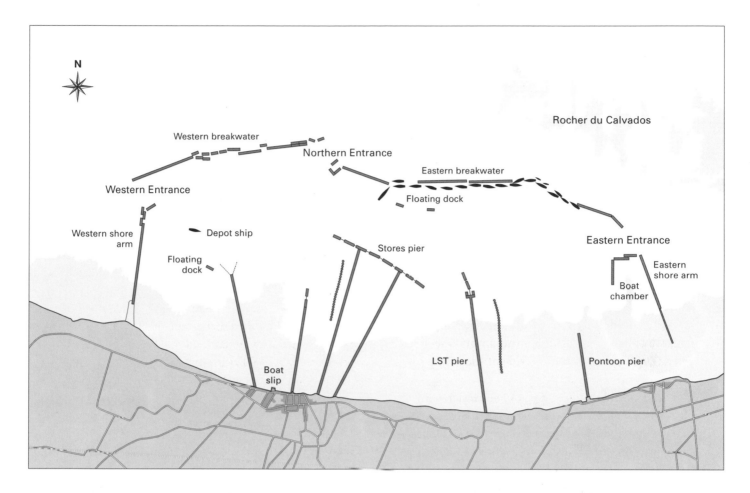

Above: The British Mulberry Harbour at Arromanches that fared better than the US at Omaha beach in the fierce July storms. The harbours were a mix of block ships and huge concrete breakwaters as well as piers that were adjustable for the rise and fall of the tides.

of nine different countries. Calibres varied, as did the availability of ammunition, some guns having only half their allocation.

The difference between the Germans and Allies was in the quantities of ordnance and equipment that were available to the combatants. Once the Allies were ashore in strength they could deploy large numbers of heavy and medium guns and howitzers which would be able to neutralize German positions. However, quantity and quality sometimes did not coincide.

The US-built M4 Sherman tank had its faults, most notably a tendency to catch fire when hit. This earned it such grim nicknames as 'Ronson', after the cigarette lighter that was guaranteed to 'Light First Time', or from the Germans, 'Tommy Cooker'. However, it was fast and manoeuvrable and easy to build and so was mass-produced by Alco, Baldwin, Detroit, Federal Machine, Fisher Body, Ford, Lima, Pacific Car, Pressed Steel Car and Pullman-Standard. Between 1942 and 1946 these companies built 40,000 Shermans.

The huge numbers meant that in Normandy in 1944, crews of tanks that had been knocked out simply returned to

depots and drew new tanks. The Sherman entered service with the British in time to see action at the battle of El Alamein in 1942. For crews that had struggled with unreliable engines and transmissions, the Sherman's rugged reliability and uncomplicated features were welcome after the flawed British designs. For the huge conscripted US Army that was built up after 1941, the M4 was a vehicle that was easy to operate.

In January 1943, a new 17pdr (76mm/2.99in) anti-tank gun was fitted to a number of Sherman M4 tanks. This combination produced the most powerfully armed British tank of World War II. Following D-Day, the British Sherman Firefly was the only tank capable of taking on the German Panther and Tiger tanks on anything like equal terms. It was issued on the basis of one tank per troop, because of the shortage of 17pdr guns. By 1945, the supply was more generous.

Above: The spartan interior of a C-47 Skytrain with US paratroops loaded with spare parachutes, main 'chutes and their weapons and equipment. Men carried huge loads out to the aircraft, knowing that they would need to be self-sufficient for some time after landing.

Initial conversion work was done with the M4A3 and the new machine was known as the Sherman IVC (Firefly). However, the bulk of conversions were done on the M4A4, designated the Sherman VC. The hull machine gun was removed to allow the tank to carry more ammunition for its main armament. The 17pdr fired a 7.65kg (17lb) shell with a muzzle velocity of 950m per second (2900ft per second). It was capable of penetrating 130mm (5.12in) of armour at 1000m (3300ft). The rate of fire was 10 rounds per minute. The Firefly was instantly recognizable by the 17pdr gun's long overhang and muzzle brake as well as the extension on the turret rear to accommodate the breech of the big anti-tank gun.

The Germans had superior tanks like the Tiger and Panther, but they were only available in limited numbers. The PzKpfw V Ausf D Panther had been rushed into action in 1943 from the production lines of Maschinenfabrik Augsburg-Nurnburg in time for the disastrous action at Kursk and many suffered from mechanical breakdowns and

problems with their tracks. It had a crew of five, weighed between 43.7 tonnes and 46.2 tonnes (43 and 45.5 tons) and was armed with a 7.5cm (2.95in) KwK42 (L/70) gun with 79 rounds of ammunition and one co-axial 7.92mm (0.31in) MG34 machine gun. Top speed from the Maybach HI230 P30 700hp (522kW) petrol engine was 55km/h (34mph). Maximum armour thickness was 120mm (4.7in) and unlike the Tiger, it was well-angled to deflect hits by solid shot. Later Panthers had a hull machine gun and an AA mount by the commander's hatch. In all 5508 Panthers were built but production rates were initially very slow with only 12 being produced each week.

So many of the German tanks were the relatively old, but battle proven and reliable, PzKpfw IV, built to a 1934 specification from the Germany Army Weapons Department. It entered service in 1939 and was in production until 1945 with a total of 9000 vehicles being built by Krupp. The same chassis was used for the up-gunned and armoured tanks and despite the increase in weight, the tank enjoyed good mobility and an excellent power-to-weight ratio.

It had a crew of five and was armed with a 75mm (2.95in) L/48 gun and two 7.92mm (0.31in) machine guns. Maximum armour protection was 80mm (3.15in) and minimum 8mm (0.31in). The PzKpfw IV Ausf H weighed 25 tonnes (24.6 tons), was 7m (23ft) long, 2.9m (9.5ft) wide and 2.65m (8.6ft) high. It was powered by a Maybach HL108TR V-12 petrol engine that developed 250hp (186kW) at 3000rpm and gave a road speed of 38km/h (24mph) and range of 180km (112 miles).

The chassis was used for a range of assault guns like the StuG IV and tank hunters like the Jagdpanzer IV, which with their low silhouette were to prove lethally effective in ambush in the lush vegetation of Normandy in June and July 1944.

For Allied tank crews, the real terror was the Tiger. Many PzKpfw IV would be erroneously reported as Tigers by nervous tank crews in Normandy. The PzKpfw VI Tiger mounted the 8.8cm (3.46in) KwK 36 gun with 92 rounds of HE or Armour Piercing Capped, Ballistic Capped (APCBC) ammunition as well as one 7.92mm (0.31in) MG 34 machine gun. Though the Tiger had none of the sloping angles of the Panther or later Tiger II, it made up for some of these design flaws by sheer strength – the thinnest armour on the Tiger was 25mm (1in) and the thickest in the most vulnerable areas was 100mm (3.94in). Its Maybach HL 230 P45 12-cylinder petrol engine developed 700hp (522kW) and gave a maximum road speed of 38km/h (24mph). The crew of five

ALLIED AIR STRENGTH

On the morning of 6 June 1944, the total Allied air strength would be:

- Heavy Bombers (Strategic Forces): 3440
- Medium and Light Bombers (Tactical Forces): 930
- Fighter Bombers and Fighters (day and night): 4190
- Troop Carriers and Transports: 1360
- Coastal Command (40 USAAF attached): 1070
- Reconnaissance: 520
- Air/Sea Rescue: 80

TOTAL: 11,590

were hand-picked and highly trained and would find the thinly armoured Shermans easy targets.

The arithmetic of quantity versus quality might make sense for the Allied planners in headquarters in Britain, but it was not encouraging for the crews who would be statistics in this lethal balance sheet.

AIR POWER

It is to be assumed that it was with some reluctance that Air Chief Marshal Sir Arthur Harris, the tough chief of RAF Bomber Command, agreed to deploy his heavy bomber bombers squadrons in a tactical role against the Normandy beachhead.

He saw the bombers as a strategic weapon that should be used against German cities and industry in Operation Pointblank and was confident that the remorseless use of bombers against the German civil, industrial and military infrastructure would bring about victory. However he proved, in Eisenhower's words 'one of the most effective members of my team – he met every request'.

In turn, Harris would tell Eisenhower that it had been an honour and delight to serve under him. Harris brought all his personal drive to the 'Transportation Plan', the bombing campaign to hit communications links to Normandy. Although he had no reservations about German civilian deaths in Operation Pointblank, saying 'if you can't hit the works, hit the workers', he was concerned that there would be French civilian deaths in the Transportation Plan due to the inherent inaccuracy of heavy bombers operating at night.

He supported the plan that reached its climax on the evening of 7 June when RAF Lancasters of 617 Squadron dropped massive 5500kg (12,000lb) bombs on a railway tunnel under the Loire which cut the last rail link between southern France and Normandy.

Bombers were classified as either heavy or medium, while fighter-bombers were conventional fighter aircraft fitted with either two underwing bombs or eight rockets. In accordance with the Overlord plan, medium bombers had been attacking the roads, bridges, railway goods yards and communications bottle necks around Normandy. This would isolate the battlefield, and prevent the Germans from moving reinforcements quickly from around Calais. By 1 June only three of the 26 bridges across the Seine were still standing, while in earlier raids, between March and June, over 1500 French locomotives, 50 per cent of the available total, had been destroyed. However, the attacks were not just confined to the Normandy area – sufficient numbers were directed at targets further afield to convince the Germans that Allied landings would be

Above: A USAAF B-17 bomber flies over the bomb and shell ravaged French coastline. The attacks on the coastal positions by bombers enjoyed mixed results, with some neutralising batteries and bunkers and some hitting farmland well inland.

further to the north. The RAF was already committed to attacking the V1 Fzg-76 flying bomb sites that were being constructed in northern France and dumped 36,580 tonnes (36,000 tons) of bombs onto identified V1 sites.

To counter the disruption to the railways 10,000 men from the *Organization Todt* were taken off defence construction tasks and 15,700 troops assigned to reconstruction work. Despite their efforts, by May, around 1500 trains were immobilized and instead of 100 military supply trains travelling from Germany to France only 32 made the journey in late May. German *Reichsbahn* officials said that the greatest damage was done by the attacks on the marshalling yards and locomotive sheds. They considered air attacks on bridges and moving trains and sabotage by the Resistance less dangerous, though still troublesome.

The heavy bomber attacks were conducted mostly by the four-engined Avro Lancaster, a bomber that could carry bomb loads of up to 10,000kg (22,000lb), but for normal bombing operations carried between 6350kg and 8200kg (14,000lb and 18,000lb). The USAAF used the Boeing B-17 Flying Fortress and Consolidated Vultee Liberator capable of carrying 2700kg and 3600kg (6000lb and 8000lb) respectively.

Though all bombers could dump tons of bombs onto target areas, they were not very accurate, so out of every 1000 bombs that were dropped on the German gun positions at Merville, only 50 fell inside the defences and only two actually hit a casemate.

Medium bombers were normally twin-engined and included types like the Douglas Boston, Martin Marauder, B-25 Mitchell. They could carry loads of 2000kg, 2500kg and 2000kg (4400lb, 5500lb and 4400lb) of bombs respectively. They would provide air support closer to the front line, and like all the RAF and USAAF aircraft, except the four-engined bombers, would have bold black and white 'invasion stripes'. These consisted of two black and three white stripes around the wings and fuselage to prevent trigger happy Allied anti-aircraft gunners shooting at them as had happened during the landings on Sicily. The ships' crews off Normandy were also assured that every aircraft they saw on D-Day would be Allied.

Fighters included the 703km/h (437mph) single-seater North American P-51D Mustang, 'the Cadillac of the Skies' and the 721km/h (448mph) Supermarine Spitfire XIV, though the two-seater Bristol Beaufighter and De Havilland Mosquito with their powerful nose mounted armament were also used in this role.

The Hawker Typhoons fitted with four 20mm (0.78in) cannon and up to 900kg (2000lb) of bombs or eight 76.2mm (3in) rockets were employed against a variety of targets including the German coastal radar stations which would be capable of giving early warning of the approaching Overlord ships and aircraft. By the evening after D-Day, (D+1) all 16 survivors of the original 92 radar sites along the northern coast of France and Belgium had been attacked and destroyed or badly damaged. The cost had been high because many sites were well protected by Flak emplacements.

Group Captain Desmond Scott commanding 123 Wing of the 2nd Tactical Air Force recalled grimly, 'As our squadrons weaved their way into the strongest parts of the Atlantic Wall, the radar site defenders fought back like demented tigers. In attacking heavily defended ground targets there was no rule of thumb, no helpful advice to give. The experienced pilot shared the same deadly flight path as the experienced.'

German radars included *Mammut*, *Wassermann* and Freya early warning radars, *Seetakt* coastal surveillance, *Giant Würzburg* for fighter control and *Würzburg* for Flak batteries.

The Allied parachute assault on the flanks of the D-Day beaches would not be possible without the vast numbers of C-47 Dakotas provided to the RAF and in use by transportation squadrons of the USAAF.

The British Army used the Airspeed Horsa attack glider that carried 24 men or equivalent cargo, while the US Army used the Waco CG-4A glider that could carry 29 men, vehicles or cargo. The British aircraft was built from plywood, a light non-strategic material while the American one was stronger and was constructed on a tubular metal frame. British glider pilots asserted that wings and even fuselage

would adequately absorb the shock of hitting an obstacle when landing.

The huge numbers of Allied aircraft would ensure that by day, the skies of Normandy would remain friendly, but night fall would allow *Luftwaffe* bombers to sneak in, and for all Allied aircraft, German flak would remain a serious threat until the end of the war.

Rommel would say of airpower: 'Anyone who has to fight, even with the most modern weapons, against an enemy in complete control of the air fights like a savage against modern European troops.'

Of the Allied aircraft total, 6080 were American and 5510 were from British or from other Allied forces. In addition there were 3500 troop transport and cargo gliders.

The Allies enjoyed a massive superiority in all types of aircraft, whether fighters, medium bombers, heavy bombers or transports. The transport aircraft were to lift the two US airborne and one British Division into the D-Day beachhead area to drop paratroopers and gliders before dawn. On the day, the Allied air forces flew 14,674 sorties at a cost of 127 aircraft lost, mostly to flak.

In France, the aircraft available to Field Marshal Hugo Sperrle's 3rd Air Force *Luftflotte III* included the Messerschmitt Bf 109 and Focke Wulf Fw 190 fighters. By D-Day, the *Luftwaffe* was a shadow of the force that had spearheaded the Blitzkrieg victories of 1939 to 1942 and had only 130 bombers in the Normandy theatre. These included the heavy Heinkel He 177, that following engine fires and other losses, Hitler had derided as 'obviously the worst junk ever manufactured', and the more versatile Junkers Ju 88.

Right: A soldier of the Canadian Regiment de Levis seen shortly after his arrival in Britain, part of the massive build-up of American and Canadian forces.

On D-Day, *Luftwaffe* fighters flew 70 sorties and the Germans estimated their losses as being three times greater than those of the Allies. Anti-shipping strikes accounted for only five Allied ships destroyed, but air-dropped mines sank 26.

Sperrle's command, with its headquarters in Paris, covered France, Belgium and Holland and could field about 950 aircraft. It was structured in three air corps and one fighter corps. *Fliegerkorps III*, commanded by Lt Gen

for anti-shipping and coastal operations. *Fliegerkorps X* was also employed in anti-shipping attacks and had 130 bombers and 30 torpedo bombers. It was commanded by Lt Gen Alexander Holle with its headquarters at Angers. Finally the *Jagdkorps II* consisted of *JagDivision 4* with 71 day fighters and 29 night fighters and *JagDivision 5* with 29 day fighters. It was commanded by Lt Gen Werner Junck with his headquarters at Coulommiers and additional headquarters at Bernay and Rennes.

Prior to D-Day, the *Luftwaffe* flew reconnaissance missions over Britain, but the Americans record only one air raid, when on the night of 30 May, bombs were dropped on a camp near Falmouth in Cornwall causing a few casualties to an ordnance battalion.

However, airpower alone would not win the battle; soldiers would be needed on the ground to eliminate the enemy. To do this, they would need ammunition, fuel and rations to keep them in the field, operating effectively.

MULBERRY, PLUTO AND LOGISTICS

As far back as 1942, the Allies realized that they could not rely on capturing a working port early in the campaign to liberate Europe. On 19 August 1942, Operation Jubilee, the disastrous raid on Dieppe, had cost the Canadians 3379 men out of a force of 5000 and had proved that a direct assault from the sea on a port was too high a price to pay. However, if they were to win, the Allies would need to be able to deliver men, weapons and consumable stores like food, fuel and ammunition by sea in huge quantities and faster than the Germans could replenish their own stores from other parts of France and western Europe.

The Allies' novel solution to a lack of port facilities in their beachhead area was to build two prefabricated harbours that could be towed in sections across the Channel and positioned off the British and American beachheads. On 30 May 1942, Churchill had set in motion the project with a terse memo to Mountbatten:

Piers for use on beaches
CCO or deputy

They must float up and down with the tide.
The anchor problem must be mastered.
Let me have the best solution worked out.

Alfred Bulowins, had its headquarters at Compiègne with 50 aircraft. Its role was close support and tactical reconnaissance. *Fliegerkorps IX* with its headquarters at Beauvais was commanded by Lt Gen Dietrich Peltz and had 130 bombers

Don't argue the matter. The difficulties will argue for themselves.

In Britain, in great secrecy, construction companies were instructed to build 'ferro concrete caissons' – in effect, gigantic concrete boxes as tall as a six-storey building, which would be sunk as breakwaters around the harbours. A senior British officer was sent to reassure the workers on the project that they were indeed doing vital war work, since a rumour was circulating at the yards that these huge concrete structures were in some way merely destined for the post-war building trade.

German aerial reconnaissance aircraft had photographed the huge structures, but as Field Marshal Keitel and Lt Gen Jodl explained to their US Army interrogator, Maj Kenneth Hechler, after the war: 'We believed their purpose was to form new quays in place of those destroyed in (a) port.' German planners were still convinced that the Allies would need a large working port to unload sufficient vehicles and supplies to prosecute the war in Europe.

'Mulberries', as the prefabricated harbours were code-named, were to be assembled at St Laurent in the US V Corps area and at Arromanches by the British beaches on the Normandy coast. The harbours consisted of an outer belt of 70 block ships, code-named 'Gooseberries', that acted both as breakwaters and also as anti-aircraft positions. Among the block ships was the old French battleship *Courbet* that was towed across the Channel and a Royal Netherlands Navy cruiser. These ships were deliberately flooded and half-submerged a short distance from the coast and were reported as 'sunk' by German coastal batteries. Though now lying on the sea bed, the *Courbet*, flying the Tricolour, was manned by French sailors who operated the AA guns.

The 'Gooseberries' were the brainchild of Rear Admiral William Tennant who from January 1943, was in command of the planning, preparation, towing and placement of the Mulberry harbours. He had a difficult time with the Admiralty who were reluctant to give up ships to be sunk as block ships, but Tennant was convinced that they would be needed to protect the harbours. At one stage, his deputy said of the Admiralty: 'We came here to get a Gooseberry and all we seem to have got is a raspberry!'

Within the block-ship belt were over 200 caissons. Once they were in position, a complex of floating causeways named 'Beetles' would be connected to 'Whale' pierheads which would allow ships to anchor beside loading ramps which moved with the rise and fall of the tide. Each harbour, made from two million tonnes (19.6 million tons) of steel and concrete, would be the size of Dover, but would have to

Operation Pluto was a remarkable feat of British engineering, distinguished in its originality, pursued with tenacity and crowned by complete success. This creative energy helped win the war.

Prime Minister Winston Churchill

be operating in two weeks. To move over 600 'Mulberry' units to Normandy would require 200 tugs (every vessel in Britain) as well as boats requisitioned from the United States. They would be moved from sites at Portland, Poole, Plymouth, Selsey and Dungeness. Each harbour enclosed an area of over five square kilometres (two square miles).

In 100 days, 2,500,000 men, 500,000 vehicles and four million tonnes (3.9 million tons) of stores were landed at Mulberry 'B', 'Port Winston', at Arromanches. Though the American port at Omaha was later badly damaged in storms, the British one survived and though intended to operate for three months in the summer was still in use eight months after D-Day.

Once the coast was secured, a fuel depot was to be set up at Port en Bessin and linked by flexible pipes to offshore booms where tankers could pump fuel ashore. Later, when Cherbourg had been secured, 'Pluto' or 'Pipe Line Under the Ocean' was established. It would allow petrol to be pumped directly from a 1,890,000-litre (500,000-gal) reservoir at Shanklin on the Isle of Wight off the south coast of Britain through four lines 450km (280 mile) long to logistic bases in France – an operation which would safer and faster than sending tankers across the Channel. The pumping stations in Britain were disguised as seaside beach huts. The plan was to extend the pipeline eastwards as Allied forces liberated more of France, and eventually build a second Pluto from Dungeness to a point near Boulogne. By the time it ceased operations, Pluto had pumped one million kilolitres (112 million gallons) of fuel to France.

However, before Mulberry could be put in place and Pluto could start pumping, in the first 24 hours of D-Day the Allies would need to land 175,000 men, 1500 trucks, 3000 guns and 10,000 trucks on the beaches. With only a few days to go, both men and vehicles were massed in woodland close to the docks on the English south coast.

Right: Jeeps, trucks and soldiers nose forward into a Landing Ship in a harbour in southern England. The Jeeps are marked with the white star within a circle that enabled Allied ground attack pilots to identify them as friendly forces.

CHAPTER FOUR

SPECIAL OPERATIONS

Though the bulk of Operation Overlord would be a huge amphibious attack supported by large scale airborne landings, there were some targets like coastal batteries and bridges that would require attacks by specialist troops. Though the gun sites could also be bombarded by warships, these direct assaults were a way of guaranteeing that enemy guns would not disrupt the landings. Each attack would become a separate epic action within the larger-scale attacks in Normandy.

ALTHOUGH 73 IDENTIFIED coastal gun positions around Normandy had been pounded from the air, Allied planners could not be certain that the guns inside the massive concrete emplacements had been destroyed. If they were even still partially effective they could cause casualties and slow down and disrupt the Allied landings by shelling ships and landing craft.

Two positions were identified as critical to the landings. At the Pointe du Hoc, which a typing error in Allied plans labelled as the Pointe du Hoe, the Germans had concrete casemates which were believed to house 155mm (6.1in) guns with a range of 23km (15.5 miles). These guns could engage shipping running in to Utah beach as well as some around Omaha.

At the eastern edge of the beaches, on Sword beach, the Germans had constructed another battery position of four two-metre (6.5ft) thick casemates on high ground about 2.5km (1 mile) inland, at Merville. The observation post

Left: British infantry and airborne troops examine a German anti-tank gun position after the landings. Though it has been hit by shell fire, the gun itself is intact and there is a slot in the concrete casemate so that it can fire along the sea front to enfilade any attackers.

Above: A flotilla of LCAs carrying US Rangers moves out from harbour into the Channel. Landing craft crews worked hard to learn how to run into the beach on a shelving shore, off load their cargo of men or vehicles and then, with engines full astern, pull back off the beach.

(OP) for the battery was at the edge of Sallenelles bay and was linked to the guns by a buried telephone cable. The battery was believed to house 150mm (5.9in) guns which, like those at the Pointe du Hoc, would be lethal to Allied shipping. At Merville, these guns were feared to have a range of over 12km (7 miles).

Allied planners also identified the Caen Canal and river Orne, running from Caen to the sea at Ouistreham, as a key feature. If the bridges across these wide water obstacles were demolished by the Germans, it would prevent the Allies breaking out eastwards and would help the Germans contain the beach head. Worse still, if the Germans held the bridges they could cross them to attack the Sword beaches near Ouistreham.

The only way in which the Pointe du Hoc could be neutralized with complete certainty was by an assault from the sea, but at this point, the cliffs were 30m (130ft) high. The men tasked with the mission of destroying the battery, the US 2nd Ranger Battalion, looked at the problem and came up with some novel solutions. At the foot of the cliffs was a narrow rocky beach. DUKWs fitted with 30m (100ft) firemens' ladders, on loan from the London Fire Brigade, would land and deploy the troops. In addition, small assault ladders and rocket propelled grapnels and ropes would be used. The Rangers practised cliff assaults on the chalk cliffs on the Isle of Wight, and Swanage in Dorset. Their plan could work, as long as the German garrison had been stunned by the air and sea bombardment that would include broadsides from the battleship USS *Texas*.

At the bridges over the Caen Canal and river Orne near Benouville there would be no air attacks or naval gunfire support. The men of the 'D' Company, the 2nd Battalion Oxfordshire and Buckinghamshire Light Infantry under

FORECASTING D-DAY

The three key Allied weather forecasting teams were the British Central Forecasting Office at Dunstable on the Bedfordshire Downs, the US Army Air Force facility at Widewing near Teddington in the Thames Valley and the Admiralty in London. The USAAF at Widewing favoured launching Operation Overlord on 5 and 6 June because they were convinced that the Atlantic low front 'L5', that had brought bad weather, would be followed by 'L6' but this would north along the coast of Greenland, not towards Norway. Dunstable and the Admiralty demurred, convinced it would go east rather than north. It was left to James Stagg to examine the data and give his advice.

Major John Howard would land in gliders almost directly on the bridges and use the shock of their midnight airborne assault to take the positions. However, if the Germans were alert to the danger, the British soldiers would die before they were out their seats in the glider – surprise was critical.

ACTION AT MERVILLE

At the Merville battery, 9th Battalion the Parachute Regiment under Colonel Terence Otway would parachute into a Dropping Zone (DZ) at Varville 3km (2 miles) south-east of the position. The men would be faced with formidable defences that included minefields, an anti-tank ditch, thick barbed wire, eight machine guns and a 2cm (0.78in) anti-aircraft gun.

Like parts in a complex jigsaw, each of these three dawn assaults had to work if the larger pieces of the D-Day operation were to fit together. All of these plans were daring and the men very well trained, but like all special operations, they needed a large element of luck.

By D-Day, the Special Air Service (SAS) that had begun as a small special forces unit in North Africa had expanded to a full brigade within the British 1st Airborne Corps under command of Brigadier Roderick McLeod.

It was composed of 1 SAS, under Lieutenant Colonel 'Paddy' Mayne, 2 SAS under Lt Col William Stirling, brother of

the SAS founder David Stirling, two Free French parachute battalions (3 and 4 SAS) and an independent company of Belgian paratroopers (5 SAS).

The SAS were now very proud of their identity and resented being part of 1st Airborne. As part of the Corps, the men were ordered to wear their SAS cap badge on a maroon Parachute Regiment beret, but many ignored the order. It produced the odd effect of some men like Mayne in the original sand beige berets and others wearing maroon. The same dilemma had faced the Ox and Bucks Light Infantry, their solution had been to wear their bugle horn cap badge with a Light Infantry green backing on the maroon beret.

However, there were other tensions within the SAS, brigade. While British veterans of the First and Eighth Armies might not speak to one another, 'the two French battalions... were prepared to fight each other on sight', recalled one veteran. The task of keeping these highly motivated but unconventional young men in hand and trained to the highest standards fell to Brigadier McLeod. He was one of the few British regulars to take an informed interest in clandestine war, and was almost the only professional British officer in

Below: Lieutenant Twm Stephens of the SAS dressed in civilian clothes, with two officers. Riding a bicycle accompanied by a railway worker and another member of the Resistance he conducted the close target reconnaissance of railway fuel tankers. They were hit by an air attack.

Above: A Commando in training holds a Fairbairn-Sykes Fighting Knife in his teeth. This was not done for effect - it left both hands free for climbing or crawling. Helmets were discarded by the Commandos in favour of woollen caps or later their distinctive green berets.

the brigade he commanded. Before the war, he had been an instructor at the Staff College, Camberley, and would be a post-war Deputy Chief of the Defence Staff.

In training in Britain, the SAS had been taught 'with indifferent success' simple phrases in French and German which led the Germans to believe that all members of the SAS were linguists. They also studied where best to place charges on generators (by practising at Kilmarnock power station), how to derail trains (at the local railway station) and how to locate underground telephone cables and junction boxes.

The Army planners saw the role of the SAS as similar to that of the conventional airborne forces who were dropped to secure the flanks of the D-Day beaches. Before he resigned

in protest, William Stirling managed to ensure that the SAS were not squandered in this role.

SAS operations in France, like many of those in Italy beforehand, were aimed at cutting or disrupting German supply lines leading north to the Normandy battlefields and later slowing their withdrawal following the Allied breakout.

SAS operations in France followed a proven procedure. First an advance party with a Phantom signals section or one or two SAS officers were parachuted into the area to establish contact with the Resistance. Phantom, or 'F' Squadron GHQ Liaison Regiment, was the signals squadron for the SAS Brigade. It consisted of a headquarters and four patrols commanded by Major JJ Astor. Two patrols were attached to 1 SAS and two to 2 SAS. Phantom operators relayed a constant stream of information back to England from SAS bases in France after D-Day. Once a Phantom signals section was in place and operating and a good DZ had been located, the main party arrived.

Squadron-sized bases were established in remote wooded areas and through the summer of 1944, parachute drops of arms, including mortars and anti-tank guns, Jeeps, ammunition, explosives and supplies were delivered to the SAS and local Resistance groups. The only drawback to operations in the summer months of 1944 was that the nights were very short, which limited the cover of darkness. The alternative approach was a 'blind' drop into an unprepared DZ. Though this sounds hazardous the location was usually reasonably close to an existing SAS base.

According to SOE agents, who worked with the SAS in France, the SAS behaved with some carelessness in the thick of enemy territory. They were sent in knowing little of France or of the Resistance war, and, according to Col Barry of SOE, regimental pride made them reluctant to accept guidance from the SOE headquarters in Baker Street, London.

ENTER THE JEDS

In the United States, the Office of Strategic Services (OSS) had decided to develop a role in France. This produced the 'Jedburgh' teams or 'Jeds'. The name was derived from the town near the training base in Scotland. Eighty-six teams, consisting of a French officer with an American or British officer or NCO, were parachuted into France and were responsible for organizing and supplying the Resistance as well as launching attacks on the Germans before D-Day. They had a strong political function, ensuring that the US secret services had some control over covert operations in France.

The RAF and USAAF used both bombers and transport aircraft to deliver the agents and soldiers for these operations. The advantage of bombers like the Armstrong Whitworth Whitley, Albermarle, Handley Page Halifax and Short Stirling Mark IV, was that containers could be stowed in the bomb bay and released quickly and accurately over the DZ. Dedicated transport aircraft like the DC-3 were more versatile and could be used to deliver paratroopers and cargo or evacuate casualties.

Below: The D-Day team, Allied Naval Commander Bertram Ramsay, Supreme Allied Commander (SAC) Dwight Eisenhower, commander Allied Expeditionary Air Force Trafford Leigh-Mallory, Deputy SAC Arthur Tedder, Commander 21st Army Group Bernard Montgomery.

Prior to D-Day, all transport aircraft were allocated to the British and American airborne divisions, but after 6 June, the SAS operations were delivered to every part of France and kept re-supplied. The British aircraft came from 33 Group, 46 Group and sometimes RAF Tempsford.

Contact between the pilot and the ground reception group as the aircraft began its run into the DZ was greatly assisted by the introduction of the S-Phone. This little radio was 457 x 203 x 101mm (18 x 8 x 4in) and weighed only 5.4kg (12lbs) with belt and batteries. The S-Phone had a range of 16km (10 miles) for ground-to-air communications if the aircraft was flying at 90m (300ft), but the range increased up to 80km (50miles) if the aircraft was at 1,800m (6,000ft).

The code names for SAS operations in France reflected a distinctly British character, partly literary and partly nostalgic for London life. In the four months following D-Day,

One day a fence was put up around the camp. The NCOs were sent for and told that anyone caught outside would be court-martialled. Nobody got out. We had the best briefing I have ever known in the forces; even the private soldiers were present. There were scale models, photographs of guns, minefields and so on.

Sergeant George Self
8th Battalion Durham Light Infantry, British 50th Infantry Division

the SAS carried out 43 operations. They ranged from 'Wolsey' and 'Benson' in the north near the Somme, to 'Defoe', 'Titanic' and 'Trueform' in Normandy, 'Samwest', 'Derry', 'Dinson/Grog', and 'Cooney' in Brittany, 'Gaff' and 'Bunyan' near Paris, 'Haft' near Le Mans and 'Dunhill', 'Dickens', 'Shakespeare', 'Chaucer', 'Gain' and 'Spenser' along

GENERAL DWIGHT DAVID EISENHOWER

Born in a farming family in Texas in 1890, Eisenhower went to West Point and became a tank instructor. He served under Gen Douglas MacArthur in the Philippines from 1933 to 1939. Between 1941 and 1942, he was on Gen George C Marshall's Operations Division staff in Washington. In June 1942, he was selected to command the Allied 'Torch' landings in North Africa. Just over a year later, he was named the Commander of the Supreme Headquarters Expeditionary Forces (SHAEF). In North Africa, he had brought together men from different nationalities and levels of experience, including difficult personalities like Montgomery and Patton, in a joint headquarters. In north-west Europe, he took over the general direction of Montgomery's and Bradley's Army Groups, specifying a methodical advance on a broad front, rather than armoured thrusts. He remained touchy about his lack of battlefield experience when dealing with men like Montgomery and Patton. On the eve of D-Day, he slipped a note into his pocket that read, 'Our landings in the Cherbourg–Le Havre area have failed to gain a satisfactory foothold and I have withdrawn the troops. My decision to attack at this time and this place were based on the best information available. The troops, the air and navy did all that bravery and devotion to duty could do. If any blame or fault attaches to the attempt it is mine alone.'

Following the war, 'Ike' ran for the US Presidency and had two terms in the White House from 1953 to 1961.

---

the Loire valley. Down the Rhone Saone valley, operations were 'Rupert', 'Loyron', 'Hardy', 'Newton', 'Barker' and 'Harrod' while in the Massif Central they were named 'Haggard', 'Bulbasket', 'Moses', 'Jockworth', 'Samson', 'Snelgrove' and 'Marshall'.

The Belgian and French SAS troops parachuting into mainland Europe had the advantage that they were either returning home, or spoke the language and so were well equipped to operate behind the lines. The arrival of the SAS gave SOE agents the military muscle to galvanize the Resistance groups they had been fostering into action against the Germans. Many Frenchmen thought that the Liberation would take only a few weeks and saw the SAS almost as reconnaissance patrols for the Allies.

Early on the morning of D-Day, the SAS was committed to several operations near the Normandy beaches.

In Operation Dingson/Grog, 160 men and four Jeeps of 4 French Parachute Battalion (4 SAS) under command of the legendary one-armed Commandant Pierre Bourgoin were parachuted into the Vannes area of Brittany. They established a base and organized three battalions of Resistance with a company of gendarmes and launched attacks against German forces which followed to the letter the orders that Bourgoin had received from 21 Army Group that 'a full-scale revolt is to be raised in Brittany'.

Left: The 54-year-old Supreme Allied Commander Dwight D Eisenhower may not have been a great tactician, but he was a superb team leader and diplomat capable of keeping some difficult or idiosyncratic personalities all working together for a common goal.

They were joined by 54 men from 4 SAS from Operation Cooney that had made a 'blind' jump into unprepared DZs between St Malo and Vannes. The force divided into 18 three-man teams and cut a number of railway lines before they joined Dingson. On 18 June, the Germans launched a sweep against the base with light armoured vehicles and infantry. The lightly armed and poorly trained *Resistants* scattered. Bourgoin was too wily a fighter to allow his men to be methodically rounded up in his heathland base and gave the order to disperse overnight.

However, before they escaped, by a lucky wireless accident, the defenders were able to contact 40 P-47 Thunderbolts and get them to support them in the late afternoon, when they had fought the Germans to a standstill. This was a tremendous encouragement, not only on this battlefield but all over Brittany. Some 40 SAS escaped and set up a new base near Pontivy, code-named Grog.

Writing about operations in north-west France Eisenhower said: 'The covert Resistance forces in this area had been built up since June around a core of SAS troops of the French 4th Parachute Battalion... Not least in importance, they had, by their ceaseless harassing activities, surrounded the Germans with a terrible atmosphere of danger and hatred which ate into the confidence of the leaders and courage of the soldiers.'

The psychological aspect of SAS and Resistance operations cannot be over estimated and the fear and insecurity that the French and British 'terrorists' induced explains in part the savage way in which the Germans reacted if they captured SAS troops or Resistance workers.

GENERAL OMAR BRADLEY

Born in Clark, Missouri, Gen Omar Bradley was the son of a farmer. He joined the US Army in 1911 and after graduating from West Point, opted to join the infantry. He rose slowly through the ranks of the peacetime army and in 1943 in North Africa was given the role of 'troubleshooter' with II Corps, following its rough handling at Kasserine. He recommended that its commander be sacked and replaced by Gen Patton. Bradley commanded II Corps as part of Patton's Seventh Army in the invasion of Sicily in 1943. Eisenhower then chose Bradley to lead the US landings in Normandy as commander of the US First Army. In Britain, Bradley concentrated on training for his troops. Following the successful landing at Utah and costly lodgement at Omaha, Bradley would lead his forces in the breakout from Normandy. He was a caring officer who also showed a real flare for planning and logistics. After the war, Bradley was promoted to five star general, and as chairman of the Joint Chiefs of Staff, developed the Cold War policy of containing the USSR. In the Vietnam war, he was one of the elder statesmen who advised President Lyndon B Johnson on policy and strategy.

Operation Bulbasket commanded by Captain John Tonkin was composed of 43 men from 'B' Squadron 1 SAS and 12 from Phantom. On D-Day, Tonkin, along with one other officer, parachuted into the Vienne area to find a suitable base and make contact with the Resistance. As he descended on his parachute he drifted towards a tree-lined road and his parachute snagged on a branch 'and I came to rest with my feet just touching the ground. I doubt if I'd have broken an egg if I'd landed on it'. His reception party was a local farmer, his son and a farm hand. A day later he met 'Samuel', in reality one of SOE French Section's outstanding agents, real name Maj Amedee Maingard de la Villes-es-Offrans, a 25-year-old Mauritian. Tonkin recalled the meeting. 'A quiet dark-haired young man carrying a Sten gun arrived. There followed one of those conversations that always made those taking part feel slightly absurd. "Is there a house in the wood?" asked Tonkin in French. "Yes, but it is not very good."' The exchange confirmed their identities.

THE SAS SABOTAGE TEAMS

On 11 June, the main party parachuted in four groups with orders to undertake sabotage attacks, before linking up with

Tonkin. They had some success, including cutting the Poitiers-Tours railway in two places and derailing a train on the Poitiers-Tours line.

One group had the terrifying experience of being dropped into the village of Airvault. One man was captured while the others made a hasty retreat.

Bulbasket operated in an area known as the Loire bend, near Poitiers. On 17 June, it received four Jeeps and a week later set up a base in some woods near Verriers. Resistance indiscretion compromised the base and it was attacked by the Germans on 3 July. They killed three men and captured 33 SAS soldiers, who were subsequently executed. Derrick Harrison reports that one wounded SAS officer was taken by the Germans to a village where the population were forced to watch as he was clubbed to death with rifle butts. His 'execution' was punishment for being a 'terrorist'. Tonkin managed to rally 11 SAS men and five Phantom signallers, but the SAS Brigade headquarters decided to end Bulbasket and the survivors were extracted by aircraft on 7 and 10 August. They were replaced by men from 3 SAS.

Operation Samwest, undertaken by 116 men of the French Battalion under Captain Le Blond, began with drops

Left: Lieutenant General Omar Bradley who commanded the US First Army that landed at Omaha and Utah. Bradley was a careful and caring commander who was soft-spoken and inclined to take deliberate, considered decisions; for this he was known as 'the GI's general'.

Above: NCOs of the British Parachute Regiment listen as an officer briefs them on the upcoming attack. For airborne forces, dropped in 'sticks' across the Norman countryside, the first priority upon landing was to find their way to their rendezvous (RV) point.

between 6 and 9 June. It was intended to prevent German forces moving from Brittany towards Normandy and so DZs were set up near St Brieuc. The local population and Resistance thought that the SAS were the liberating Allies and made them welcome. Security became slack and some of the French soldiers began having meals in local restaurants. Arming and recruiting 30 members of the local Resistance was also a problem because many 'turned out to belong to different groups who hated each other nearly as much as they hated the Germans', an SOE officer later observed. On 12 June, the Germans mounted a full-scale attack against the SAS base and though the SAS took 32 casualties, the Germans suffered 155. Survivors escaped and joined the Dingson base.

Operation Houndsworth was undertaken by 'A' Squadron 1 SAS under Maj Bill Fraser, and operated from the wooded hills west of Dijon. Fraser was a highly experienced soldier and one of the 'Originals' from 'L' Detachment. He had won the Military Cross during the raid on Agedabia airfield in December 1941. Between 6 and 21 June, the rest of the squadron parachuted into France. Their mission was to disrupt enemy communications, sever railway lines and arm the local Resistance. By the end of June, the force consisted of 144 men with nine Jeeps and two 6-pdr (57mm/2.24in) anti-tank guns.

THE LEADERS

Gen Dwight D Eisenhower, the Supreme Commander Allied Expeditionary Force, chose as his senior staff four Britons

After blackening our faces, sharpening our knives and checking our equipment for the 100th time, we got into formation and walked to the airfield. This was about 10pm. On the way, we were swinging along, some of us singing, and a little old Cockney lady ran up and said, 'Give 'em hell, Yanks'. A lump came into my throat, both of fear and pride.

Lieutenant Parker A Alford
3rd Battalion, 501st Parachute Infantry Regiment, US 101st Airborne Division

Right: M4 Shermans modified for deep wading are packed onto a landing craft in Portsmouth. The hooded structures on the rear of the tanks' decks allowed air to enter the engine and the exhaust fumes to escape without seawater flooding it and 'drowning' the tank's engine.

and two Americans. Of the two Americans, Gen Omar Bradley would lead the US invasion forces and Gen Walter Bedell-Smith, who had begun his army career in the ranks, would eventually be Eisenhower's Chief of Staff.

In 1941, Bedell-Smith was Secretary of the Joint Chiefs of Staff, thereafter Secretary of the Anglo-American Combined Chiefs of Staff and in 1942, was appointed Eisenhower's Chief of Staff. Bedell-Smith had served in France in World War I and by 1918 had been promoted to Major. It was with his appointment by Gen George Marshall to a staff post in Washington that his true talents became obvious. He was known as 'Beadle' or the 'Beetle' behind his back and could be humourless, abrupt with subordinates and often difficult to work with. Eisenhower described the 49-year-old Bedell-Smith as 'the general manager of the war'.

Having worked in North Africa with the quietly competent Air Chief Marshal Sir Arthur Tedder, Eisenhower chose him as his deputy. Tedder would integrate the Allied tactical and strategic air assault on northern France and Normandy. Gen

Left: A GI laden with all the equipment for the landing swigs from his aluminium canteen mug. Some GIs were drowned due to their kit's weight.

Bernard Montgomery, the very experienced and very opinionated commander of the British ground forces, would make some forceful but valuable contributions to the planning. He insisted that five divisions rather than three be used for the landings over a wider front, supported by airborne landings on the flanks.

In contrast, Admiral Bertram Ramsay was a polite, but highly experienced Royal Navy officer who as Flag Officer Dover had been closely involved with Operation Dynamo – the evacuation of Dunkirk in 1940.

Nominated Supreme Commander of the Allied Expeditionary Force in 1943, Eisenhower had served in staff posts in the US Army during World War I and the inter-war years. In June 1942, he was appointed commander of US troops in Europe, and as a Lt Gen, commanded the Anglo-American 'Torch' landings in North Africa. He had his critics among the US military establishment who saw him as inexperienced, and who were even more vocal after the savaging of the US Army II Corps by the Afrika Korps at Kasserine in Tunisia in 1943. However, as Supreme Commander, he demonstrated a talent for staff work and leadership which would be essential if the British and Americans and their allies were to work together effectively at D-Day.

Air Chief Marshal Sir Trafford Leigh-Mallory commanded 12 Fighter Group during the Battle of Britain and then afterwards, commanding 11 Group, pursued an aggressive policy against the *Luftwaffe* across the Channel. In 1942, he became head of Fighter Command and a year later commander of the Allied Expeditionary Air Force.

Leigh-Mallory, advocate of the 'Big Wing' tactics in the Battle of Britain and later costly fighter raids into northern France, was a forceful RAF officer who would coordinate the air attacks on German forces in the Normandy area. As Commander-in-Chief Allied Air Forces for Operation Overlord, his greatest contribution would be his part in the Transportation Plan that cut road and rail links in northern France and isolated Normandy.

His efforts to bring USAAF and RAF heavy bombers under his command were resisted by Harris and Gen Spaatz commanding the 8th and 15th Air Forces, but Allied fighters and bombers enjoyed complete superiority over the Normandy front and the Transportation Plan was very effective.

These men who made up the SHAEF headquarters were about to commit tens of thousands of men and women, vast resources of material and wealth, to an operation which had never before been undertaken on such a vast scale.

H-HOUR MINUS 12

Up to 3 June, the weather had been good, and then it had broken. The landings were originally scheduled for the 4 and 5 June, and so for many, there had been an exhausting anti-climax when they were cancelled. Some men were actually at sea when the order was given to return to port. The bad weather and pre-battle nerves left them nauseous. Gen Bradley foresaw the impact of the delay. 'Now the sharp edge of those troops would be dulled and seasickness would take its toll in another day on the choppy Channel.'

For men who had not boarded landing ships, the cancellation sent them back to their tents to sort out bedding. Sergeant Ian Grant of No 45 Royal Marine Commando remembered that 'the decision to abort was not accepted with pleasure... men were sullen and critical of the higher echelons of command.'

However, at sea, Lt Gregson of the Royal Artillery recalled: 'We were well out in the Channel and it was dark and rough, when the code message came through, "Return to Base". The tension evaporated and I for one heaved a sigh of relief that the great trial of strength was postponed for the moment.'

At Eisenhower's headquarters, the weather patterns were studied closely and at 21:30 hours on 4 June, his chief meteorological officer, Group Captain JM Stagg forecast a brief break for the next day. 'Mercifully, the almost unbelievable happened,' said Stagg. 'I told him on Sunday we could expect an interlude between two depressions. I convinced him the quieter period would arrive on Monday and continue into Tuesday.'

After consultation with his senior commanders, the Supreme Commander took the decision that the attack was 'on' for 5 and 6 June. It was a lonely decision, as his deputy, Air Chief Marshal Tedder, and the other air force commanders were unenthusiastic, since they feared that a low cloud base would prevent them from delivering accurate attacks. The naval officers were in favour of launching the operation and Montgomery snapped, 'I would say, go.' Bedell-Smith

Left: In a display of youthful bravado, US paratroopers at an airfield in England pose with shaved heads and scalp locks. When some were captured on D-Day, their appearance prompted the Germans to liken them to the inmates of Sing Sing, the notorious US gaol.

watched Eisenhower and was struck by 'the loneliness and isolation' of the Supreme Commander's position. After a long silence he said quietly, 'I am quite positive we must give the order... I don't like it, but there it is.' Afterwards, Eisenhower would admit, 'I've had to do things that were so risky as to be almost crazy.'

What were the words that finally committed the American, British and Canadian troops to this huge attack? At 04:00 hours on 5 June he said, 'OK, let's go.' Other witnesses assert that it was a more robust – 'OK, let her rip.'

As Eisenhower took the decision, the weather was appalling, with wind and rain lashing the French windows of the library at Southwick House, his D-Day headquarters on the chalk hills above Portsmouth. Stagg would be vindicated, when on the afternoon of D-Day, excellent flying weather would allow the Allied air forces to attack German reinforcements moving towards the beaches and impose the critical delay that Montgomery had demanded.

THE WEATHER FROM GERMAN EYES

Across the Channel, the veteran tank officer Major Hans von Luck of the 21st Panzer Division recalled: 'The general weather conditions worked out every day by naval meteorologists and passed on to us by Division, gave the "all clear" for 5 and 6 June. So we did not anticipate any landings, for heavy seas, storms, and low flying clouds would make large scale operations at sea and in the air impossible.'

If Eisenhower had decided against 6 June, the next dates when conditions were right would have been 17 and 19 June. History might have been very different because on 19 June the Channel was hit by the worst storms experienced for decades, though a day earlier conditions had been good. The storms were so severe that they effectively wrecked the US Mulberry 'A' harbour at Omaha.

Despite tight security, the population of southern England had a shrewd idea that the Second Front was coming. The roads that had been full of military traffic were now silent and huge stocks of ammunition, fuel, rations, vehicle spares, trucks, tanks and guns had been amassed in every area of open ground adjoining airfields and ports. The night sky was noisy with aircraft.

The way in which last hours were passed on British soil, for the soldiers, airmen and sailors varied according to age and each serviceman's temperament. Having been briefed, they had been confined to camps, the perimeters of which were patrolled by military police.

For the soldiers who were to be among the first ashore, there was suddenly little to do. Freshly cooked food had been available and in some camps there were improvized cinemas. Many men read, played dice or cards or sat, smoked and day dreamed. Some men became 'rich' in these card games, stuffing specially printed paper French franc 'invasion money' into their uniforms, aware that this wealth would only be realizable if they survived D-Day and the days that followed.

Others checked their kit and equipment for the last time – did it fit snugly, was the weight correctly distributed, how accessible were magazines, grenades and ammunition? Many of the British Commandos, disdaining helmets, would go ashore in their distinctive green berets that had been awarded to the force following Operation Jubilee at Dieppe in 1942. However, paratroopers checked that their helmets would fit snugly and be secure when they hit the slipstream of the plane as they jumped.

Knowing that in the next few hours and perhaps days, regular meals would be unlikely, they carefully stowed their one-day ration packs. The Americans carried one 'D' Ration – three large chocolate bars – and one tinned 'K' ration that came as a single meal. British and Canadian troops had tins of self-heating soup and cocoa for the crossing and '24 Hour' rations for when they had landed in France.

FIELD MARSHAL
SIR BERNARD LAW MONTGOMERY

Field Marshal Sir Bernard Law Montgomery had fought on the Western Front in World War I and been badly wounded and was awarded the DSO. He returned to France in 1939, commanding the 3rd Division and took part in the withdrawal to Dunkirk in 1940. He was a small man with a rather piping voice and as a non-smoker and strict tee-totaller, he was a rather austere figure in the British Army. He came to prominence when commanding the Eighth Army in North Africa where he defeated Rommel's *Afrika Korps* at El Alamein in October 1942. Despite having accurate Ultra intelligence on the very poor state of the *Afrika Korps* he was reluctant to press them following the victory at El Alamein. Under Eisenhower's command, the Anglo-American First and British Eighth Army eliminated the Germans in Tunisia. Montgomery commanded the British sector in Sicily and led the Eighth Army into Italy. In January 1944, he was recalled to plan the invasion of Europe.

On the night of the invasion, at about 11p.m., I received a phone call from a Frenchwoman whom I did not know and she said to me, 'Captain Fromm, all of us wish you the best of luck in the next few hours.' I was somewhat perplexed by this.

Hauptmann Curt Fromm
6 Company, 100 Panzer Brigade, 22 Panzer Division

Maps and aerial photographs were studied so that the position of enemy bunkers, obstacles, minefields and landmarks were familiar. Paratroopers looked at the shape of field patterns and the position of buildings on the aerial photographs, so that they could orientate themselves when they landed at night on the DZ.

Some men, aware that in the next hours or days they might be dead or gravely injured, had written carefully worded letters to wives and sweethearts. When, overnight, the US 4th Cavalry Regiment pulled out of the Sussex village of Singleton en route for their holding area before embarkation for France, a housewife opened her curtains in the morning to see 'odd packages on the windowsill'. These packages were soldiers' wallets, containing photographs of families and girlfriends and other little personal treasures, with notes asking her to look after them until they could call again.

LETTERS OF FAREWELL

A young British officer, Lt Ian Hammerton, commanding a Flail Tank Troop, remembered that men wrote 'letters of farewell we hoped would never have to be sent'. Many of the letters were simple compositions giving no hidden truths or emotions, aware that they would be read by censors, but rather gratitude and affection. One young soldier wrote to his 'next of kin', his mother.

Dear Mum
…You may not hear from me for a week or two, as we shall be busy for a bit. Don't worry, whatever you read in the papers. I'll make up for it as soon as I can with a nice long one.
Love and kisses,
Charlie

Right: Loaded with weapons and equipment and their simple flotation devices, GIs move towards a Landing Craft Infantry (LCI) moored to a rough jetty, ready to embark for D-Day. Besides their ammunition they carried rations and simple first aid kits.

Above: DUKW amphibious trucks with British or Canadian infantry move towards the ships carrying them across the Channel. The picture was taken on exercise, since the sea is calm. On 5 June 1944, the weather was poor, leading to a 24-hour postponement of the landings.

Personal letters and documents that might have intelligence or propaganda value, if they were captured, were burned. Knowing that training was at an end and that they now shared a common fate simplified relations between soldiers and NCOs and officers. Class distinctions were meaningless. The men might risk their lives for their officer, be he a fresh-faced Subaltern or tough, experienced Brigadier, and in return he was expected to give the lead and value the lives entrusted to him.

Commander MOW Miller RN, who would lead an LCT squadron to Normandy, had watched the spring change to summer in 1944. He recalled: 'When the blossoms began to fall we realized that the nightmare would soon be reality and

the next year's apple-blossoms a doubtful dream that many of us might never see.'

Now on a wet and windy summer evening, paratroopers, who would be landing at night, smeared their faces with camouflage cream – in some cases an improvized mix of linseed oil and cocoa powder. Some of the Americans had their hair cut in Mohican style scalp locks and made 'war paint' patterns on their faces with camouflage cream. For Lt Martin Pöppel of the German 6th Paratroop Regiment the first US paratroopers captured in the early hours of 6 June were a surprise. He recalled: 'More prisoners were brought in, great hulking figures. Is this the American elite? They look as though they could be from Sing Sing [a tough US prison]'.

For the Allied paratroopers who would be crossing the Channel, there was the prospect of riding in a cramped transport plane, loaded with weapons and equipment and at the other side, disembarking under fire across open beaches. For them, it would be a leap in the dark.

For the men who would be landing from the sea, there was the final truck ride to the ports, embarkation onto the landing ships and then in cramped conditions, the beginning, for some, of a second rough journey in the Channel, which only the stomachs of a few hardened sailors could tolerate. A soldier of the East Yorks Regiment recalled that as the launch carrying them from the harbour quay to the assault ship moved off, the soldiers spotted an immaculate Military Police officer.

'From the safe distance on the boat, knowing nothing could be done about it, the lads blew resounding raspberries and in a good-humoured sort of way shouted insults and profanities at the Redcap, but he never batted an eyelid. The officer came up to the salute and I swear I saw a smile on his face.'

Aboard the USS *Chase*, photographer Robert Capa divided the GIs into three groups, the gamblers, the planners and the writers of last letters. The gamblers were on the upper deck clustered around a blanket watching as thousands of dollars changed hands on the roll of two dice.

The planners were below deck studying rubber terrain maps of the coast on which they would land. He said, 'The platoon leaders picked their way between the rubber villages and looked for protection behind the rubber trees and in the rubber ditches'.

The last group, the letter writers, 'hid in corners and put down beautiful sentences on paper leaving their favourite shotguns to kid brothers and their dough to the family.'

Paratroopers waited until dusk before boarding their Dakota transports.

The next day would change the course of the war. Alan Moorehead explained: 'The mind projected itself forward as far as the embarkation, as far as the landing. Then there was a blank, a kind of wall over which the mind would not travel.'

In the words of Field Marshal Erwin Rommel in conversation with his Adjutant, Capt Helmut Lang on 22 April 1944, for the Allies, as well as for Germany, this day, which he knew would come sooner or later, would be '*Der langste Tag*' (the longest day).

CHAPTER FIVE

H–HOUR

The airborne assault on Normandy was critical to secure exits from Utah beach for the Americans and the left flank for the British. Within this larger tactical task were several smaller ones, in which bridges were to be captured or destroyed, and coastal batteries neutralised. But before this could be done, the scattered paratroopers had to assemble into cohesive groups - a task that would have to be done quickly and silently at night in unfamiliar territory.

The first men to go into action on D-Day were the 13,400 paratroopers and 'glider riders' of the US 82nd and 101st Airborne Divisions and the 6255 men of the British and Canadian 6th Airborne Division. Their missions were to secure the right and left flanks of the invasion beaches before the main landings took place.

Also committed to action in those early morning hours was the SAS, who were engaged in several operations near the Normandy beaches. One of these operations, code-named 'Titanic', appeared to live up to its inauspicious name when seven men of 1 SAS were dropped south of Carentan, Normandy. They were part of a deception plan designed to convince the Germans that large scale airborne, rather than sea-launched, landings were taking place. Captain John Tonkin remembered two SAS officers emerging from Colonel Paddy Mayne's tent at Fairford, Gloucestershire 'as white as sheets' after they had received their orders for Operation 'Titanic'.

Left: Pathfinder officers of the 22nd Independent Parachute Company at Harwell on June 5, standing in front of a C-47 waiting to take them to France. Left to right, Lieutenants Robert de Latour, Donald Wells, John Vischer and Captain Robert Medwood.

Above: British troops board an Airspeed Horsa glider with its fuselage adorned with combative graffiti. One man carries a fireman's axe in case the glider crashed and it became necessary to break their way out. The gliders were largely built from wood and canvas.

The deception schemes involved 29 RAF Stirling and Halifax bombers of Nos 90, 138, 149 and 161 Squadrons. Six of these aircraft dropped weapons containers filled with sand, dummy paratroopers (made from sand bags on scaled down parachutes) and pyrotechnic devices called Pintail Bombs which fired Very lights. The Pintail Bombs landed before the dummy parachutists and fired the Very lights, simulating a reception group on a drop zone. Each dummy had a small arms fire simulator attached to it, so after a delay, they would explode, producing the sound of rifle or machine gun fire for about five minutes.

When 19-year-old *Gefreiter* Walter Hermes, a motorcycle despatch rider with the German 21st Panzer Division ,reported to the Sergeant Major's office, the senior NCO asked, 'Do you want to see our first prisoner? He's standing right there behind the door.' Hermes said: 'I quickly turned round and saw not a man, but a life-size dummy made of some kind of rubber and hung all over with firecrackers. I said, "By God, if the Allies expect to win the invasion with this sort of thing, they're crazy. They're just trying to scare us."'

The war diary of the 352nd Division recorded that a US paratroop officer captured at 04:35 hours by the 916th Grenadier Regiment confirmed the explosive content of the dummy paratroopers.

SAS DECEPTION

Meanwhile, the SAS landing was widely scattered and the men were unable to trace their real weapons containers among all the dummies. Without them they could do little, and so went into hiding. On 10 July, they were discovered by a German patrol and in the firefight, three men were wounded. Later, a larger group of German paratroopers returned to the location heavily armed with light machine guns, MP40 submachine guns, and rifles. The paratroops were all young with 'white faces and appeared jumpy'. To

A TORPEDO FOR BARBED WIRE

The Bangalore torpedo, named after the munitions factory in India where it was developed in World War I, consisted of a cast iron tube 40 to 50mm (1.5 to 2in) in diameter and 2.4m (8ft) long. It contained between 4.5kg (10lb) and 5.4kg (12lb) of Amatol high explosives with a primer and safety fuse. Tubes could be linked together using a 'male' pin and 'female' bayonet slots. At the front, a pointed wooden nose plug could be fitted to prevent the torpedo snagging on wire or vegetation as it was pushed into the wire obstacle. Ideally, the torpedo was not set to explode on the ground, but amongst the wire where the blast would be more effective. At the rear, a safety fuse initiation set with a primer, detonator and safety fuse was fitted. When the torpedo exploded, shrapnel fragments from the iron casing shredded the barbed wire and, depending on the strength and proximity of the pickets, created a gap 0.76 to 3m (2 to 10ft) through the obstacle.

resist would have been hopeless, and the group were surrounded and obliged to surrender.

Operation Titanic may have seemed like a failure, but combined with a scattered drop during the night by the men of the US 82nd and 101st Airborne Divisions, 'Titanic' was enough to convince General Kraiss, the acting commander of the German 352nd Division in reserve behind Omaha beach, that a major airborne threat had developed. He called out his reserve regiment at 03:00 hours and they cycled off into the darkness to search the woods south-east of Isigny. These men were thus not available for what would have been the *coup de grace* counter attack against the Americans at Omaha beach.

To the east, the critical attack on the Merville battery was about to take place. The commanding officer of the 9th Battalion, 3rd Parachute Brigade, Lieutenant Colonel Terence Otway, had 35 officers and 750 men for the task. They were superbly trained and

equipped with anti-tank guns, Jeeps, scaling ladders, Bangalore torpedoes and explosives.

They had rehearsed the attack on a full-scale reproduction of the German position that had been created by bulldozers at West Woodbury near Newbury, England. The plan of attack called for the majority of the battalion, with its equipment, to land by parachute and glider near the battery. A reconnaissance party would have cleared and marked the way through the minefield protecting the position. The men would then launch a conventional infantry attack while simultaneously, a 60-man force, including men from 591st Parachute Squadron, Royal Engineers, would land on the casemates in three gliders.

As part of the plan, ten minutes before the paratroopers attacked, 100 RAF Avro Lancaster bombers would pulverize the battery with 635,000kg (1,400,000lb) of bombs.

However, the situation facing the men at dawn on 6 June was very different. The reality was that at 23:20 hours on 5 June, the Dakotas of 519 Squadron, carrying the men of 9th Parachute Battalion, took off from RAF Broadwell. At the same time, tug aircraft towing the seven stores gliders lifted off from RAF Down Ampney. Three gliders

Below: Private Frank Gardner, Captain Brian Priday, second in command of D Company, 2nd Battalion the Oxfordshire and Buckinghamshire Light Infantry, and Lance Corporal B. Lambley at Pegasus Bridge on 6 June.

> As I dropped, I looked round and I could see other 'chutes coming down. I hit the deck and got out of my 'chute, got my Sten gun out and looked round again, but couldn't see anybody! But there was one thing implanted in my mind – I must get to that RV. And the Colonel's orders were: 'You are to have no private firefights. You get to the RV AND THAT IS IT.'
>
> *Private Les Cartwright*
> *9th Battalion, 3rd Parachute Brigade*

carrying the assault troops left RAF Brize Norton at 02:30 hours on 6 June.

Wind, poor navigation and enemy flak caused the paratroopers and gliders to be scattered over a wide area. The pilots had confused the rivers Orne and Dives and over half the battalion landed well to the south and east of their drop zones (DZs).

150 MEN AGAINST A BATTERY

At 02:50 hours, a force that should have been 635-men strong stood at only 150 – each Company was effectively only 30

men. Col Otway's equipment for the attack consisted of one machine gun and a few lengths of Bangalore torpedo.

The men assembled near the village of Gonneville to await the RAF bombers. They arrived and dropped their huge payload but completely missed the battery and instead destroyed Gonneville, causing even more disruption to the paratroopers.

Luckily, the reconnaissance party had landed well, had cut the wire and cleared the minefield by hand, making three lanes through this dangerous obstacle.

Undaunted, in a triumph of courage and improvization, the small force under Otway attacked and neutralized the German position. Of the three gliders that were supposed to land on the battery, one had broken its towrope en route and had managed to return to England. The pilot of the second, seeing the fires in Gonneville, assumed this was the target, thought it had been destroyed, so decided to land well away. Otway's men were unable to signal to the pilot since their

Below: A map showing the landing points of the British airborne forces on D-Day, including the bridges over the River Orne and the Caen Canal, the latter more famously known as Pegasus Bridge. The glider troops and paratroopers came under fierce attack on D-Day.

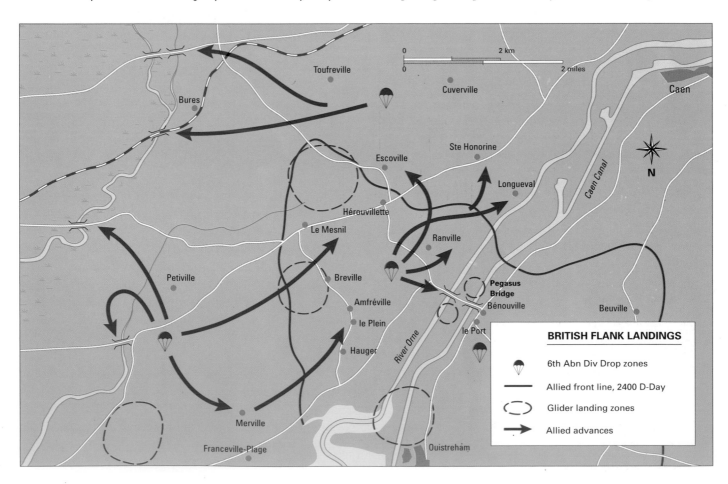

flares had been lost in the disrupted parachute drop. The third glider came in low over the battery and was engaged by German 2cm (0.78in) anti-aircraft fire. It crashed nearby and the survivors were immediately attacked by a fighting patrol moving up to reinforce the battery. This crash actually played into the Allies' hands by providing a distraction for Otway's force who, using their Bangalore torpedoes, were able to breach the remaining wire and attacked the battery from the rear.

The fight lasted 30 minutes and resulted in 65 paratroopers killed and 30 wounded. They took 22 prisoners. What the British did not know was that many members of the German garrison (drawn from 1716th

A British glider pilot clutching his red beret. Unlike their US counterparts, British glider pilots were fully-trained soldiers expected to 'do their bit'.

Above: GAL Hamilcar gliders carrying light armoured vehicles coming in to land near Ranville during the second phase of the British airborne landings by the 6th (Air Landing) Brigade on the afternoon of 6 June. Note the steep angles of approach for the gliders.

Artillery Regiment and commanded by Lieutenant Rudolf Steiner and Batterie Feldwebel Buskotte along with men of the 736th Grenadier Regiment, were hiding in the command and stores bunkers, which had appeared on aerial photographs simply as grass mounds.

Otway then discovered that the concrete casemates did not house the powerful 15cm (5.9in) artillery they expected to find, but World War I-vintage captured Skoda 100mm (3.94in) field guns, with a modest range of 8km (5 miles). These were destroyed, and a success signal was transmitted. The paratroopers then withdrew since they did not know if HMS *Arethusa*, waiting out to sea, had received it or would now bombard the battery. She had and so did not open fire.

It was now that the surviving men of the German garrison emerged to reoccupy the position. A second attack was needed, this time carried out by men of 3 Commando, backed by fire from HMS *Arethusa*, to finally secure the Merville battery.

A short distance down the hill from Merville battery, another airborne assault was taking place according to the rehearsals carried out on Salisbury Plain in England. The difference for the men of 2nd Oxfordshire and Buckinghamshire (Ox and Bucks) was that this time the attack was for real and among their ranks would be the first man to die on D-Day.

The bridges across the Caen Canal and River Orne spanned two formidable water obstacles, and were defended by a garrison of 50 men who were believed to be conscripts from occupied countries but with a backbone of German NCOs and officers. Nearby were elements of the 736th Grenadier Regiment from the 716th Infantry Division. They were known to have a small number of tanks, and were also expected to have prepared the bridges for demolition.

The full force assigned to Major Howard was D Company with two platoons of B Company and a detachment of Royal Engineers from 249th (Airborne) Field Company whose task was to neutralize the demolitions. They would be carried in six Horsa gliders, towed by Halifax bombers of Nos 298 and 644 Squadrons.

The bombers took off at 22:56 hours from RAF Tarrant Rushton and all the gliders were released at 1900m (6000ft),

Below: German infantry pass the shattered remains of an Allied troop carrying glider in Normandy. Gliders wrecked on their one way trip to France made for striking, but misleading, propaganda photographs in the German press.

on the French coast, to the east of Merville. The tugs then flew on to bomb a cement factory in Caen as a cover. Five of the six glider pilots found their correct Landing Zone (LZ). Horsa No 94 landed 13km (8miles) away near two bridges on the River Dives that looked like the target area. The men aboard from D Company fought their way back to the 6th Airborne Division perimeter suffering four casualties.

Meanwhile at the Caen Canal bridge, Staff Sergeant Wallwork landed Horsa No 91 carrying Maj Howard and Lt Den Brotheridge and A Platoon. A barbed wire fence halted the glider 47m (150ft) from the bridge at 00:16 hours. Horsa No 92, piloted by SSgt Boland and carrying Lt DJ Wood and B Platoon came in a minute later, landing a few metres away and finally No 93, with Lt Smith and carrying C Platoon landed nearby but skidded into a pond, trapping six men. After the action, Air Chief Marshal Leigh-Mallory, who could be a stern critic, said that these landings by the Army Glider Pilots were probably the finest feat of flying in World War II.

On Bénouville Bridge (soon to be known as Pegasus Bridge), Private Helmut Römer, the sentry on duty on the swing bridge, assumed that all the noise was made by an

PARACHUTING TO WAR

The British used the X-type parachute that measured 8.5m (28ft) across with a circular 55cm (22in) vent in the centre. All early types were made of silk, but later, cotton parachutes known as 'Ramtex' were introduced. Finally, nylon canopies were manufactured towards the end of the war. There were 28 rigging lines each 6.3m (25ft) long, made of nylon or silk with a minimum breaking strength of 181.4kg (400lbs). The web harness supported a minimum breaking strength of 1361kg (3000lbs). All metal fittings were of forged stainless steel. Men who had jumped with the X-type said that the shock of landing was similar to jumping off a 4.5m (15ft) wall.

Equipment like mortars, radios and small arms were delivered in a Central Landing Establishment (CLE) container. A wood and metal box with a hinged side opening, the CLE container was 1.82m (6ft) long and 381mm (15in) in diameter and could carry up to 272kg (600lbs). It landed without damaging its contents, since the lower end had a shock absorbing metal pan, and at the top end was a 3m or 4.8m (10 or 16ft) parachute. CLE containers could fit into a bomb bay and so as bombers became bigger, so did the containers, growing up to 3.3m (11ft) long. Wicker panniers were used for some loads, while motorcycles were packed into wooden crates. Jeeps and anti-tank guns were slung in the bomb bay of aircraft such as the Handley Page Hastings. Crash pans and shock absorbing structures were bolted under the axles.

The US Airborne used the T-7 parachute developed from the T-4. The parachute had a three-point harness, using snap hooks and a wide canvas waistband to hold the pack snug against the wearer's back. Like the German parachute, the T-4 was a 'canopy-first' design that gave the user a considerable jolt when it deployed. It did, however, allow men to be dropped from lower altitudes and so therefore spend less time in the air, itself a considerable safety feature.

The DZ for paratroopers and containers, destined for the French Resistance, was normally open ground 731.5m x 183m (800yds x 200yds) at the edge of a wood where containers could be opened and their contents distributed in cover. Agricultural carts were positioned to recover the containers quickly. On the open ground was a Eureka radar homing beacon and a man with a signalling torch. Aircraft were fitted with an answering device code named 'Rebecca', which showed range and orientation to port or starboard on a vertical scale. For the final run in and visual fix for the pilot on the DZ, three bonfires spaced at 92m (100yd) intervals were ignited by the Resistance and the parachute containers were dropped from a height of 92m to 184m (300 to 600ft).

aircraft crashing, and didn't react. The men of the Ox and Bucks stormed out and threw grenades into the embrasures of the bunkers protecting the right bank approaches to the bridge and the men rushed the bridge. The surprise was complete but as Lt Brotheridge dashed across the bridge he was hit by a burst of machine gun fire and was fatally wounded. His grave is not in a Commonwealth War Graves cemetery, but close to where he was buried immediately after the fighting was over in Ranville churchyard.

The airborne engineers, under Captain Neilson, quickly removed the explosive charges attached to the bridge and made it safe.

A BRIDGE AT MIDNIGHT

At the Orne bridge to the east of this fighting, Horsa No 95, flown by SSgt Pearson with Lt 'Tod' Sweeny and E Platoon landed 400m (1300ft) from the objective. No 96, flown by SSgt Howard landed closer to the bridge and Lt Fox and his men from F Platoon stormed out. They captured their objective with no casualties and found that it had not been prepared for demolition.

The signal for the capture of the canal bridge was 'Ham' and that for the river, 'Jam'. Howard began to transmit the concise but triumphant message 'Ham and Jam'. 'As I spoke,' he recalled later, 'I could hardly believe that we had done it.' The operation had been completed in ten minutes.

The men held the position and saw off counter attacks both by road, where a Piat gunner destroyed a German light armoured vehicle, and along the canal when a small patrol boat appeared. On the river bridge, 'Tod' Sweeney's men shot up a vehicle that approached his bridge and out of the wreck stumbled Maj Hans Schmidt who as bridge commander demanded to be shot as he had 'lost his honour'. The British soldiers were intrigued to find that the Major's transport also held ladies' lingerie and perfume. Clearly the officer had other things on his mind on the night of 5 June.

At 03:00 hours, men of the 7th Parachute Battalion joined Sweeney's men to bolster the defences. At 13:30 hours they

Above: Grim-faced airborne troops dig in with a pickaxe at the edge of the Ranville LZ where 250 gliders landed, bringing light artillery, armoured vehicles and much needed reinforcements for the 6th Airborne Division.

heard the skirl of the bagpipes as Lord Lovat's piper, Bill Millen, accompanied men of Lord Lovat's 1st Special Service Brigade. The Commandos had landed at Sword beach and worked their way inland.

On the left bank of the canal by the swing bridge an enterprising Frenchman had built a café – an ideal spot to catch the trade of passing ships. In June 1944, the owners were a couple, the Gondrées. It became Regimental Aid Post (RAP) for the Ox and Bucks, but word soon filtered round that 99 bottles of champagne, hidden by Mnsr Gondrée, were being uncorked by the delighted French couple to celebrate the Liberation. Howard recalled that men in the vicinity suddenly found it necessary to make short trips to the RAP. Here, Madame Gondrée had been kissed by so many airborne soldiers that their brown camouflage cream had rubbed off on her face. The café was the

first house to be liberated on D-Day and is now a shrine to airborne operations.

FOUR DROP ZONES

On the left flank of the D-Day airborne landings, the 6th Airborne Division, under Major General 'Windy' Gale and composed of the 3rd Parachute Brigade under Brigadier Poett and the 5th Parachute Brigade under Brigadier Hill,

Apart from the firefight, a great deal of noise emanated from platoons shouting code-names to identify friends in the dark. There was an unholy babble of 'Able-Able-Able', 'Baker-Baker-Baker', 'Charlie-Charlie-Charlie' and 'Sapper-Sapper-Sapper' coming from all directions; on top of automatic fire, tracer and the odd grenade it was hell let loose and most certainly would have helped any wavering enemy to make a quick decision about quitting.

Major John Howard
Oxfordshire and Buckinghamshire Light Infantry

had four Drop Zones (DZ). To the north and west of Pegasus Bridge was DZ 'W' for elements of the 7th (Yorkshire) Battalion, and to the east of the brigde, DZ 'N', where the 7th, 12th and 13th (Lancashire) Battalions would land. Their task was to secure the area for the gliders of the 6th Air Landing Brigade, who would follow on the evening of D-Day. To the south, near Escoville, the 8th Parachute Battalion would land at DZ 'K' and to the north, near Varaville, the Canadian 1st Parachute Battalion and British 9th Battalion would land at DZ 'V'. The men landing at DZ 'W' and 'N' were to move to secure the bridges captured by Maj Howard. The Canadians and British at DZ 'K' and 'V' were to demolish the bridges over the River Dives at Troarn, Bures, Robehomme and Varaville, while the 9th Battalion would eliminate the battery at Merville.

The DZs were in an area of rolling farmland with lightly wooded hills. To the south was the large forest, the Bois de Bavent. Capturing the high ground near Bréville to the east was important to ensure the security of the British left flank. The Germans were quick to understand this and fought hard to hold it, which they did for six weeks after D-Day. The German 346th and 711th Infantry Divisions in the area were quick to counter attack and the lines became mixed among woodland and hedges.

Between 00:10 and 00:20 hours 60 Pathfinders of the 22nd Independent Parachute Company had jumped to mark the DZs with lights and Rebecca-Eureka radio homing beacons. Among them was Lt Bob de Latour who was later featured in the 22 July edition of the British magazine, *Picture Post*, as the 'first' Allied soldier to land in France. With fellow Pathfinders Don Wells, John Vischer and Bob Midwood he was photographed synchronizing his watch on the evening of 5 June. The 9 September edition of the same magazine would carry the postscript that the young officer, by then a Captain, had been killed on 20 June in the tough fighting near Ranville.

Bad weather and flak scattered the Pathfinders and they landed too far to the east of the proposed DZs. When the main force arrived, their drop was

Right: The grave of Lt Den Brotheridge in Ranville churchyard. He was killed at Pegasus Bridge - the first British soldier to die on D-Day. The Gondrée family placed the dedication by the headstone.

consequently not as concentrated as was hoped and many men drowned when they landed in the flooded valley of the River Dives.

In the 5th Brigade area, Lt Col Pine-Coffin began to assemble the men of the 7th Battalion using a hunting horn. By 04:00 hours, a wide perimeter around the bridges had been established.

The glider LZ had been cleared sufficiently for gliders carrying stores and anti-tank guns to land. Of the 68 Horsa and four larger Hamilcar gliders, only 52 landed safely, either because of flak damage or bad weather.

However, the paratroopers were able to recover 44 Jeeps, 55 motorcycles, 15 six-pounder and two seventeen-pounder anti-tank guns. A light bulldozer had come in aboard a Hamilcar and was invaluable in clearing the LZ for the second, larger glider wave that evening.

Above: 'Pegasus Bridge', the bridge across the Caen canal at Bénouville, seen after its liberation. The canal and the Orne River bridges captured by British glider troops would have been a formidable obstacle if they had remained in German hands.

At first light, the Germans launched vigorous counter-attacks against the airborne troops. In addition to local regiments from the 716th under Lieutenant General Wilhelm Richter and 711th Infantry Division under Major General Josef Reichert, the 21st Panzer Division was deployed. Its armour was a major threat to the lightly armed and equipped paratroops, who possessed few anti-tank weapons or indeed heavy weapons of any kind.

Richter had fought in World War I and in World War II in Poland, Belgium and Flanders. Following the invasion of the USSR, he commanded the 35th Artillery Command in the drive on Leningrad and later in fighting near Moscow. On D-Day, his division received the full weight of air and sea bombardment and the brunt of attacks by the British Second Army. Despite this punishment, it still was able to block the way to Caen.

In the afternoon of D-Day, Reichert, accompanied by Generals Hans von Salmuth and Hofmann, moved forward to a battery position at Mont Canisoy. From here they could see the eastern end of the invasion beaches. Reichert saw the transports stationed offshore and landing craft bringing reinforcements to the beaches.

'I still did not believe that this was the main invasion,' he recalled. 'I thought it was a Dieppe-type raid, aimed at creating a situation where various German units would be sucked into a vortex and that this would be followed by a major invasion elsewhere.'

The illusion fostered by Fortitude South, the Allied deception plan, was still working.

At Bénouville, A Coy 7th Battalion lost all its officers, who were either killed or wounded, as tanks and infantry attacked the village. At Ranville, the 13th Battalion was persistently attacked by the 125th Panzer Grenadier Regiment but held their positions until relieved by the Commandos in the afternoon.

The 1st Canadian Parachute Battalion landed well, destroyed their target bridges and established defensive positions around the north-east of the Bois de Bavent and Robenhomme.

However, the 8th Battalion were badly scattered and only 120 men gathered at the DZ. They had no engineers and only enough explosives to destroy two of the three target bridges. However, airborne sappers were making their way to the bridges and met up at Bures. Engineers under Maj 'Rosie' Roseveare borrowed a Jeep from a medical officer to

A FLYING TANK
THE TETRACH LIGHT TANK (A17)

Privately developed by Vickers from 1937, the Tetrach, originally known by the company project name 'Purdah', was accepted for service by the British Army in 1938 as the Light Tank Mk VII. Production started in 1940 but was soon halted when it was realized that light tanks were increasingly vulnerable on the modern battlefield.

The Tetrach had a crew of three, was armed with a 2pdr (40mm/1.57in) gun, one 7.92mm (0.31in) Besa machine gun and had armour protection of between 4–14mm (0.16–0.55in). It was 4.11m (13ft 6in) long, 2.31m (7ft 7in) wide, 2.10m (6ft 11in) high and weighed 7.6 tonnes (7.5 tons).

The tank was powered by Meadows flat-12 petrol developing 123kW (165bhp) at 2700rpm, and had a top speed of 64km/h (40mph) and range of 225km (140 miles)

Unlike earlier vehicles in this class, the Tetrach used a modified Christie suspension in which the front wheels could be steered so as to bend the track for gentle turns. This design feature overcame the problem of loss of power found with steering a vehicle by skidding the tracks on the ground. If a tighter manoeuvre was necessary the controls automatically braked one track to allow the tank to make a conventional skid turn. The suspension was formed by pneumatic shock absorbers on each of the four road wheels. A foot-pump was necessary to maintain the correct pressure.

The General Aircraft Hamilcar that carried the tank had a crew of two and was 20.72m (68ft) long with a wing span of 33.53m (110ft). Besides the Tetrach, its other possible payloads were two Bren Gun Carriers or two Scout Cars. Used exclusively by the British, 412 Hamilcars were built during the war.

drive to the distant Troarn. En route they crashed through heavy fire at a German road block but reached the bridge, which they then demolished, blasting a 6m (20ft) gap in the masonry structure.

JEEP RIDE TO DANGER

For 22-year-old Sgt Bill Irving RE, the ride was memorable. 'The further we went the more fire there was and the faster Roseveare drove the Jeep. I was sitting at the front, blazing away with my Sten gun at anything that moved. One German with a machine gun rushed into the road to really have a go at us and changed his mind because he got the hell out of it. Roseveare was driving like mad, zig-zagging from side to side.'

The intrepid Roseveare recalled the firefight in Troarn. 'The fun started, as there seemed to be a Boche in every doorway shooting like mad.' Sadly, the Bren gunner, who had been positioned as a rear gunner in the explosives laden trailer, was thrown clear during the dash to the bridge.

At around 21:00 hours, the 6th Airlanding Brigade commanded by Brigadier Kindersley and more divisional troops arrived in 256 gliders.

The 142 that landed at LZ 'N' were mainly carrying the 1st Battalion the Royal Ulster Regiment. However, uniquely, 30 big Hamilcar gliders landed carrying 20 Tetrach light tanks and nine Bren Gun Carriers of the 6th Airborne Armoured Reconnaissance Regiment.

The 104 Horsa gliders that landed at LZ 'W' brought in the rest of the 2nd Battalion Ox and Bucks and eight 75mm (2.95in) light guns of the 211th Airborne battery.

At 09:30 hours, Gen Gale, who, jumping with the Pathfinders became the first general to land in Normandy on D-Day, Brig Poett and Brig Kindersley crossed Pegasus Bridge to inspect the position and congratulate Howard.

By the end of 6 June, the British and Canadian airborne forces had achieved all their missions, despite the fact that only 3000 of the 4800 men who had landed had fought as planned. The Orne bridges had been taken and held, Ranville and the DZs were secure, a link up had been made with the Commandos of the 1st Special Service Brigade, the Merville battery had been neutralized and the bridges to the east across the Dives demolished. Only seven out of the 260 parachute aircraft used in the operation had been lost but 22 out of 98 gliders failed to reach their LZs. Some never made it to France as towropes sheared and they ditched in the Channel and many landed in the wrong place.

Of the 196 men of the Glider Pilot Regiment who flew on D-Day, 71 became casualties.

On the right flank of the Allied landings, the US 82nd Airborne Division 'All American', commanded by Maj Gen Matthew B. Ridgway and the 101st Airborne Division 'Screaming Eagles' under Maj Gen Maxwell Taylor went into action before dawn. Their mission was to secure the causeway exits from Utah beach across the flooded areas inland. They were to gain control of the crossings over the rivers Merderet and Douvre and prevent German forces from advancing along the N13 road. The paratroopers were to secure LZs for the follow-up glider landings at dawn and dusk.

The 101st was assigned three DZs. The 502nd Parachute Infantry Regiment (PIR) was to land on DZ 'A', to the immediate west of St Germain de Varreville, the 506th PIR on DZ 'C', west of St Marie du Mont and the 501st PIR on DZ 'D', east of St Côme du Mont and north of the road and rail crossings over the rivers Douve and Groule. DZ 'C' would be cleared to accept glider resupply.

DZ 'O', west of St Mère Eglise, would be the drop zone for the 505th PIR while the 507th and 508th PIR would land at DZs 'T' and 'N', west of the river Merderet. Resupply and reinforcements from the 325th Regiment would come by glider to LZs cleared south of St Mère Eglise. A total force of 13,000 men would be delivered to the area and the paratroop lift alone would require 822 transport aircraft.

From the outset, the plans were opposed by Leigh-Mallory who said that flak in the area, including the heavily defended Channel Islands and around Cherbourg, was too heavy and that the DZs and LZs in the area were unsuitable for paratroopers

Left: A paratrooper of the 101st Airborne Division, the 'Screaming Eagles', armed with a folding butt M1A1 Carbine.

Right: Laden with equipment and his parachute, a soldier of the 101st Airborne Division armed with a 'Bazooka' 2.36in (60mm) M1A1 anti-tank launcher boards a Douglas C-47 Skytrain. Hours later hundreds of men would be jumping out of similar doorways over Normandy.

and gliders. He asserted that the US forces would take at least 75 percent casualties. Montgomery, backed by Bradley, persisted in advocating the plan.

Only two weeks before D-Day, Allied planners learned that a fresh German division, the 91st Air Landing Division (which included the élite 6th Paratroop Regiment) commanded by Lt Gen Wilhelm Falley, had been moved in to the area of the 82nd Airborne DZ. Falley had fought with distinction on the Eastern Front where he had been decorated with the Knight's Cross. He was wounded in 1942 and while recovering, served on the staffs of Infantry Schools at

GENERAL FRIEDRICH DOLLMANN

Dollmann had served in World War I, but unlike his contemporaries, in the four years of World War II he had seen virtually no action. However, he was an adept 'political soldier' and as a Bavarian, he had ingratiated himself with the leaders of the Nazi Party, many of whom came from southern Germany, and this had furthered his career. Life in France had been enjoyable and by D-Day he was 62, overweight and suffering from poor health. He had also failed to keep up to date with weapons development and modern tactics. He had no conception of the weight of Allied firepower or knowledge of armoured tactics. When he ordered the Panzer Lehr and 12th SS Panzer Divisions to move to the front he instructed them to do so in daylight, but to maintain radio silence. These orders led to chaos in the Panzer Lehr. Allied ground attack fighters destroyed 40 loaded fuel trucks and 84 half-tracks and self-propelled guns and numerous other vehicles. The enraged divisional commander commented, 'As if radio silence could have stopped the fighter-bombers and reconnaissance planes from spotting us!' When the port of Cherbourg fell on 26 June, Hitler accused Dollmann of negligence and on 29 June he was replaced by the experienced and highly competent *SS-Obergruppenführer*, Paul Hausser. By now the pressure had become too great for the unfit Dollmann, who had a massive heart attack and died on the morning of 29 June. Hitler authorized a laudatory obituary.

Döberitz and Posen. Returning to the USSR commanding the 246th Infantry Division, he had helped halt the Soviet winter offensive of 1943 and 1944.

TALKING TO THE TROOPS

The American airborne plan was modified but Leigh-Mallory continued to express doubts. A week before D-Day, with perhaps an eye to history, he wrote to Eisenhower

Below: 'Stand Up. Hook Up.' US paratroops in a C-47 start the final ritual before the orders 'Stand in the Door… Red On… Green On. GO!" that will send them out into the slipstream over northern France. Static lines ensured the paratroopers' parachutes deployed safely.

stating that slow-moving troop carriers and tugs and gliders flying at a fixed altitude would be an easy target for flak. Worst still, flooded and swampy ground would be potentially lethal for heavily laden paratroopers moving in the dark. It would, he wrote, be a 'highly speculative operation'. Eisenhower read the letter and over-ruled him.

On the evening of 5 June, Kay Summersby, Eisenhower's British driver, took him out to the tented camp of 502nd Parachute Regiment, 101st Airborne, at Greenham Common, Newbury. Here, Eisenhower talked with Maxwell Taylor and then, in some of the most memorable film of the operation, informally chatted with the young paratroopers. Their faces were smeared with camouflage cream as they listened intently.

The conversation was informal and very typical of Ike.

'What's your job, soldier?'

'Ammunition bearer, sir.'

'Where's your home?'

'Pennsylvania, sir.'

'Did you get those shoulders working in a coal mine?'

'Yes, sir.'

Among the soldiers with whom Eisenhower talked was Lt Wallace C. Strobel, the jumpmaster of Company E. It was the young officer's 22nd birthday and though his face was anonymous under the camouflage cream, as jumpmaster, he wore a label with the number 23. Strobel survived the war and recalled that the Supreme Commander simply asked, 'What's your name, Lieutenant?' and 'Where are you from?'

One of the paratroopers, seeing a frown of concern on Eisenhower's face, cracked it into a grin when he said. 'Now

Above: A famous image of Eisenhower giving a pep talk to men of the 101st before they embarked for France on 5 June 1944. Eisenhower was clearly nervous – he realised what a gamble the Allies were taking with the invasion, and what defeat could mean for the Allied powers.

quit worrying, General, we'll take care of this thing for you.' As he turned away, Eisenhower's eyes were moist with tears.

Back in his staff car, he said quietly to Kay Summersby, whose discretion and support would be invaluable, 'I hope to God I know what I'm doing.'

In part, Leigh-Mallory's fears would be realized. Thick cloud made it hard for the pilots of the Pathfinder aircraft to navigate accurately and the Pathfinders were dropped in the wrong areas. Flak did not prove as great a hazard as had been feared but pilots' attempts to avoid it meant they either flew too fast or at the wrong altitude for safe delivery of the

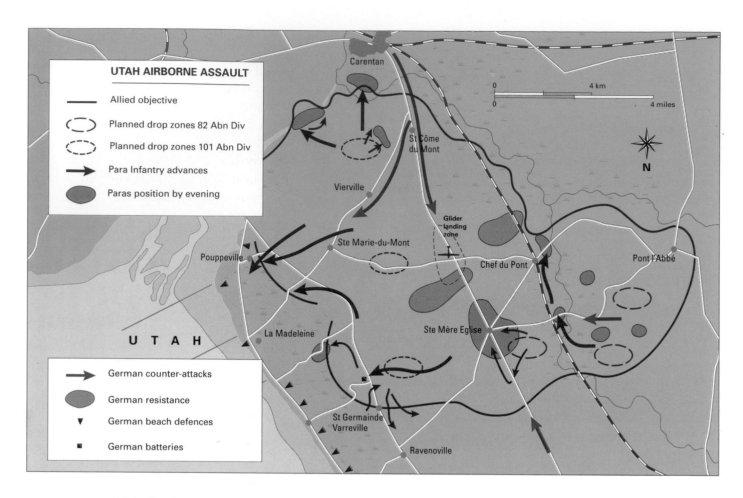

UTAH AIRBORNE ASSAULT

—— Allied objective

⬭ Planned drop zones 82 Abn Div

⬭ Planned drop zones 101 Abn Div

→ Para Infantry advances

⬭ Paras position by evening

→ German counter-attacks

⬬ German resistance

▼ German beach defences

▪ German batteries

paratroopers. Critically, they scattered the soldiers over a wide area, which meant that they were unable to form balanced and cohesive groups. For paratroopers on the ground, there was the terrible experience of hearing Dakota pilots flying too low. They knew their comrades' parachutes wouldn't deploy properly.

A sight that has never left my memory… was a picture story of the death of one 82nd Airborne trooper. He had occupied a German foxhole and made it his personal Alamo. In a half-circle around the hole lay the bodies of nine German soldiers. The body closest to the hole was only three feet away, a grenade in its fist. The other distorted forms lay where they had fallen, testimony to the ferocity of the fight. His ammunition bandoleers were still on his shoulders, empty… Cartridge cases littered the ground. His rifle stock was broken in two. He had fought alone and like many that night, he had died alone.

Private John E. Fitzgerald
502nd PIR, 101st Airborne Division

Above: The US airborne landings securing the western flank of the Allied bridgehead before the beach landings began. A major factor for the American paratroopers was the extensive flooded areas in which a number of paratroopers drowned.

COUNTER ATTACK ON UTAH

Below the American paratroopers, the area was defended by the 243rd and 709th Static Infantry Divisions which though largely composed of second line troops were equipped with some tanks, self-propelled guns and the normal allocation of artillery. These forces were beefed up with the 91st Division that had a battery of 12 8.8cm (3.46in) Pak/Flak guns. Ironically, one of the early German fatalities was Gen Falley who was speeding back to his headquarters at St Saveur from a war-gaming exercise in Rennes to the south.

The commanders and senior officers from the 91st, 77th, 709th, 352nd and 716th Divisions had been attending the study day at Rennes, the subject of which was 'defence against the airborne and seaborne invasion of the Cotentin peninsula'. Many of the senior officers who were not on the study day ordered by Gen Dollmann, commander of the Seventh Army and organized by Gen Meindl of the II Parachute

As I dove for the ditch, all hell broke loose. We had been ambushed. The German behind the hedge had his weapon set on full automatic and it sprayed bullets all over the area. Instantaneously, shots started coming from the buildings in Ste Côme-du-Mont and from the hedges… It was obvious that we were badly outnumbered and that the Germans were well emplaced and planned to defend Ste Côme-du-Mont stubbornly. So there we were, 200 yards north of Ste Côme-du-Mont, meeting superior fire from a major force. We had no automatic weapons, no radios, only our semi-automatic rifles and a few pistols. We hardly knew each other, but we were getting well acquainted, and we were working well together.

Captain Sam Gibbons
501st PIR, US 101st Airborne Division

Corps, were away from their headquarters. The absence of so many senior officers on D-Day fired the paranoid mind of Adolf Hitler who ordered an investigation to establish if this was the work of the British Secret Service.

Interrogated after the war, Lt Gen Karl von Schlieben, who commanded the 709th Division, was convinced that had Gen Falley survived he would have ensured that a balanced counter-attack was delivered against Utah beach supported by artillery, flak and armour.

Of the two American airborne divisions, the 82nd got off with fewest casualties. It landed west of Ste Mère Eglise and astride the Merderet. The 505th PIR landed on its assigned DZ, the 1st/505th moved west to secure the road and rail bridges and the 2nd/505th moved to cover the northern approaches to Ste Mère Eglise. The 3rd/505th under Lt Col Edward 'Cannonball' Krause approached Ste Mère Eglise and the colonel decided to assault the town. The defending troops were Austrians from a flak transportation unit and, taken by surprise, were driven out. The citizens remembered them as fairly genial occupiers with little taste for the war.

The town was taken at 04:00 hours and the Stars and Stripes that the 3rd/505th had flown when they liberated Naples was unfurled and hung from the Marie. The German 91st Division launched several aggressive counter-attacks and, though the Americans were outnumbered five to one, they held the town, though by the end of the day, only 16 out of 42 were still alive. The men who fought their way into the town were startled to find the bodies of their comrades in F Coy 2nd /505th who had landed directly on the roofs and trees. One Private John Steele had snagged his parachute on the tower of the town church and hung limply in his harness playing dead – the Germans ignored him during the fighting and he survived to be taken prisoner.

The division's other two regiments were scattered west of the river Merderet and had landed in areas of grassy swamp that looked in aerial photographs like pasture. Many men drowned in the darkness, struggling with their parachute harnesses and equipment in the flooded river valley. Among the men to survive was the Deputy Divisional Commander, Maj Gen James 'Jumpin' Jim' Gavin. He gathered a force of 100 men and held the small village of la Fière that became a

Below: The church of Ste Mère Eglise today, with a dummy depicting Private John Steele. Steele pretended to be dead as he hung snagged on the tower, unable to move, and saw the fighting below. He was later taken prisoner.

Above: The spoils of war. US paratroops hold a captured Swastika flag, that in former times would have been used to signal German positions to Luftwaffe ground support aircraft. These paratroopers were lucky – they linked up with the beach landings on 7 June 1944.

The 101st Airborne drop was distributed over an area of almost 650sq km (400sq miles) between Ste Mère Eglise and Carentan. The pilots of the IX Troop Carrier Command (TCC), commanded by Maj Gen Paul Williams, had flown a complex dog-leg flight plan and unacquainted with flak, had jinked and manoeuvred and ended up losing touch. Fog and clouds added to the confusion. On D-Day the IX TCC flew 1606 sorties, towed 512 gliders and lost 41 aircraft and nine gliders.

By dawn only 1100 men of the 101st Airborne Division's 6600 had reached their reporting points and only a further 1400 had assembled by the end of D-Day. Some had been dropped over 40km (25 miles) from their planned DZs. On the ground, the men discovered that orientation at night in small fields bordered by high thick hedges was extremely difficult. The scattering of the force had one advantage though – it confused the Germans, who were unable to identify a pattern to the landings and so prepare a counter-attack.

General Maxwell Taylor landed south of Ste Marie du Mont. Divisional history would say that the 'commander of 14,000 men found himself on a battlefield without a single one of those men within sight or hearing, any order he might have given would have been received only by a circle of curious Norman cows'.

Compared to Gavin, Taylor was an old man, 43 years old. He had participated in operations in North Africa and Sicily and in September 1943 had entered Italy behind German lines to assess the ability of the Italians to support an American airborne drop in the vicinity of Rome. He determined that it would be a disaster and Eisenhower cancelled it. Writing about Taylor's mission, Eisenhower asserted: 'The risks he ran were greater than I asked any other agent or emissary to undertake during the war.'

Taylor had assumed command of the 101st Airborne Division in England when its commander, Gen Bill Lee, 'the

western outpost for Ste Mère Eglise. The division drop was divided by the river and swamp and so the bridges at Chef du Pont and la Fière became critical for liaison and communication. On D-Day, Gavin was a 37-year-old Brigadier General. He had already seen action in North Africa, Sicily and Salerno and was senior airborne adviser for COSSAC. In August 1944 he was promoted to command the 82nd Airborne Division, the youngest man to hold this position in the US Army in World War II.

Much of the equipment dropped from the gliders was lost as the paratroopers had not had time to prepare or mark the LZs. Some 60 percent of the equipment of the 456th Artillery and 80th Anti-tank Artillery Battalions was lost. Some ended up as an unexpected gift for the German 6th Parachute Regiment who were quick to investigate the contents of the scattered supply containers and discover the wonders of US rations – chocolate, Virginia tobacco, condensed milk and instant coffee.

father of American parachute operations', suffered a heart attack. Lee had shaped the division and in his opening address to his men in training in the US had inspired them with the words: 'The 101st has no history, but it has a rendezvous with destiny.'

Losses in men and equipment due to the flooding near the coast were heavy. The 456th Parachute Artillery Regiment lost 11 of its 12 75mm (2.95in) guns, but put the remaining gun to good use.

As they gained confidence and began to pick out landmarks, the men of the 101st moved towards their planned objectives.

101ST IN ACTION

Maxwell Taylor collected together a small force from the 501st PIR and moved towards Ste Marie du Mont. Col Sink of the 506th PIR could only assemble 50 men to take Pouppeville. Lt Col Strayer of the 2nd/506th PIR gathered a force made up of elements of his battalion, the 3rd/506th PIR and strays from the 82nd Division's 508th PIR. It was a tiny force, since only ten transport aircraft out of a total of 84 had managed to drop the 2nd/506th PIR on the correct DZ. They then moved eastwards to secure Exit No 2 from Utah, a move critical to the later breakout from the beaches.

Col Ewell, commanding the 3rd/501st, collected about 100 men and moved off to secure Exit No 1 on the causeways off Utah. Looking at his group he realized that it had more officers than men and chuckled, 'never have so few been led by so many'.

The 3rd/501st, who landed on DZ 'D', was probably the most unlucky battalion. The local German commander had recognized that the area was a potential DZ and thus had it covered by machine guns and mortars. The second-in-command of the 3rd/501st was an early casualty and by the time the area had been secured, the unit was down to five officers and 29 men, out of an original strength of about 1000 men.

AIRBORNE ARTILLERY

The 75mm (2.95in) Pack Howitzer M1A1 on Carriage (Airborne) M8 was a US design. For parachute drops, the howitzer could be broken down into nine loads. It had a muzzle velocity of 381m/sec (1250ft/sec) and a maximum range of 8930m (9760yds), firing a 6.25kg (13.76lb) M41A1 shell. It originally weighed 588kg (1296lb) but with rubber tyres, this increased to 608kg (1340lb). By the end of the war, some 4939 75mm (2.95in) M1A1 Pack Howitzers had been built.

HITLER'S D-DAY TIMETABLE

05:00 The first reports of the landings reach Hitler's summer retreat at the Berghof, Berchtesgaden, Bavaria. He has taken a sleeping tablet so no-one wakes him.

09:00 Hitler is woken and immediately calls a planning conference.

12:00 Hitler chairs an upbeat conference at the tea house on the Kehlstein. The feeling is that a landing will allow the German forces to get to grips with the Allies. The Normandy landings are still thought to be a diversion.

16:55 Hitler sends orders to Field Marshal Von Rundstedt stating that 'the enemy beachhead must be cleaned up no later than tonight'.

23:00 In a final situation report, Hitler states that the Normandy landings are a diversion.

Despite these heavy losses, the battalion moved off to the primary objective – the wooden bridges across the Douve, which they took and held against heavy attacks. The 1st/501st set off towards the road and rail bridges across the Douve but encountered the German 3rd/1058th at the hamlet of les Droueries, near Ste Côme-du-Mont.

Elements of the German 1058th Regiment also held the lock at la Barquette, the objective for the 2nd/501st commanded by Lt Col Johnson. On the way in he had narrowly escaped injury or death when the green light signalling the order to jump had come on in his C-47 Skytrain. At the same moment, a container of supplies fell, blocking the exit and delaying the jump until the aircraft was north of la Barquette.

The men landed safely and captured the lock. When they came under fire from German batteries east of Carentan and Saint-Côme-du-Mont, they were able to call in supporting fire from the cruiser USS Quincy.

Though widely dispersed, the landings by the 82nd and 101st Airborne had distracted the Germans and secured the exits along the causeways from Utah beach. To the east the British had enjoyed greater success and at Pegasus Bridge achieved a coup that would be celebrated after the war as a battle honour for both the Parachute Regiment and the Royal Green Jackets.

It was now the dawn of D-Day. The way had now been prepared for the amphibious landings.

CHAPTER SIX

UTAH BEACH

The operation at Utah beach was the least costly in human lives of all the Allied landings on D-Day. This was in part because of the initiative of Brigadier General Theodore Roosevelt. He was an old man of 57 and one of the most senior officers to land on D-Day. When he came ashore at Utah, he quickly realised that it was the 'wrong' beach, the landing craft having drifted south during their run in to the shore. However, this section of the beach was far less heavily defended, and Roosevelt ordered that the landings should continue.

A LANDING ON THE EAST COAST of the Cotentin Peninsula had not been envisaged in the initial plan for D-Day. In early 1944, when the Allied planners increased the sea-assault force from three to five divisions, an open stretch of sandy coast backed by grassy dunes and a concrete sea wall known as les Dunes de Varreville became Utah beach. About 6.4km (4 miles) to the south was the twin mouths of the rivers Douve and Vire that effectively separated Utah from the other invasion beaches. At low tide, the flat sand was 1km (0.5 mile) wide and it was here that the 8th Regiment commanded by Colonel James A Van Fleet would land.

In the German evaluation of possible Allied landing sites, their Seventh Army had not only identified the Normandy coast, but also the Cotentin Peninsula. They had even anticipated the flanking locations of the airborne attacks that would support the amphibious assault. However, they had also considered that amphibious landings supported by paratroopers would be made in Brittany to capture the port of Brest.

Left: A surviving gun position in a Widerstandnest *(Resistance Nest) covering Utah Beach. These positions were sited to give interlocking fire along the beach, and were in effect self-contained forts with a mixture of weaponry for long range and local defence.*

The US Army 8th Regiment, along with the 12th and 22nd Regiments, was made up from the infantry element of the 4th US Infantry Division, commanded by Major General Raymond O Barton. They were known as 'The Ivy Leaves' because of their distinctive divisional patch. General Bradley had visited the division in England and described it as 'superbly trained'. It would become the first American unit to enter Paris and, in 1945, Gen Patton wrote to Barton that 'no American division in France has excelled the magnificent record of the 4th Infantry Division, which has been almost continuously in action since it fought its way ashore on the 6th of last June.' On June 6 the follow up formations after the 4th Division had secured the beach would be the 90th, 9th and 79th Infantry Divisions.

THE PLAN

The American plan was that following the air and naval bombardment, Duplex Drive (DD) amphibious Sherman tanks would land first. They would be followed by the 2nd Battalion 8th Regiment carried in 20 Landing Craft, Vehicle and Personnel (LCVP), also known as Higgins Boats after the US boat builder who made them. Each boat would carry a platoon of 31 men.

The second wave of 32 LCVPs carrying 1st Battalion 8th Regiment plus combat engineers and naval demolition teams would land five minutes later.

The third wave would arrive 15 minutes later and included eight Landing Craft Tank (LCTs) with bulldozer tanks and conventional M4 Shermans.

Finally the fourth wave would arrive carrying men of the 237th and 229th Engineer Combat Battalions (ECBs).

For the plan, Utah was subdivided into a northern beach GREEN, with the sea approaches identified by the phonetic word for 'T' - TARE, so the different beaches were designated TARE GREEN and a southern 'U'- UNCLE, so UNCLE RED.

Opposite them at the base of the Cotentin Peninsula were ranged the German 709th Infantry Division commanded by Lieutenant General Karl W von Schlieben and elements of the 352nd Infantry Division under Lt Gen Dietrich Kraiss. The Germans had flooded the low-lying farmland behind the beaches and so made it impassable to vehicles and a hazardous drop zone for paratroopers. On the beach between high and low water there were three lines of obstacles, mainly

Right: A USAAF B-26 Marauder medium bomber in distinctive D-Day stripes over the invasion fleet in the hours after the weather improved in the afternoon of June 6. Only two German fighters appeared over the landing beaches on D-Day.

steel spikes and wooden posts with fused shells or Teller anti-tank mines as well as tetrahedra and Czech hedgehog anti-tank obstacles. Inland and along the coast, the Germans had built a group of *Widerstandsnesten* (WN) (Resistance nests) with platoon-strength garrisons from the 709th that covered the five road exits from the beach through the flooded farmland.

The average age of the defenders was 36 while that of the Allied invasion force was ten years younger. In the whole German Army in 1944 the average age was now 31, which contrasted to that of the German Army in 1917 which was 27.

In the analysis of Lt Gen Max Pemsel of the Seventh Army, the German 709th and 716th Infantry Divisions, though 'static' formations, had been 'well acquainted with their sectors for years, [and were] well-trained for defence, [but with] not much combat experience'. Many of the men within the division suffered from stomach ailments and were grouped in special 'Stomach and Ear Battalions' or 'White Bread Battalions' where their health problems could be centrally monitored.

Others units like the 795th Georgian Ost Battalion was made up of former Eastern Front prisoners-of-war. The

Above: US soldiers packed into Higgins Boats or LCVPs prepared to move off from a troopship. For the first wave to land on D-Day, the trip on the flat-bottomed craft was a grim journey where fear and sea sickness ensured that few except the hardened Navy crew did not vomit.

Georgian soldiers were commanded by German or Baltic NCOs and officers and were expected to understand their orders and instructions delivered to them in German.

Lt General Karl von Schlieben a veteran of fighting in this theatre, remarked ruefully: 'We are asking rather a lot if we expect Russians to fight in France for Germany against Americans.' On the day, many took the opportunity to surrender or run away.

However, if the men of the 1st Battalion 919th Grenadier Regiment, 709th Infantry Division in the *Widerstandsnesten* on the south-east coast of the Cotentin Peninsula could hold long enough they would ensure that an invasion force would be trapped and destroyed on the long, flat sand beaches.

The *Widerstandsnesten* numbered four to ten from south to north along the beaches and covered the exits through the flooded land behind the coast. The nests themselves were self-contained forts that could deliver lateral fire along the shore. One of them, WN5, would feature prominently in the Utah landings because it covered Exit 2. Further along the

coast, WN7 was a formidable position with three 3.7cm (1.46in) tank turrets, casemates housing a 7.5cm (2.95in) gun facing north and two with a 5cm (1.97in) KwK and a 4.7cm (1.85in) K36(t) covering approaches from the south. The position also had two 5cm (1.97in) mortars and was protected by seven dug-in flame-throwers and four machine gun positions.

At 04:30 hours, 132 men of the US 2nd and 4th Cavalry, under Lieutenant Colonel Dunn, landed on the islands of Saint Marcouf that commanded the approaches to Utah. Enemy activity had been seen on the islands in May and it was thought that it had an observation post or minefield control point. The Germans had not garrisoned the islands but had mined them extensively and along

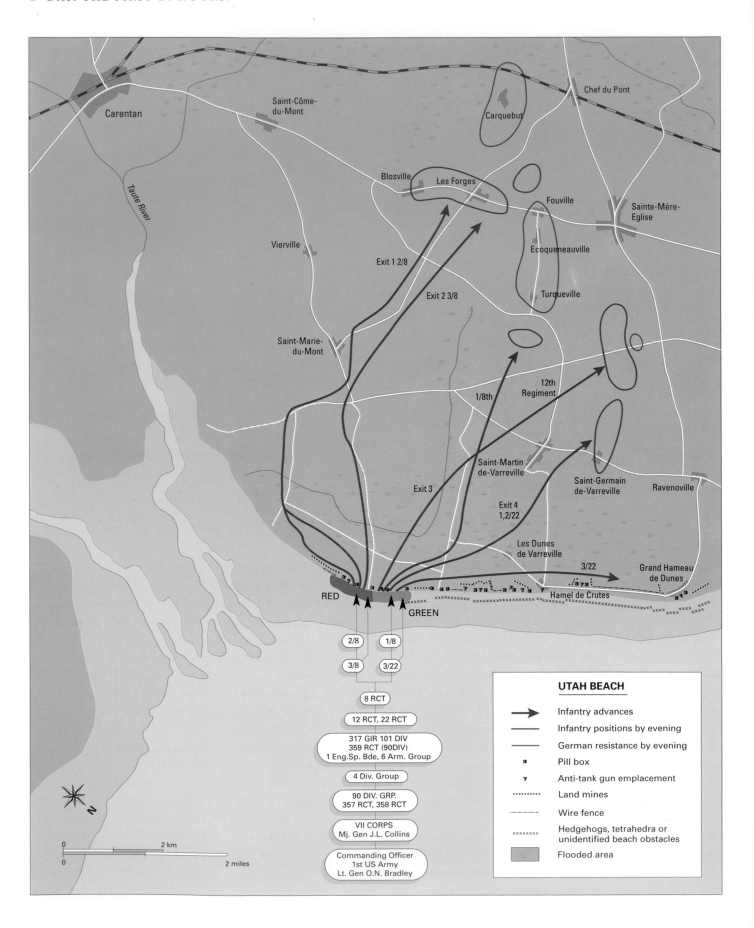

Carentan

Taute River

Saint-Côme-du-Mont

Carquebut

Chef du Pont

Blosville

Les Forges

Fouville

Sainte-Mére-Eglise

Vierville

Ecoqueneauville

Exit 1 2/8

Exit 2 3/8

Turqueville

Saint-Marie-du-Mont

12th Regiment

1/8th

Saint-Martin de-Varreville

Saint-Germain de-Varreville

Ravenoville

Exit 3

Exit 4 1,2/22

Les Dunes de Varreville

3/22

Grand Hameau de Dunes

Hamel de Crutes

RED

GREEN

2/8   1/8

3/8   3/22

8 RCT

12 RCT, 22 RCT

317 GIR 101 DIV
359 RCT (90DIV)
1 Eng.Sp. Bde, 6 Arm. Group

4 Div. Group

90 DIV. GRP.
357 RCT, 358 RCT

VII CORPS
Mj. Gen J.L. Collins

Commanding Officer
1st US Army
Lt. Gen O.N. Bradley

UTAH BEACH

→ Infantry advances

—— Infantry positions by evening

—— German resistance by evening

▪ Pill box

▾ Anti-tank gun emplacement

········· Land mines

—— Wire fence

✕✕✕✕✕ Hedgehogs, tetrahedra or unidentified beach obstacles

Flooded area

N

0   2 km
0   2 miles

Above: Landing craft move to and from Utah Beach while on the foreshore beached craft and wrecked vehicles can be seen among the obstacles and infantry. The causeways through the flooded country behind the beach are visible in the top right of the picture.

the shore bombardment. Their initial targets were the known major gun batteries. The cruisers then closed to engage bunkers and coastal defences.

At 06:00 hours, the destruction was further compounded by a sortie by 270 Martin Marauder medium bombers of the USAAF IX Bomber Command which dropped 4404 110kg (250lb) bombs. Of the force, 67 failed to release their bombs because of poor visibility and some of the bombs fell on farmland inland from the beaches because the crews had been told to delay several seconds before releasing to avoid hitting the invasion force offshore. This was an error that would be compounded at Omaha. Smaller calibre bombs had been chosen to ensure that craters did not impede movement on the beaches.

As the run in by the landing craft began, of the two guide ships Landing Craft Control (LCC) off Uncle Red, one hit a mine and the other fouled its propeller 5km (3 miles) offshore.

Just before the landing craft grounded on the sand, 'drenching fire' was directed at the coastline by destroyers and 33 Landing Craft Gun LCT (G) and Landing Craft Tank Rocket LCT (R). The LCT (R) fired 1000 0.9kg (2lb) rockets in three salvos.

The current carried the invasion shipping southwards along the coast before the LCVPs finally hit the beach. The

with artillery fire this killed two US soldiers and wounded 17 on D-Day.

At 03.00 hours, 21km (13 miles) offshore, troops of the 8th Regiment began to transfer from the troop ships of Task Force 'U' to LCVPs in preparation for the three-hour journey to the beach. In the rough weather, some men were injured or drowned as they made their way into the craft and during the run to the shore many men were violently sea sick from a combination of the rough weather and tension.

With an awesome roar at 05:50 hours, the Offshore Bombardment Force 'A', under Rear Admiral Moon, began

Left: A map of the landing at Utah Beach clearly showing the estuary that cut the beach off from the other landing areas on D-Day, and the large-scale flooding of the areas behind the beach. Movement was restricted to elevated causeways which were extremely exposed.

men of the 2nd Battalion 8th Regiment were the first to land on Uncle Red at 06:30 hours.

According to the plan they should be opposite Exit No 3, while the 1st Battalion landing a few minutes later should be in front of the German position at St Martin-de-Varreville. In fact, they landed 1.6km (1 mile) south, opposite Exit No 2.

If they had landed at their intended location, they would have run into an obstacle belt on the shore and then have been forced to fight through WN6, a powerful defensive position commanded by Lt Schön.

Brigadier General Theodore Roosevelt Jnr, the 57-year-old Assistant Divisional Commander, a position he described as 'a spare Brigadier', who landed in the first wave, realized that there had been a mistake, but also that the German opposition was weak. Earlier, he had watched the preparatory air attacks from his landing craft and recalled: 'Flight after flight dropped its bombs on the German emplacements. There'd be a ripple of thunder, blazes of light, clouds of dust, and the planes would pass us on their way home. One fell by me, flaming like a meteor.'

Ashore, Roosevelt spotted a windmill that enabled him to recognize where he had landed. Realizing that opposition was modest he ordered his troops to push inland and signalled to the ships offshore that landing craft should continue to land at the new beach. His radio was out of action for three hours and consequently he commented: 'Most of our work was done on foot. As the succeeding waves

Above: With Utah Beach secured, an orderly line of M4 Shermans modified for deep wading moves towards the shore while White half tracks that have already landed queue to move through the exit in the sand dunes. Meanwhile infantry wade ashore to support the vehicles.

landed I pushed them inland if they halted and redirected them when they started to go wrong.'

The son of the former President Teddy Roosevelt, he had pressed to be assigned to a formation that would land at D-Day. He came ashore with the first wave on Utah beach and led his troops off the beach, over the sea wall and inland, where they established secure positions. He then returned to the beach, leading other groups over the sea wall to the secure positions over and over again. For these actions he was awarded the United States' highest gallantry decoration, the Medal of Honor.

'WE'LL START THE WAR RIGHT HERE'

Gen Eisenhower recognized Roosevelt's ability to instil vitality into a combat unit and decided to give him command of the 90th 'Tough Ombres' Infantry Division on 12 July 1944. Roosevelt never assumed his new command, as he died of a heart attack in his Jeep on the evening of 11 July 1944. He was buried in the American Cemetery in Normandy on Bastille Day, 14 July 1944.

Gen Patton, a man careful with his praise, recorded in his diary that Roosevelt 'was one of the bravest men I ever knew'. At Utah he had the tactical knowledge and the rank to capitalize on the navigation error and did so with the memorable words: 'We'll start the war right here.'

For Sergeant William Clayton of the 4th Infantry Division, there was a strange sense of unreality. 'It was just like a big play, until they started shooting, you know – a few shells came and you realized it was not a play. But other than that, it was beautiful.'

The first eight DD tanks of the 70th Tank Battalion launched offshore from LCTs reached the beach at 06:45 hours. The tanks had been launched only 3.2km (2 miles) from the shore instead of the planned 6.4km (4 miles) and consequently, of the 32 DD tanks carried in eight LCTs, a total of 28 made it to the beach to give direct fire support. They were followed by tank dozers and other vehicles.

Engineers of the 4th ECB began to clear minefields and obstacle belts.

On Tare Green, the northern beach, the 1st Battalion came ashore and swung right and captured WN5, the strongpoint near the defended village of La Madeleine on Exit No 2 leading to St Marie-du-Mont.

WN5 was held by the 1st Platoon, 3rd Coy 919th Grenadier Regiment commanded by the bespectacled 23-year-old Lieutenant Arthur Jahnke. The young officer had been posted to France after being wounded on the Eastern Front where his leadership had earned him the Knight's Cross. He was a serious soldier, nicknamed by the soldiers under his command the 'Ruski' because of his service in Russia and he had worked hard preparing the defences for his position.

His weaponry included two 5cm (1.97in) guns, a former French Renault R67 tank turret with 3.7cm (1.46in) gun

Below: US Army medics work on a GI wounded in the first moments of the landing. The medics would aim to stabilize and rehydrate the casualty so that he could be evacuated back to England aboard a modified landing ship and treated in hospitals that had been readied.

concreted into a bunker, machine guns covering the beach and landwards approaches, and barbed wire and minefields. On either flank of his position were four *Goliath* remote-controlled tracked demolition vehicles. The first version had been designed and built by the Hansa-Lloyd-Goliath Werke Carl FW Borgward and was powered by two converted electric starter motors. It carried 60kg (132lb) of TNT and was directed towards its target by its operator through signals transmitted along a cable. It had a road range of 1.5km (1 mile) and maximum speed of 10km/h (6mph).

Bombing and naval gunfire would smash many of these defences, installations and the cable links for the *Goliaths* before the American battalion put in its attack. Later, one demolition vehicle would cause casualties, when ignorant of its function, a US soldier put a hand grenade into an access hatch and detonated the 60kg (132lb) payload, killing or wounding 15 to 20 men unfortunate to be near it. On Sword beach, British Sappers were able to disarm captured *Goliaths* and used them to tow or transport stores.

By the middle of the afternoon the beach had changed from nothing but obstacles to a small city. It was apparent that we NCD units had done our job well because as far as I could see one side of the beach was all the way opened, there was nothing holding the landing craft back. We figured our day was well spent, even though no one knew who we were… The coxswains didn't like us because we always had so many explosives with us. When we went inland the Army officers wanted to know, 'What is the Navy doing in here?'

Sergeant Orval Wakefield
US Navy Construction/Demolition Battalion

Below: An infantry section wait for orders in foxholes on Utah beach later in the day. The beach is already becoming crowded with jeeps, trucks and tanks as the great flow of logistics needed to keep the Allied armies fighting gets under way.

In the early hours of 6 June, a fighting patrol from Jahnke's small garrison had ventured out and captured 19 men of the 2nd Battalion 506th Parachute Regiment, part of the 101st Airborne. His erstwhile prisoners now watched as their captor was held near the battered remains of his strongpoint by beach-landed US troops. Inland, the German 10th Battery, 1261st Army Coastal Artillery Regiment, commanded by Col Triepel, opened fire with its 17cm (6.7in) guns. Shells fell among the men and vehicles and Jahnke, having survived the massive US bombardment was wounded by 'friendly fire'.

CLEARING THE BEACH

The 1st Battalion pushed on to Exit No 3, and by the evening, had reached Turqueville, opposite a strong German concentration at Ecoqueneauville.

By 08:00 hours four battalions were ashore and two hours later, the number had increased to six. The beachhead was 4km (2 miles) long and 6.4km (4 miles) deep.

The 2nd Battalion pushed off the beach and turned left to avoid the flooded areas and cleared WN2, a defensive position south of Exit No 2, commanded by Lt Ritter. The battalion then advanced through Pouppeville and St Marie-du-Mont, finally reaching a position on the crossroads at Les Forges on the Route National 17.

The 3rd Battalion, which had landed at Uncle Red, had continued down Exit No 2 through the village of Houdienville, linking up with the 2nd Battalion at Les Forges at the end of the day.

Around noon, patrols from the 4th Division made contact with men of the 3rd Battalion 301st Airborne and reached St Mère Eglise in the afternoon.

In the following waves landing on Tare Green, the 12th Regiment pushed over 10km (6 miles) inland through the flooded area to take a position at the end of the day covering the north-west flank of the beach head.

The 1st and 2nd Battalion 22nd Regiment had also landed at Tare Green, swung right past La Madeleine, crossed a flooded area and by the evening were to the right of 12th Regiment straddling the road at St Germain de Varreville.

Finally, after landing, the 3rd Battalion 22nd Regiment had swung sharp right and rolled up four *Widerstandsnesten* to the north of Utah. By nightfall they had reached the coastal village of Hamel de Cruttes about 10km (6 miles) from the invasion beach.

Above: A grin from a US Ranger equipped with the anti-tank weapon known popularly as the 'Bazooka' or more correctly as the 60mm (2.36in) Rocket Launcher M1A1. The weapon could also be used against bunkers and fortifications.

By the end of 6 June the 4th Division had achieved almost all of its objectives. Some 23,250 men and 1700 vehicles had been landed and the causeways were open. The Division had suffered 197 casualties of whom 60 were missing at sea and many of the rest had been injured by mines.

At St Côme du Mont, Lt Col Friedrich, Freiherr von der Heydte, the veteran German paratroop officer, commanding the 6th Parachute Regiment, climbed the church tower. 'An overwhelming picture presented itself to the regimental commander... Before him lay the coast and the sea. The horizon was strewn with hundreds of ships, and countless landing boats and barges were moving back and forth between the ships and shore, landing troops and tanks. It was an almost peaceful picture; in the combat report which I submitted at the time to the Parachute Army, I wrote that it reminded me of a beautiful summer day on the Wannsee. The noise of battle could not be heard, and from the church tower… there was no sign of German defence activities. Only a shot rang out here and there whenever the sentries of the German battalions came into contact with Allied paratroopers.'

Helmut Berndt, a correspondent with the *Kriegsmarine*, reported: 'Most of the bigger ships lie at anchor; through the haze they resemble an imaginary city with winking towers in the mist – "The Golden City", as the troops call it.'

Inland, the German naval personnel of the Crisbecq also known as the St Marcouf battery, part of the 1261st Army Coastal Artillery Regiment, observed the 'Golden City' and would fight an epic defence against its formidable firepower. The battery at full strength consisted of three officers, seven NCOs and 287 men commanded by Ensign First Class Walter Ohmsen.

Construction work had begun in 1941 for a battery of six 15cm (5.9in) guns. On D-Day, all but one of these guns had been moved to Fontenay-sur-Mer and it had been rearmed with three more powerful Czech-built Skoda K52 21cm (8.26in) guns. They had a range of 33km (20miles) and their Type 683 casemates allowed them to cover an arc of 120 degrees. However, they had a slow rate of fire because to reload they had to be at an elevation of eight degrees and then re-aimed. On D-Day, only two of these guns were operational. Regular air attacks had delayed the construction of the three remaining casemates that would house the other guns and protective armour plate had not been delivered to cover the embrasures.

The battery was protected against air attack by six 7.5cm (2.95in) and three 2cm (0.78in) flak guns that could also be used in the ground role. The perimeter was surrounded by a double barbed wire fence and minefield with 17 machine guns in Tobruks.

It had an Observation and Fire Control Post that also provided range data for a battery at Azeville some 2km (1.2 miles) to the south-west.

On the night of 5 June, Allied bombers dropped 610 tonnes (600 tons) of bombs on the position, destroying the AA guns and killing many of the men who were off duty in billets in adjoining houses. While Ohmsen was struggling to re-establish control in the dust and chaos of the attack, isolated groups of paratroopers from the 501st and 502nd PIRs of the 101st Airborne Division attempted to storm the

Above: US Rangers test their London Fire Brigade extending ladder during training in England. At the Pointe du Hoc they were unable to get close enough to the cliff, but heroic Rangers perched at the top of the ladders used light machine guns to engage the German defenders.

battery. They were beaten off and 20 were captured. Their mission had been to attack the 1/1261st battery at St Martin des Varreville about 6.4km (4 miles) to the west but they had been dropped well away from their objective. Ohmsen was startled to discover that some of the paratroopers were carrying maps that plotted the positions of his machine gun posts more accurately than his own.

At dawn, the naval gunners saw the shipping massed off Utah. Staff Sergeant Baumgarten recalled the calm contact report sent by Ohmsen to Admiral Hennecke, the naval commander in Cherbourg.

'Several hundred ships sighted in the Bay of the Seine.

Question: Any German vessels at sea?

No. None of our ships at sea. Any vessels sighted bound to be enemy ships. Permission to open fire. Ammunition to be used sparingly.

Message ends. Out'

The battery opened fire, sinking the destroyer USS *Corry* and hitting a cruiser and damaging other ships. (It is also claimed that the *Corry* hit a mine after being hit by shellfire). *Retribution* came quickly and fire from the 304cm (12in) and 355mm (14in) guns of the battleships USS *Nevada*, *Arkansas* and *Texas* knocked out one gun at 08:00 hours by a hit to the immediate front of the casemate and the second by a direct hit at 09:00 hours.

PROBING THE DEFENCES

On 7 and 8 June the US 4th Division that had landed at Utah probed the defences but were beaten back. By 8 June one gun had been repaired and was back in action, but was again knocked out by naval gunfire. The battery was reinforced by the 6th/919th Regiment under Lt Geissler. Ohmsen was also able to contact Lt Kattnig commanding the four 10cm (3.94in) Schneider gun battery at Azeville to call down fire onto his position. On the night of 11 June, Ohmsen received orders to evacuate the battery and move towards positions closer to Cherbourg. A medical orderly volunteered to remain behind with 21 wounded but 78 men slipped away in the darkness. The battery was taken by the 2nd/39th Infantry Regiment 9th Infantry Division on 12 June.

The battery at Azeville held out until 9 June and then after a heavy preliminary bombardment by the 44th Field Artillery Battalion that fired 1500 shells the 3rd/2nd Infantry Regiment attacked and overwhelmed the position. It was a hard fight with the Americans employing armour, pole charges and flame-throwers. When the battery finally fell it had expended all its main ammunition.

To the east of Utah, a different battle was fought on the 30m (100ft) high Pointe du Hoc in the position manned by the German 2nd Battery, 1260th Army Coastal Regiment. The area between Grandchamp Maisy and Vierville-sur-Mer was defended by the 716th Static Infantry Division, a unit that had a large number of non-Germans.

The site had been identified by the Germans as a good location for a defensive coastal battery and six captured French 155mm (6.1in) guns, designated 15cm GPF K418(f), were dug into open pits. They had a range of 19.5km (12 miles) and so could cover both Omaha and Utah and the approaches to the small ports of Isigny and Carentan.

The increased threat from Allied bombers led to concrete casemates being constructed for the guns. Two were still under construction on 6 June, but eight personnel bunkers, ammunition stores and 2cm (0.78in) flak positions had been built. The position was protected on the landward side by barbed wire, minefields and Tobruks, housing machine guns. A Type R636 Observation and Fire Control Post had been located at the tip of the headland and linked into the radar station at Pointe de la Percée 5km (3 miles) to the east.

With its prominent position, the battery was easy to locate from the air and it was attacked on 15 April, 22 May, 4 and 5 June. On the morning of 6 June, 700 tonnes (687 tons) of bombs were dropped and the battery was shelled by the 355mm (14in) guns of the battleship USS *Texas*.

The responsibility for the amphibious assault on the position lay with Gen Gerow's V Corps and hence with the 1st Infantry Division and the right flank assault formation the 116th Infantry Regiment detached from the 29th Division. The men for the task would have to be capable of climbing the cliffs before attacking the battery and the obvious choice for this were the Rangers.

Modelled on the British Commandos, this force had been formed in 1942. The historic name recalled the force of American Colonists that had been formed in the 18th Century with the formal title of 'His Majesty's Independent Company of American Rangers'. Fifty were selected to accompany British and Canadian forces to Dieppe in the attack in August 1942. The Rangers would thus have the distinction of being the first US soldiers to see action on land in the European Theatre of Operations (ETO) in World War II and sadly some of their number would be the first to be killed.

Two years later, they were a well-honed élite formation. The men designated for the task were from three companies in the US 2nd Ranger Battalion commanded by Lt Col James Rudder, a total force of 225 men.

They were to land at 06:30 hours. On receipt of the success signal at 07:00 hours, the remainder of the 2nd Battalion with the whole of the 5th Ranger Battalion would land to secure the area until relieved by forces landing at Dog Green on Omaha. If the plan failed, the reinforcement group would land at the western end of Omaha and hook round to assault the battery overland. It was a carefully thought through plan with plenty of allowances for losses and the errors of the 'fog of war' – allowances that would be vital on D-Day. However, Admiral Hall's intelligence officer had grimly prophesized: 'It can't be done. Three old women with brooms could keep the Rangers from climbing that cliff.'

In the pre-dawn light, a combination of a strong tide and navigation errors pushed the Royal Navy guide boat, ML 304, too far to the east towards the Pointe de la Percée, which looked like the Pointe du Hoc. Col Rudder alerted the Royal Navy officer by breaking out of formation and the Navy officer thought that the Rangers were attempting to

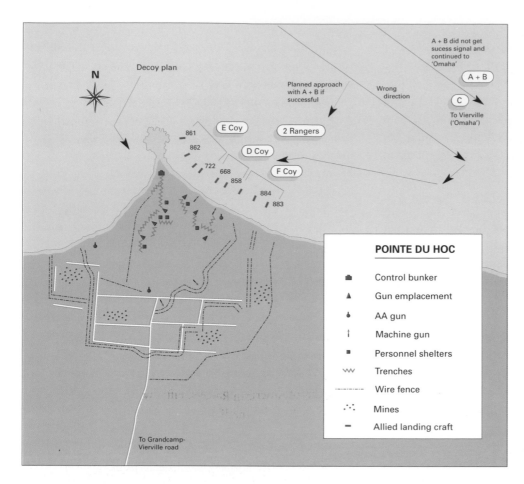

Decoy plan

A + B did not get
sucess signal and
continued to
'Omaha'

Planned approach
with A + B if
successful

Wrong
direction

A + B

C

To Vierville
('Omaha')

N

861
862
722 668
858
884
883

E Coy
2 Rangers
D Coy
F Coy

To Grandcamp-
Vierville road

POINTE DU HOC

🚢 Control bunker
▲ Gun emplacement
♦ AA gun
╵ Machine gun
■ Personnel shelters
〰 Trenches
⋯ Wire fence
∴ Mines
— Allied landing craft

Left: The US Ranger attack on the Pointe du Hoc battery showing the position of the landing craft and defences. Unknown to the Allied planners, the guns themselves were not in position.

closed to the shore and engaged the Germans with machine gun fire. In these critical minutes, the Rangers scrambled up and reached the top of the cliffs. A 12m (40ft) crater on the cliff was used along with 5m (16ft) telescopic ladders and toggle ropes to reach the summit. A violent firefight followed in the trenches and cratered landscape of the battery, the official American account called it a 'wild and frenzied scene'. When Corporal Kenneth Bargmann reached the top of the cliffs, 'it looked like the moon. There was nothing but craters. You ran from hole to hole like a rabbit.' When they finally reached the casemates to their disbelief the Rangers discovered that they were empty.

They then established a defensive perimeter and sent out patrols, one of which found the missing guns in an orchard about 1km (1.5 miles) to the south-west near Criqueville-en-Bessin. The Germans had removed them after the air raid on 15 April and stored them under camouflage. The two man patrol, led by Sgt Len Lommell, used Thermite grenades to attack the elevation and traversing mechanism. The intense heat generated by the grenades melted the mechanism. When the grenades ran out, Lommell then smashed the sights with his rifle while his companion stood guard. A second patrol later joined them and added to the destruction with their own Thermite grenades.

The Rangers would receive only one reinforcement during their siege. Sgt Leonard Goodgal of the 506th PIR, 101st Airborne had landed in France during the night and found himself close to the Pointe du Hoc. Hearing the sound of

abort the missions. When the mistake became clear, the landing craft turned about but in the swell, lost a DUKW to 2cm (0.78in) flak fire and LCA 91 to machine gun fire. As the landing craft came under fire its skipper Lt NE Fraser RNVR returned fire with the craft's Vickers machine gun.

FIGHT ON THE BEACHES

The Rangers, now down to only 180 men, arrived at their objective 40 minutes late. Since they had not received the success signal, the reinforcement group offshore moved away to be landed at Omaha.

At the battery, the gunners were fully alert and opened fire killing 15 men on the narrow shingle beach and then began to throw grenades and even rocks at the small group. The DUKWs were unable to drive close enough to the cliffs on the heavily cratered beach to deploy the ladders, but at 07:08 hours, the Rangers climbed them to give covering fire. The rocket propelled grapnels did not work because the ropes were saturated.

An attack by 18 medium bombers, as well as fire from the destroyers HMS *Talybont* and USS *Satterlee*, forced the defenders to take cover. The crew of the Fairmile ML 304

Right: The view today from the German positions at Pointe du Hoc looking down on the beach below from the cliff's top. Such a view clearly shows the huge advantage the defenders enjoyed over the assaulting Rangers struggling up the cliff face.

gunfire he 'marched to the sound of the guns' and joined Rudder's beleaguered force.

Forty men from the German 1st/914th Regiment, part of the 352nd Infantry Division, launched a heavy counter attack against the Rangers at 23:30 hours on 6 June and followed up again at 01:00 hours and 03:00 hours on 7 June. The Americans were forced back into a pocket 200m (650ft) deep on the cliff edge. On Omaha, the US 116th Infantry Regiment with the 5th Ranger Battalion attempted to break-through to the isolated group but were stopped 900m (1000yd) short. At the Pointe du Hoc, the Rangers endured not only attacks by the German infantry but also accidental bombardment by Allied aircraft and ships.

On the night of 7 June, Gen Kraiss ordered the 352nd Division to withdraw to positions on the River Aure and US forces broke through to the Rangers. Col Rudder's force of 225 that had landed at dawn on D-Day had been reduced to 135, a casualty rate of 60 percent.

Rudder, who was wounded during the fighting, would be awarded the Distinguished Service Cross for his action at the Pointe du Hoc and go on to command the 109th Infantry Regiment from 8 December 1944 until the end of the war. He

I went up about, I don't know, 40, 50 feet. The rope was wet and kind of muddy. My hands just couldn't hold, they were like grease, and I came sliding back down. As I was going down, I wrapped my foot around the rope and slowed myself up as much as I could, but still I burned my hands. If the rope hadn't been so wet I wouldn't have been able to hang on for burning.

I landed right beside Sweeney there, and he says, 'What's the matter, Sundby – chicken? Let me – I'll show you how to climb.' So he went up first and I was right after him, and when I got to the top, Sweeney says, 'Hey, Sundby, don't forget to zig-zag.'

Private Sigurd Sundby
US 2nd Ranger Battalion

would lead the regiment through the battle of the Bulge in Luxembourg. Under his leadership, the 109th Regiment would cripple the German thrust on the southern flank and prevent any significant advance. For this action his Regiment received a Presidential Citation.

CHAPTER SEVEN

OMAHA BEACH

Omaha beach was not an ideal site for a landing but the Overlord planners knew that without troops going ashore at Vierville-sur-Mer there would be a risk that the landing at Utah would be isolated and perhaps cut off. The men tasked with the landing were assured that they would be supported by a massive bombardment from the air and sea and that the German troops ashore were not high grade. They would be disappointed on both counts.

THE POTENTIAL OF the long and open sand beach between Vierville-sur-Mer and Colleville-sur-Mer as a landing site for an Allied amphibious assault had been recognized by the Germans when they planned their coastal defences.

Like Utah, they sited *Widerstandsnesten* (WN) along the 10km (6 mile) shore but concentrated them around the five gullies that cut through the bluffs overlooking the beach. The slight concave curve of the coastline meant that positions at the western end, WN70, WN71, WN72 and WN73 and at the eastern end WN60, WN61 and WN62 had excellent fields of fire that interlocked on the beach. As well as these coastal positions, three *Widerstandsnesten*, WN63, WN67 and WN69 were sited deep behind the bluffs.

Houses on the coast road had been dismantled to improve fields of fire and the materials used for the construction of fortifications. Minefields had been laid between the

Left: Men of a follow-up wave landing observe the Omaha coastline with the bluffs close to the seashore. Wrecked vehicles can be seen on the beach, remnants of earlier assault waves. Already engineers are busy clearing the beach of obstacles and mines.

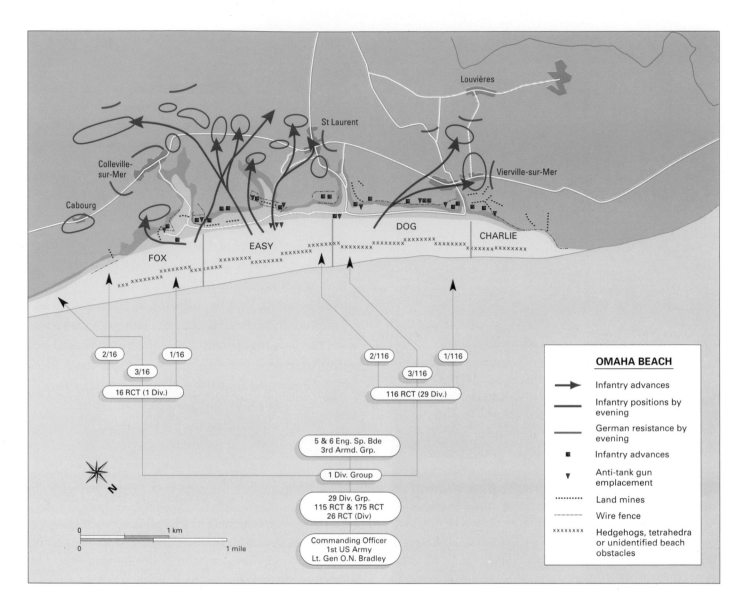

Above: Omaha beach, showing the positions that the assault troops had reached by the end of the day. It had been a very hard fight and the breakout had been costly, but the Americans had cleared the bluffs that dominated the beach.

Widerstandsnesten and in the gullies and remote control flamethrowers had been dug in to cover dead ground. It was a perfect killing ground, but the Allied planners knew that a landing would have to be made at Omaha to ensure that Utah was not isolated on a flank, away from the Anglo-Canadian beaches.

With hindsight, critics have said that the American planners had learned no lessons from Dieppe two years earlier and went for a frontal assault. They then imposed a strict timetable on the landings that would keep feeding men and vehicles onto a shrinking beach that was still under fire as the tide rose.

Perhaps the grimmest suggestion was that a bloody victory in the Presidential election year would not only be good for Roosevelt, but would also convince any waverers among the Allies that the United States was committed to the

'Germany first' strategy of defeating Nazi Germany before Imperial Japan.

The best route off the beach was around the metalled road to the hamlet of Vierville to the west. This had been blocked with an anti-tank wall and the Germans had sited WN70 on the bluff, armed with infantry weapons, and WN71, with two 7.5cm (2.95in) guns, one in an open pit and one in a casemate, two mortars and one 2cm (0.78in) flak gun. WN72, at the entrance to the gully, was a real fortress with two 8.8cm (3.46in) guns that covered the shore, one 5cm (1.97in) gun and five 5cm (1.97in) mortars. However, WN71 and WN73 were under-strength and men from construction pioneer units were added to beef them up.

The dirt track up the St Laurent exit was protected by four *Widerstandsnesten*. WN64 had two 7.5cm (2.95in) guns, five 5cm (1.97in) mortars and a 2cm (0.78in) flak gun. WN65 had one 8.8cm (3.46in) gun and a 5cm (1.97in) mortar in a casemate. WN68 had only infantry weapons, but WN66 was formidable. Protected by an anti-tank ditch it had two 7.5cm (2.95in) guns, three Renault tank turrets concreted into bunkers or Tobruks, and six 5cm (1.97in) mortars.

DEPTH POSITIONS

In depth were the strongpoints WN67 and WN69, the latter with a battery of rockets. The German 1st Battalion of the 352nd Division's Artillery Regiment, under Colonel Ocker, was in position around Houtteville with their observation posts in WN59, WN61 and WN62 where forward observer Lieutenant Frerking could correct fire.

The Colleville exit, which was nothing more than a path, was protected by three *Widerstandsnesten*. WN60 had two 7.5cm (2.95in) guns, a bunker with a Renault tank turret, four 5cm (1.97in) mortars and a 2cm (0.78in) flak gun. WN61 was armed with an 8.8cm (3.46in) gun, one 5cm (1.97in) and Renault tank turret bunkers and a 5cm (1.97in) mortar. Finally there was an anti-tank ditch in front of WN62, the command post of Lt Frerking, which was armed with two 7.5cm (2.95in) guns in casemates, two 5cm (1.97in) guns in hardstandings and a 5cm (1.97in) mortar. The anti-tank ditch would prove an effective obstacle and even at 11:40 hours on D-Day it was still causing US tanks to bunch up as their drivers struggled to find a place to cross. Inland, on the road to Colleville, WN63 was armed with a 7.5cm (2.95in) gun. It was in this area that the 2nd/916th would concentrate during defensive alerts.

All the *Widerstandsnesten* were surrounded by barbed wire and the Allied planners were aware of an intricate pattern of minefields both on the foreshore and inland. Between high and low water the beach was densely covered with obstacles including the 2.75m (9ft) wide Element C at the front, with ramps and stakes closer to the shore and tetrahedra and hedgehogs close to the high water mark. The obstacle belts that were a total of 50m (165ft) thick had been carefully thought out, each varied in height so the lowest were closer to the shore where the water would be shallower. At high tide, each belt, about 15m (50ft) apart, would be covered at the same potentially lethal depth. The anti-tank ditches that had been dug to cover the eastern exits from the beach would have filled with water, while at the western end,

the German defenders had built an anti-tank wall or *Panzermauer* to block the road.

Grenadier Robert Vogt of the 1st/726th Regiment recalled the construction work. 'We did all this at low tide when the sea retreated a few kilometres. We put in a wooden stake and then, at a distance of, I'd say four of five metres, another stake. On top of these we attached a third stake with clamps – all of it done by hand – and secured by more clamps. Teller mines were attached to the tips of the stakes or beams, so that, at high tide, the mines were just below the water's surface, so that even a flat-bottomed boat would touch them and be destroyed.'

The work parties simply used high-pressure hoses to blast a hole in the wet sand before inserting the stakes. It was in the course of this work that an RAF air reconnaissance Spitfire flying low across the beach surprised German soldiers at work. With its cameras running it caught the terrified soldiers as they dashed for cover behind the obstacles.

The Allied planners and intelligence staff believed the positions to be manned by 1st/726th and 3rd/726th Grenadier Regiment under Col Korfes, who were part of the 716th Static Infantry Division commanded by General Richter. It was believed to be under-strength with only 7771 men, or 35 percent of the established strength of a division. Many of the men were thought to be non-German troops, either Poles or Slavs. Though Ultra intercepts indicated troop movements in the area, they did not

Right: Wearing the basic assault order including a gas mask, water bottle and mess tin, a German soldier armed with a Kar 98K rifle peers cautiously from behind cover on Omaha.

Above: Smoke hangs over the German positions at the base of the bluffs at Omaha beach as US soldiers wade ashore. The picture gives no idea how ghastly the beach was, littered with bodies and body parts as well as weapons and equipment, and the water red with blood.

identify the formation or its size. In fact, the division was the 352nd Infantry Division that had been based in the St Lô area. It was at full strength, had combat hardened troops and two of its regiments, the 914th, under Lt Col Heyna, and the 916th, under Col Goth, which covered the western end of Omaha beach, would prove to be formidable opponents. The 726th were still in place at the eastern end of the beach and it may have been that the radio traffic of the 914th and 916th was masked by that of the 726th.

Aware of the potential strength of this position, Allied planners proposed an intense pre-landing bombardment. Before dawn at 05:55 hours, 329 B-24 Liberators would hit the beaches and this would be followed by a naval bombardment by the battleships USS *Texas* (flagship) and *Arkansas*, the French cruisers FFS *Montcalm* and FFS *Georges Leygues* and HMS *Glasgow*. In addition, 11 destroyers would provide close range support. The command ship, the USS *Ancon*, would be in position about 21km (13 miles) offshore at 02:50 hours.

The beach had been divided into sectors that from west to east were 'Charlie', 'Dog', 'Easy' and 'Fox'. Dog was subdivided from the sea and land into 'Green', 'White' and 'Red', Easy into 'Green' and 'Red' and Fox into 'Green'.

FORETELLING THE FUTURE

Following the dress rehearsal exercises held with live ammunition on Slapton Sands in Devon in the build-up to the landings, Brigadier General Norman Cota, the Assistant Divisional Commander of 29th Division, briefed the headquarters staff on what would probably happen at Omaha – he was grimly prescient.

'This is different from any of the other exercises that you've had so far. The little discrepancies that we tried to correct on Slapton Sands are going to be magnified and are going to give way to incidents that you might first view as chaotic. The air and naval bombardment and artillery support are reassuring. But you're going to find confusion. The landing craft aren't going to be on schedule and people are going to be landed in the wrong place. Some won't be landing at all. The enemy will try, and he will have some success, in preventing our gaining a lodgement. But we must improvize, carry on, not lose our heads. Nor must we add to the confusion.'

Cota did not like the plan for Omaha and, like Lord Lovat and No 4 Commando at Dieppe two years earlier, favoured a landing before first light.

BOMBS GONE

At Omaha, as with the pilots at Utah, in the poor weather, the crews of the B-24 Liberators were concerned that if they dropped too early they would hit the invasion fleet as it approached the shore. To prevent this they delayed a few critical seconds before they toggled their payloads over the 13 designated targets and 1310 tonnes (1285 tons) of bombs exploded harmlessly on agricultural land over 3km (2 miles) inland.

Whereas Utah beach was protected by the coast of the Cotentin Peninsula, Omaha was more exposed and poor weather and the swell made accurate shooting difficult. Most of the barrage of 3000 rounds fired by Force 'C' overshot their targets and was too brief to be effective. When the Royal Navy rocket firing landing craft moved in for the final barrage of 127mm (5in) rockets, they fired too early and many fell harmlessly in the sea.

To Staff Sergeant William Lewis in his DUKW, the bombardment appeared impressive. 'I remember the battleship *Texas* firing broadsides into the shore while we were close by. It was God awful, terrible explosions – muzzle blast in our ears – when they fired. The smoke ring passed by us and it looked like a funnel of a tornado, growing larger and larger and finally dissipating. Then they fired another one.'

The men of the first assault wave, huddled in the landing craft that now started their course for the shore, were wet and cold and suffering from sea sickness. They were apprehensive but had no idea of the grim fate awaiting them.

Each LCA or LCVP accommodated 31 men who, for the first wave, were organized into a mixed team capable of breaching obstacles and neutralizing enemy positions. Led by an officer, the team was as follows:

Below: Soldiers shelter behind an M4 Sherman while others attempt to hide behind the Czech hedgehog steel girder anti-tank obstacles. All are in the 'killing ground' for the German defenders and are under direct and indirect fire from the resistance nests.

I picked up my artillery binoculars with amazement when I saw that the horizon was literally filling with ships of all kinds. I could hardly believe it. It seemed impossible to me that this vast fleet could have gathered without anyone being the wiser. I passed the binoculars to the man alongside me and said, 'Take a look.' He said, 'My God, it's the invasion.'

Major Werner Pluskat
352nd Artillery Regiment, 352nd Division

- One NCO and five riflemen in the bow
- A wire cutting team of four men
- Two Browning Automatic Rifle (BAR) teams of two men
- Two Bazooka teams of two men
- A 60mm (2.36in) mortar crew of four men
- A flame thrower team
- A demolition squad with prepared TNT charges
- A medic and section commander in the stern
- The coxswain

The US assault waves were led by the 1st, 2nd and 3rd/116th Regimental Combat Team (RCT), part of the 29th Infantry Division 'The Blue and Gray Division' under Major General Charles 'Uncle Charlie' H Gerhardt, who were destined for Dog on the left. Anticipating casualties on the day, the 116th RCT had been reinforced by 500 'over-strength men'. The 1st, 2nd and 3rd/16th RCT, part of the 18th RCT would hit Easy, Red and Fox. Both the 16th and 18th were part of the 1st Infantry Division known as 'The Big Red One' because of its distinctive shoulder patch. The division was commanded by Maj Gen Clarence R Huebner.

In August 1943 Huebner had replaced Maj Gen Terry de la Mesa Allen who had commanded the division in North Africa and Sicily. It was initially difficult taking over a division from a popular commanding officer who had taken it to war. Worse still, the popular deputy, Brigadier General Theodore Roosevelt Jr, had also been replaced and sent to a desk job in London. It took time for Huebner to put his stamp on the Big Red One but his approach, which combined stiff discipline with fairness, earned him the nickname of 'The Coach'. During training, he shrewdly insisted that battalion commanders should be familiar with one another's areas so that any last-minute changes in orders would not jeopardize the landings. It would pay dividends on the day.

The 1st Division had been chosen for Omaha by Gen Bradley because at the time, it was the US Army's most experienced and battle-tested division. However, many men were bitter that having survived two landings they may not survive another in Normandy.

The 29th Division, who would also land at Omaha, had been in England since October 1942. There, among other US soldiers, it had earned the derisive nickname of 'England's Own' because of its long residence in Britain. In Bradley's words, they 'had staked out squatters' rights on Omaha beach'. When the veterans of the 1st Division learned that the National Guard 29th boasted a battle cry, 'Twenty-Nine – Let's Go!' coined for them by Gerhardt, they quipped, 'Go ahead Twenty-Nine – we'll be right behind you.'

The commanding officer of the 29th had only been posted to the division in July 1943. He was ordered to prepare it for amphibious operations and 'to correct the situation of too many 29th Division men in the guardhouse'. Gerhardt imposed strict discipline and insisted that 'this war will be won at battalion level'. He drove this home at a meeting with his battalion commanders. 'A year from today, one out of every three of you will be dead, and the toll will be higher if

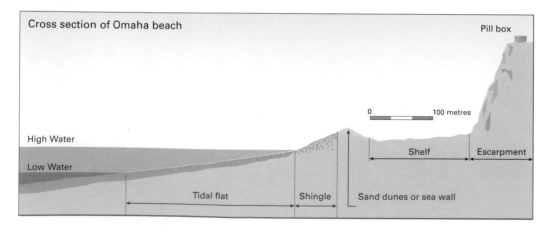

Cross section of Omaha beach

Pill box

High Water

Low Water

0   100 metres

Shelf

Escarpment

Tidal flat

Shingle

Sand dunes or sea wall

Left: A cross section of the Omaha beach. Men who had landed and made it to the cover of the sea wall and sand dunes needed to draw on reserves of almost super human courage to stand up and cross the 'shelf' to attack German positions. However, with support from warships that had moved as close as they could to the shore, the Americans were eventually able to get off the beach.

senior commanders don't know their stuff and don't get out of their chairs!'

LOW MORALE

The 29th began to worry about what the fighting would be like. Rumours circulated that platoon and company commanders would not live long in action. The word reached Bradley that the unit was 'infected with a despondent fear of the casualties it was predicted they would suffer in the assault. Some talked of 90 percent'.

> Where Channel and shore met was a wavering, undulating line of dark objects. Some of the larger ones, recognizable as tanks and landing craft, were erupting in black smoke. Higher up the beach was another line of smaller forms, straight as though drawn with a ruler, for they were aligned along a bank of shingle stone and seawall. Scattered black forms were detaching themselves from the surf and labouring toward the line.
>
> *Captain Charles Cawthon*
> *Commanding Officer HQ Company, 2nd Battalion, 116th Infantry*

Above: The terribly exposed sweep of Omaha beach at low tide seen a day or so after the landings, showing a number of vehicles knocked out in the initial assault, including a Sherman tank. The Germans had not expected the Allies to try an attack on a rising tide.

He decided to visit the 29th and attempting to raise morale, referred to casualty figures in Mediterranean. 'This stuff about huge losses is tommyrot. Some of you won't come back – but it'll be very few.'

Prior to embarkation, the Regimental Commander gave the men of the 116th Regiment 'The Stonewall Brigade', a pep talk.

'There is one certain way to get the enemy out of action and that is to kill him. War is not child's play and requires hatred for the enemy. At this time we don't have it. I hope you get it when you see your friends wounded and killed. Learn to take care of yourself from the start. Remember the Hun is a crafty, intelligent fighter and will not have any mercy on you. Don't have it on him.'

Despite these optimistic words and encouragement, within hours of landing, both the regiment and the division as a whole would suffer the heaviest casualties of any unit involved in the landings on D-Day.

For a 14-year-old English girl living in Tavistock, Devon, the change in atmosphere surrounding the 29th Division, which had been based in the area, remained a haunting memory. 'A couple of months before D-Day things went subdued and there was a great air of secrecy and solemnity where before there had been fun and light-heartedness. Everyone I knew seemed to disappear and I felt that a phase of my life was over.'

The first waves landing on Omaha would include two battalions of eight DD tanks from the 741st and 743rd Tank Battalion. Engineer demolition teams would also land in this wave; their task was to clear obstacles and minefields and so open the gullies to allow men and vehicles to move up to the plateau behind the beach. Maj Kenneth Lord Assistant G3 (operations officer) with the 1st Infantry Division recalled that with days to go before D-Day, air reconnaissance

Below: Omaha and the bluffs with the anti-invasion obstacles still in place, and tanks and vehicles on the foreshore. Engineers would clear the obstacles and begin work to ready the area for the construction of a Mulberry Harbour.

revealed that more obstacles had been emplaced along the shore. The destruction of these obstacles would be the task for the extra engineer units who would be in the first wave.

'We had to change our entire loading plan. We went to the underground headquarters at Plymouth and worked around the clock for three days, until we had finished. We imagine it was a great shock to those engineers to find they were in the first wave.'

At H-Hour, to support the infantry, 32 gun tanks would be landed with 16 armoured bulldozers that would push obstacles aside. According to the plan, the high ground should have been captured by 07:30 hours, an hour after landing. The 116th would then clear the area to the River Aure beyond the N13 road as far west as Isigny. The 16th would link up with the British on the right at Port-en-Bessin. By last light the beachhead was intended to be 26km (16 miles) wide and 8km (5 miles) deep.

'DONKEY'S EARS'

In WN62, Lt Frerking watched through his powerful stereoscopic artillery binoculars, known as 'Donkey's Ears', the

MG42 'SPANDAU'

The MG 34 gun, loosely known by the Allies as the Spandau, was the weapon with which the German forces entered the war. The MG 42 replaced the more complex MG 34 during the war. It used stamping and spot-welding to speed the manufacturing process. When examples were captured by the Allies in Tunisia in 1943 it was thought that this relatively crude finish was the result of production problems in the German small arms industry. The 7.92mm (0.31in) calibre gun was 122cm (48in) long with a 533mm (21in) barrel and weighed 11.6kg (25lb) in the light role. The sustained fire tripod mount added an extra 19.2kg (42lb). With a muzzle velocity of 756m/sec (2480ft/sec), it fired 50-round belted ammunition and had a maximum range of 2000m (2200yd) and a cyclic rate of 1550 rounds per minute. The high rate of fire made a very distinctive noise and GIs likened it to the sound of ripping calico.

approaching ships with rising incredulity. It seemed impossible to envisage such a huge concentration of vessels in such a small area. The 352nd Division war diary concurred. 'The choice of the landing place, the strength, and the continuous naval artillery fire, as well as large numbers of approaching landing craft reported again and again, gave rise to the idea at the Command Post that we had to deal here with a systematic landing by major forces. The invasion had really started!'

Though following the airborne landings the German defenders expected a seaborne assault, they calculated that it would come in after 08:00 hours when the tide started to turn.

At 06:30 hours, the first waves of US landing craft were about a 0.5km (0.25 miles) from the beach, which had seemed strangely quiet, when they were hit by the full weight of fire from the *Widerstandsnesten* emplacements. Company A of the 116th lost 96 percent of its effective strength before it had fired a single shot. The landing craft carrying the HQ of the 743rd Tank Battalion was hit just short of the beach, killing all but one officer. The craft carrying engineers were hit. About half their number were killed and most of their equipment lost. Of the 16 armoured bulldozers only two reached the beach and they were quickly used by the infantry as cover. As machine gun fire raked the landing craft carrying Sgt Golas and men of the 2nd Ranger Battalion towards

Charlie, he said with mock surprise: 'Gee fellas they're shooting back at us.'

The weather seemed to be on the side of the defenders as the swell and overcast skies disrupted the landing order and caused craft to deliver troops to the wrong beaches. The DD tanks of 741st Tank Battalion were launched and began to make their way towards the shore. The maps issued to the tank commanders and landing craft also showed a drawing of the foreshore at sea level with reference points. These had been updated from aerial photographs as recently as 22 May. Fatally, the DD crews did not run straight towards the shore with the waves breaking behind them but began to align their flimsy craft on the spire of the church at Vierville. The waves now began to hit the canvas screens from the side, they collapsed and soon the tanks flooded and sank. A Navy Lieutenant, seeing the fate of the 741st, decided to bring his LCTs into the beach to give the 743rd a better chance. However, they would be leaderless as the battalion commander's LCT was sunk off the beach and all officers except one Lieutenant were killed or wounded. The tanks that landed opposite the Vierville gully then came under fire from the German positions.

The men on shore would have no direct fire support. With tight fire discipline, the German defenders had waited until the landing craft were well within range and as the ramps went down opened fire. To their rear, 10.5cm (4.13in) howitzers delivered indirect fire.

The 29th Division was a National Guard formation and within the 1st Battalion, Company 'A', 'B' and 'D' had been recruited from the Virginia towns of Bedford, Lynchburg and Roanoke. One of the survivors, Sgt Robert J Slaughter recalled that: 'We landed in column of companies. 'A' Company at about 06:30, 'B' Company some ten to 15 minutes later and 'D' Company about 07:10, though we were probably all late. We hit the eye of the storm. The battalion was decimated. Hell, after that we didn't have enough to whip a cat with.'

On the morning of 6 June, the town of Bedford lost 23 men out of a population of 3000. All were serving in 'A' Company and among the dead were brothers from three families.

For one young German private with the 352nd Infantry Division on the shore it would be his first encounter with combat. Captured and interrogated after the landings he recalled: 'It was the first time I shoot [sic] at living men. I don't remember exactly how it was: the only thing I know is that I went to my machine gun and I shoot, I shoot, I shoot.'

It was now apparent that we were coming ashore in one of the carefully registered killing zones of German machine-guns and mortars. The havoc they had wrought was all around in an incredible chaos – bodies, weapons, boxes of demolitions, flamethrowers, reels of telephone wire, and personal equipment from socks to toilet articles. Hundreds of brown lifebelts were washing to and fro, writhing and twisting like brown sea slugs. The waves broke around the disabled tanks, bulldozers and beached landing craft… There was a wide stretch of sand being narrowed by the minute by the tide, then a sharply rising shingle bank of small, smooth stones that ended at the sea wall. Against the wall were soldiers of the first assault team. Some were scooping out shelters; a number were stretched out in the loose attitude of the wounded; others had the ultimate stillness of death; but most were sitting with their backs against the wall.

Captain Charles Cawthon
Commanding Officer HQ Company, 2nd Battalion, 116th Infantry

At 06:30 hours, the USS *McCook* action report stated baldly: 'First landing craft containing men and material made landing on beach. Enemy fire severe from unknown points.'

To the east, where Dog became Easy, two battalions of the 116th landed either side of the gully leading to les Moulins. Here, smoke from burning buildings and scrub following the naval bombardment helped to screen them. On Easy, Red, however, the 2nd/16th suffered the same fate as the 1st/116th landing opposite WN62. Enemy fire caused heavy casualties and minefields forced infantry to move in single file along narrow paths.

STALLED ON THE DEFENCES

The Americans had decided not to use the British specialized armoured vehicles (the Funnies), that could have quickly flailed through these obstacles or blasted bunkers. While there was a logic to not mixing Churchill tanks with Shermans – spares and maintenance could have been a problem – they would have saved time and lives. ARK bridge layers would, for example, have enabled the tanks to cross the anti-tank ditch at WN62.

Left: The Omaha defences were well built and survive today, a mute tribute to the bravery of the men who took them on. Many have been used as the foundations for memorials to the units that landed at 'Bloody Omaha'. This one covers the gap in the bluffs at Vierville.

As the tide rose, wounded men drowned and those ashore were crammed into a constricted stretch that had become a virtual shooting gallery for the German defenders. Pte First Class Gilbert Murdock of the 116th Regiment remembered,

'…many were lost before they had a chance to face the enemy. Some of them were hit in the water and wounded and then drowned. Others, wounded, dragged themselves ashore and upon finding the sand lay quiet and gave themselves [morphine] shots, only to be caught and drowned within a few minutes by the on-racing tide.'

Some of the wounded at Omaha owed their survival to 25-year-old Pte Carlton Barrett, who was part of the reconnaissance platoon of HQ Company 18th/1st Infantry. On D-Day, he waded ashore in neck-deep waves and then returned under fire to rescue floundering comrades who were close to drowning. Ashore during the day, he worked as a guide, a runner and assisted the wounded and those unable to care for themselves. For his actions and inspiration he was awarded the Medal of Honor.

At 08:30 hours, the beachmaster, the officer controlling the landing craft from the shore, suspended landings because there was no more space for men and vehicles. A German officer at Vierville telephoned Gen Kraiss at the 352nd headquarters to report that the landings at Omaha had been stopped and anticipated that the US forces would attempt to withdraw.

He stated: 'At the water's edge at low tide near St Laurent and Vierville, the enemy is in search of cover behind coastal zone obstacles. A great many motor vehicles – and among these ten tanks – stand burning at the beach. The obstacle demolition squads have given up their activity. Disembarkation from landing craft has ceased; the boats keep farther seawards. The fire of our battle positions and artillery was well-placed and has inflicted considerable casualties on the enemy. A great many wounded and dead lie on the beach.'

From the sea, Sgt Alan Anderson of the 116th Combat Team, 467th AAA Battalion 'could see machine guns ripping into the ramps of some of the larger vessels unloading men further out in the Channel and the men were tumbling, falling dead in the water, just like corn cobs off a conveyor belt'.

As we approached the beach the ramp was lowered. Mortar and artillery shells exploded on land and in the water. Unseen snipers concealed in the cliffs were shooting down at individuals, but most havoc was from automatic weapons. The water was turning red from the blood… There were dead men floating in the water and there were live ones acting dead, letting the tide take them in. I was crouching down to chin deep in the water when mortar shells began falling on the water's edge. Sand began to kick up from small-arms fire from the bluffs… While lying half in half out of the water, behind one of the log poles, I noticed a GI running from right to left… An enemy gunner shot him and he stumbled for cover. He screamed for a medic. One of the aid men moved quickly to help him, and was also shot. I will never forget seeing that medic lying next to the wounded GI and both of them screaming. They died in minutes.

Sergeant Robert J Slaughter
1st Battalion, 116th Infantry Regiment, US 29th Infantry Division

It was on the basis of the optimistic German report and the distraction of airborne forces scattered in areas to their rear, that Kraiss did not send reinforcements to Utah and Omaha; at the latter beach the Germans might have turned a bloody battle into a tragic defeat.

Offshore, Gen Bradley was receiving pessimistic reports from V Corps, including estimated casualties of 3000. Closer to the beaches, Col Benjamin Talley, Assistant Chief of Staff of V Corps was aboard a DUKW and could see that the shore was jammed with riflemen who were still under fire. He reported this at 09:30 hours. He was particularly concerned that the LCTs were milling around offshore like 'a stampeding herd of cattle'. Bradley considered diverting his follow up formations to Utah or even the British beaches.

SEARCH FOR A CIGARETTE

Lt William Jones had made it to the beach, but the half-track mounting quad 12.7mm (0.50in) Brownings on which he should have ridden into action had sunk as it drove off the landing craft. Finding himself ashore and alive he had one craving. 'The only thing I wanted was a cigarette and I asked this medic that was running across, "You got a dry cigarette?" And he handed me a cigarette and was hit with something, I don't know what it was, but his entire body, his insides and everything, was

Above: Troops wade ashore waist-deep in water on Omaha. As predicted by Allied meteorologists the weather improved in the afternoon and this allowed the USAAF and RAF to dominate the battlefield and prevent the Germans from reinforcing their defences.

blown all over me. It must have been a mortar that hit him, I don't know.'

On Omaha, the stunned and demoralized US troops were beginning to coalesce into ad hoc combat groups. Offshore, the US Navy destroyers had moved as close as 800m (900yd) to give direct fire support to the men on the beaches. Some were so close to the shore that they grounded during these attacks.

Lt John Carroll of the 16th Infantry remembered the impact of the fire from the warships. 'They were 600 yards (550m) offshore and firing flat trajectory at the German gun emplacements above us with eight to 12-inch (200 to 304mm) shells. The emplacements were being completely destroyed, and chunks of cement as big as a foot square (0.1 sq m) were falling all around us and on us. The shells were coming in no higher than 100 feet (30m) over our heads. They hit and blew that cliff right out.'

On the beach, leadership came from experienced soldiers, NCOs and officers like Col George Taylor, commanding the 16th RCT, who brutally summed up the fate of men on the shore: 'Two kinds of people are staying on this beach, the dead and those who are going to die. Now let's get the hell out of here.'

Carroll employed a leadership technique that was never taught at Officer Candidate School, let alone West Point. 'I remember distinctly taking my trench knife and pressing it into people's backs to see if they were alive. If they were alive I'd kick them and say, "Let's go!." Later it dawned on me, after I'd checked a few, that some of them were alive, but they couldn't turn around – just absolute terror!'

Twenty-six-year-old Sgt Joe Pilck of the 16th Regiment 1st Infantry Division heard the exhortations from officers, but confessed: 'I can't say if I was scared or not. Mostly I was thinking of getting captured because it looked like the invasion was a failure.'

Striding along the beach, Brig Gen Norman Cota encouraged the men to begin to move. 'Don't die on the beaches, die up on the bluff if you have to die, but get off the beaches or you're sure to die.' He then saw men of the 5th Ranger Battalion, who had landed at Dog, on the right flank at 08:00 hours.

Cota found the battalion commander, Col Schneider, at his command post. Cota and Schneider stood up to converse while under fire. During their conversation, the general gave the élite force its motto when he said to the colonel: 'We're counting on your Rangers to lead the way.' This has since been shortened to the crisp 'Rangers lead the way'.

Cota supervised blowing a gap through the concertina wire with a Bangalore torpedo and then led 40 men up the gully into Vierville and by 10:00 hours some 200 had followed them and were in position to repulse a German counter-attack.

Below: A Browning .30 machine gun crew from the US 1st Infantry Division moves off the shore past the grim human wreckage of the earlier waves. At the rear of the group a man loaded with ammunition boxes follows the gunner.

Above: Soaked and sick, a US casualty is helped ashore from a rubber dinghy that has been used to bring stores to the beach. A number of casualties were caused by drowning, the heavy equipment given to GIs for the landing dragging the unwary or unconscious under water.

Right: A chart showing the timetable for the landing of troops and equipment on Omaha beach. Most of the DD Shermans intended to help support the initial landings were lost before they neared the shore, as the heavy swell of the sea buckled their canvas floatation screens.

Elsewhere, 22-year-old Pte Carl Weast watched leadership in action. 'Capt Whittington was one of the first ones over that goddamn sea wall. The officers went first. Later on I heard our adjutant criticizing Capt Whittington for unnecessarily exposing himself to enemy fire and I

> When you run over unconscious men, or men lying on their bellies, it's tough to keep your balance. There is no room. You go into the water, but the water is washing bodies in and out. Everywhere there are body pieces – a testicle here, a head there, an ass here. Crap all over the place. Intestines, intestines, intestines. That's what Omaha beach was.
>
> *Corporal Samuel Fuller*
> *16th Regiment, US 1st Infantry Division*

remember he [Whittington] says, "You saw it happen back on the goddamn beach. Now when you know how the hell you lead men from behind, you tell me. It just doesn't work."'

Sgt Victor Fast, with the 5th Ranger Battalion, recalled that as he and his men made their way up the gully into Vierville, they were under fire from both sides as well as negotiating their way through an S-Mine anti-personnel minefield. When they came under sniper fire from the church steeple at Vierville, Col Schneider called for naval gunfire and the church was promptly demolished, with the sniper still in his position.

BRIGADIER COTA'S ATTACK

The redoubtable Cota had established his command post shortly after 08:30 hours and began the task of reorganizing the disordered units. Uniquely in World War II, a general

LANDING DIAGRAM, OMAHA BEACH
(SECTOR OF 116TH RCT)

	EASY GREEN	DOG RED	DOG WHITE	DOG GREEN
H − 5			Co C (DD) 743 Tk Bn	Co B (DD) 743 Tk Bn
H HOUR	Co A 743 Tk Bn	Co A 743 Tk Bn		
H + 01	Co E 116 Inf	Co F 116 Inf	Co G 116 Inf	Co A 116 Inf
H + 03	146 Engr CT	146 Engr CT / Demolitions Control Boat	146 Engr CT	146 Engr CT / Co C 2d Ranger Bn
H + 30	AAAW Btry / Co H / HQ Co E / Co H — 116 Inf — AAAW Btry	HQ 2d Bn / Co H / HQ Co F / Co H / HQ Co 2d Bn — 116 Inf — AAAW Btry	AAAW Btry / Co H / HQ Co G / Co H — 116 Inf — AAAW Btry	Co B / HQ Co A / Co B — 116 Inf — AAAW Btry
H + 40	112 Engr Bn	Co D 81 Cml Wpns Bn / 112 Engr 149 Engr Beach Bn	149 Engr Beach Bn / 121 Engr Bn	HQ 1st Bn 116 / 149 Beach Bn / 121 Engr / Co D 116 Inf
H + 50	Co L 116 Inf	Co I 116 Inf	Co K 116 Inf	121 Engr Bn / Co C 116 Inf
H + 57		HQ Co 3d Bn — Co M 116 Inf		Co B 81 Cml Wpns Bn
H + 60		112 Engr Bn	HQ & HQ Co 116 Inf	121 Engr Bn / Co A & B 2d Ranger BN
H + 65				5th Ranger Bn
H + 70	149 Engr Beach Bn	112 Engr Bn	Alt HQ & HQ Co 116 Inf	121 Engr Bn / 5th Ranger Bn
H + 90			58 FA Bn Armd	
H + 100			6th Engr Sp Brig	
H + 110	149 Engr Beach Bn	AT Plat 2d Bn / AT Plat 3d Bn / 29 Sig Bn		AT Plat 1st Bn / Gn Co 116 Inf
H + 120	467 AAAW Bn / AT Co 116 Inf / 467 AAAW Bn	AT Co 116 Inf / 467 AAAW Bn / 149 Engr Beach Bn	467 AAAW Bn	467 AAAW Bn
H + 150		DD Tanks	HQ Co 116 Inf / 104 Med Bn	
H + 180 to H + 180		461 Amph Trk Co	Navy Salvage	
H + 225	461 Amph Trk Co			

KEY TO SYMBOLS: LCT — LCVP — LCM — LCA — LCI — DUKW — DD TANK

had led an infantry attack and demonstrated that he had retained a grasp of infantry tactics at squad level.

Further east, two battalions of the 116th RCT had worked their way uphill and moved towards St Laurent. On Fox, a platoon had broken through the defences and created a gap through which 300 men advanced towards Colleville. One of the men who made this possible was 27-year-old First Lieutenant Jimmie Monteith Jr of I Company, 3rd/16th Infantry, 1st Division. As his soldiers landed, Monteith realized that the only cover available was the edge of the bluffs and organized an assault across the beach. He then returned under fire to bring two tanks forward through a minefield and directed their fire against enemy positions which they destroyed. He then returned to his

Below: His face puffy with swelling, a young GI receives treatment from a medic. Many men who had suffered minor injuries would fight on with their comrades as the forces advanced inland off the beaches, rather than return on a landing craft to England.

company and led them in the attack up the gully. Consolidating the position at the end of the day, Monteith was killed. He was subsequently posthumously awarded the Medal of Honor.

At 07:45 hours, the German soldiers in WN70 reported that three tanks were rolling up the hill, three tanks had penetrated WN66 and the upper casemate of WN62 had been destroyed by a direct hit. By 09:15 hours, the war diary of the 352nd Division recorded that WN65 to WN68 and WN70 had been captured.

The Germans intercepted a US signal in clear at 09:35 hours that read: 'To all commanders of the units. Everything is going OK, only a bit too late.'

Radio communications were now working because of the bravery of men like 23-year-old Technical Sergeant John Pinder of HQ Company 16th Regiment 1st Infantry Division. He had been wounded as he struggled ashore carrying a heavy radio but managed to complete his task. Refusing medical assistance, he returned to the sea to

BAZOOKA – A DEADLY JOKE

The 60mm (2.36in) Rocket Launcher M1A1, or the later two-piece M9, was based on a pre-war, American-designed, shoulder-fired recoilless weapon. A trigger produced an electric impulse that fired a 1.5kg (3.4lb) fin-stabilized rocket. The development of shaped charged warheads turned the rocket launcher into a potent tank-killing weapon for the infantry. The launcher was 1.5m (5ft) long, had an effective range of about 140m (450ft) and the warhead could penetrate up to 203mm (8in) of armour at 90 degrees. The launcher could also fire HE and White Phosphorus rockets. As a rocket weapon it had a low muzzle velocity of 83m/sec (270ft/sec). It was widely known among US troops as the 'Bazooka' after the wind instrument played by Bob Burns, an American comedian in the 1940s. During World War II, 476,628 Bazookas and 15,603,000 rockets were produced.

recover more urgently needed radio equipment. On his last trip, he was wounded in the legs by machine gun fire but still managed to get his radio into action. As he worked, a third burst of fire killed him. He was awarded the Medal of Honor.

At 13:00 hours, radio messages from the beach reached Bradley that men had reached the top of the bluffs and there was now no longer any question of the beach not being held. By last light, the Americans had pushed 1.5km (1 miles) inland had captured Vierville and Colleville and 34,000 men were in the beach head area. However, out of a planned 240 tonnes (236 tons) only 100 tonnes (98.5 tons) of stores had been landed.

At 17:00 hours, Gen Clarence Huebner disembarked from the USS *Ancon* and landed on Easy Red, struggling through the waves under small arms fire. At the divisional command post, he joined Brig Willard Wyman of the 1st Infantry Division to urge the division to leave the beaches and move inland.

Inland, Lt Col Fritz Ziegelmann of the German 352nd Infantry Division reported that the Allied soldiers who had been take prisoner were:

Right: With the fighting over and the beach secure, a GI in the German field fortifications that were built around the resistance nests looks at the body of one of the defenders. The cost of securing Omaha was in sharp contrast to the landing at Utah.

'Good human stock (each soldier being amply provided with tobacco)

Good small arms and plenty of ammunition

Practical clothing and equipment (excellent maps, including panoramic maps of the field of view of the attacker – front towards the south – maps on handkerchiefs and so on)

Good, standardized motor vehicle accessories.'

At the end of the day, WN74 to WN91 were still in German hands and resisting. However, the beachhead at Omaha was secure, though at a cost of more than 4000 US casualties.

Among the men who offered spiritual solace to the wounded and dying was an RAF Chaplain, Geoffrey Harding. He had landed with an RAF radar team. Their equipment had been destroyed on the beach and so Harding spent the next 36 hours with the American wounded, winning the Military Cross.

The 29th Division had suffered 2440 casualties and the 1st 1744, and the two divisions had taken 2500 prisoners. Omaha was secure, but at a terrible human price.

CHAPTER EIGHT

GOLD BEACH

At the western end of the Anglo–Canadian beaches, Gold was the objective for the XXX Corps. The German planners had dismissed it as a potential site for a major landing because of the steep bluffs and rock strewn shore, which would make any landing difficult. Once ashore, the British forces were to swing right to link up with the American V Corps at Omaha. They would also drive inland, with the liberation of the historical town of Bayeux as an objective to be secured before the end of D-Day.

IN SEPTEMBER 1943, A FORMIDABLE German coastal battery was commissioned on the cliffs at Les Longues between Omaha and Gold. Manned by the *Kriegsmarine*, it had four 15cm (5.9in) *Torpedobootskanone* C/36 guns taken from decommissioned destroyers. The guns had been made at the Czechoslovakian armaments plant at Skoda, Pilsen, and had a range of 19.5km (12 miles) that covered the approaches to the future Omaha, Gold and Juno beaches.

The guns were in Type M272 casemates that gave them an elevation of minus four degrees to plus 40 degrees and an arc of fire of 130 degrees – which was possible because of cut-outs at the sides of the embrasure. The casemates had been textured and landscaped for camouflage and protection. They were about 330m (1100ft) from the cliff and had not been built in a straight line but in a slight convex arc that enabled the guns to cover a wider area. As with all naval designs, ammunition was kept in magazines within the casemates.

Left: The two-storey fire control and observation post at Les Longues battery that is still in excellent condition today. The scars of the Allied bombardment are clearly visible. The battery was not captured until 7 June, but it was put out of action by Allied naval gunfire.

At the cliff edge, a two-storey semi-underground Type M262 Observation and Fire Control bunker had been constructed. It had optical range and direction finding equipment, map room and accommodation. Telephone cables buried 2m (6.5ft) deep ran from the OP to the guns.

The battery, manned by 184 sailors, had seven personnel shelters and six bunkers with Tobruks. A mortar pit was located behind the No 2 gun casemate. A 2cm (0.78in) flak gun was sited to cover the cliffs and as anti-aircraft protection. The whole position was protected by barbed wire and minefields. The battery was bombed on 28 May and 3 June when it received 150 tonnes (148 tons) of bombs. They did no damage.

GERMAN GUNS IN ACTION

On the morning of 6 June, the guns went into action against the invasion fleet. They engaged the USS *Arkansas* and then switched to Gold beach where they straddled the XXX Corps HQ ship HMS *Bulolo*. The cruiser HMS *Ajax* moved into position and at 12km (7 miles) fired 114 shells from her 152mm (6in) guns. Two direct hits knocked out guns No 3

and No 4 and near misses damaged the other two. Within 20 minutes, the battery was silent.

During the day, the battery crew worked on No 1 gun and during the afternoon opened fire again. The French cruiser FFS *George Leygues* began a duel that lasted until 18:00 hours when the battery was finally silenced. The battery had been a D-Day objective of the 231st Brigade of the British 50th (Northumbrian) Division, but it was not captured until the next day.

The effectiveness of naval counter battery fire here and on the Cotentin Peninsula raises the question of why airborne and amphibious assaults were necessary at Merville and the Point du Hoc.

The German defences at Gold at Le Hamel and La Rivière were held by two battalions of the 726th Regiment

Below: Commandos prime No36 grenades before landing at Gold. The grenades, often covered in a coating of sticky grease, needed to be cleaned before springs and mechanisms were checked. Then the detonator assembly was carefully inserted and the grenades were primed.

from the 716th Static Infantry Division with its headquarters at Trévières. A third battalion was held in depth to counter-attack or provide reinforcements. Supervised by 270 German officers and NCOs, a unit of 1000 *Osttruppen* in the 441st Battalion held the coast between Ver and Asnelles. Three companies of the 200th anti-tank battalion in St Croix, Grand-Tonne, Fresne-Camilly and Putot were fully mobile.

CENTRE OF RESISTANCE

The main potential areas of German resistance inland were the two batteries around the village of Ver-sur-Mer, immediately inland from La Rivière. The 1260th Artillery Regiment manned the battery of four captured Russian K390(r) 12cm (4.72in) guns close to the mansion at Mont Fleury. Two guns were in casemates and a further two were under construction. At La Mare Fontaine, further inland, the 1716th Artillery Regiment with its headquarters at Crepon had four FH18 10.5cm (4.13in) howitzers in casemates. However, both batteries were subject to heavy air attacks prior to D-Day and were bombarded and neutralized on the day by the cruisers HMS *Orion* and *Belfast*.

At the western end of the area, at St Côme de Fresné, on the cliffs above Arromanches, a 560MHz *Würzburg-Riese* radar station had been built. With a parabolic 7m (23ft) dish mounted on an octagonal concrete base it had a range of

Above: HMS Bulolo, the headquarters ship for XXX Corps, in Malta harbour. It had anchored at 05:56 off Normandy but was obliged to shift position when it came under fire from the battery at Les Longues at 06:25. On D-Day signallers aboard the ship handled 3219 signals.

30km (18.5 miles). It was used for fire control and low altitude coordination of fighter aircraft. Its weakness was that following the airborne raid on the *Würzburg* radar station at Bruneval in February 1942 British electronic warfare experts had established techniques for jamming its signals. The station at Arromanches, along with others in Europe, was destroyed during the air attacks prior to D-Day but still retained its fortifications for local defence.

British planners had divided the beach into four zones 'I', 'J', 'K' and 'L' identified by signallers' phonetic alphabet as 'Item', 'Jig', 'King' and 'Love'. These were in turn broken down into 'Red' and 'Green'.

To the west, Item was not a viable landing area because of offshore rocks and steep bluffs. However, between Arromanches and La Rivière, the sea broke on gently sloping sand and clay, known as the Sable de Heurtot. To prevent landings on these beaches, the German defenders had developed a complex belt of over 2500 mined obstacles.

At Jig Green, at the western end of Gold beach, were two *Widerstandsnesten*, one at Aisnelles sur Mer, delivering flanking fire onto the beach, and the second, armed with six

149

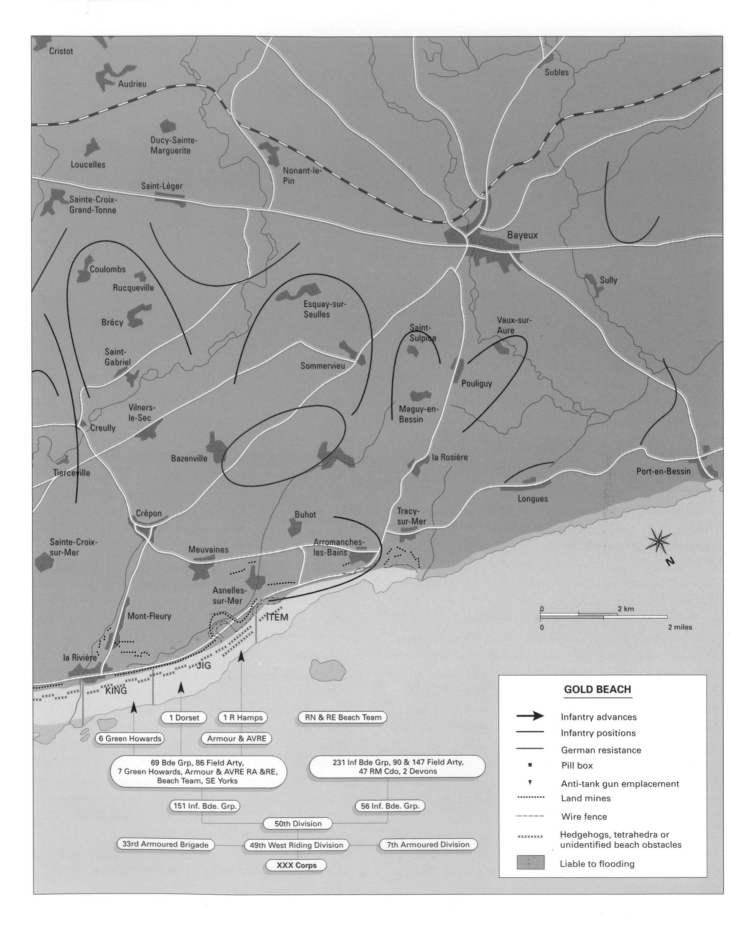

Cristot

Audrieu

Subles

Ducy-Sainte-Marguerite

Loucelles

Nonant-le-Pin

Saint-Léger

Sainte-Croix-Grand-Tonne

Bayeux

Coulombs

Sully

Rucqueville

Esquay-sur-Seulles

Brécy

Vaux-sur-Aure

Saint-Gabriel

Saint-Sulpice

Sommervieu

Pouliguy

Vilners-le-Sec

Maguy-en-Bessin

Creully

la Rosiére

Bazenville

Port-en-Bessin

Tierceville

Longues

Crépon

Buhot

Tracy-sur-Mer

Sainte-Croix-sur-Mer

Meuvaines

Arromanches-les-Bains

Asnelles-sur-Mer

Mont-Fleury

ITEM

la Rivière

JIG

KING

GOLD BEACH

1 Dorset

1 R Hamps

RN & RE Beach Team

6 Green Howards

Armour & AVRE

69 Bde Grp, 86 Field Arty,
7 Green Howards, Armour & AVRE RA &RE,
Beach Team, SE Yorks

231 Inf Bde Grp, 90 & 147 Field Arty,
47 RM Cdo, 2 Devons

151 Inf. Bde. Grp.

56 Inf. Bde. Grp.

50th Division

33rd Armoured Brigade

49th West Riding Division

7th Armoured Division

XXX Corps

	Legend
→	Infantry advances
—	Infantry positions
—	German resistance
▪	Pill box
▼	Anti-tank gun emplacement
....	Land mines
--·--·--	Wire fence
xxxxxxxx	Hedgehogs, tetrahedra or unidentified beach obstacles
▨	Liable to flooding

0   2 km

0   2 miles

machine guns, along the coastal road to the east. Both positions were protected by minefields and barbed wire. In front of them, on the shore, the obstacles began with Element Cs in deep water about 230m (250yd), with 2.5m to 3m (8ft to 10ft) high ramps and posts tipped with mines or shells about 22m (25yds) closer to the beach. Finally, concrete tetrahedra and steel Czech Hedgehog anti-tank obstacles were sited closer to the high-water mark. The Hedgehog was made from three or more steel girders bolted together at their centres and stood about 1.7m (5.5ft) high.

Jig Red had rows of tetrahedra with a *Widerstandsnester* on the border with King Green. This position with three open gun emplacements was covered by a long minefield six rows deep that stretched the length of King Green and half of Jig Red. In front, the shore was blocked with two rows of tetrahedra. Finally, at King Red the houses of La Rivière had been turned into strong points with windows bricked up. The battery at Mont Fleury provided support.

MEN FROM NORTHUMBERLAND

For the assault on Gold beach, XXX Corps had assigned the 50th Northumbrian Division, commanded by General DA Graham. Its lead formations would be the 231st Brigade that would land on Jig and the 69th Brigade, which would attack King. The 8th Armoured Brigade would land with DD tanks to support the 6th Battalion The Green Howards and the 5th Battalion East Yorkshire Regiment on King and the 1st Battalion Dorset Regiment and 1st Battalion Royal Hampshire Regiment on Jig.

XXX Corps, commanded by Lieutenant General GC Bucknall would have a hard fight on D-Day and in the following weeks. It had been set unrealistic objectives for D-Day and would have to fight across rolling terrain with woods that were ideal cover for anti-tank actions, with an armoured force which lacked infantry, who could have stalked the anti-tank positions. When Montgomery relieved Bucknall of his command and replaced him with the forceful Lt Gen Brian Horrocks, the performance of XXX Corps improved. However, this may in part be attributable to the overall collapse of German resistance in northern France.

At H-Hour minus seven, RAF bombers commenced their air attacks on the German defences, concentrating principally on the coastal batteries in the area. Seventy minutes

Left: Gold Beach showing the penetration inland by the end of D-Day. The original objective for the troops landing on D-Day was the main road to the south of Bayeux, which planners hoped they would reach by D+24 hours.

The AVREs on the beach all seemed to have been knocked out. We did not find the gaps we expected. The beach was raked with enfilading fire, and there was an anti-tank gun in a concrete and steel emplacement in Le Hamel. The Germans did not show much sign of giving up. I realized we should have to gap our way through ourselves, using Bangalores which we had with us. Casualties began to pile up. While gapping our way off the beach, I saw the OC [Officer Commanding] limping badly. He had been hit by mortar fragments as he left his LCA. He told me to take command of the Battalion. 'A' Company, who should have landed close to Le Hamel, climbed the sea wall and silenced the opposition, had almost ceased to exist.

Major Warren
1st Battalion Hampshire Regiment, British 50th Infantry Division

before H-Hour, the RAF attacks stopped and five minutes later the USAAF arrived over the beach head to combine their attacks with the shore bombardment.

The shore bombardment by Force 'K' began, conducted by the cruisers HMS *Orion*, *Ajax*, *Argonaut* and *Emerald*, the Dutch gunboat HMNS *Flores* and 13 destroyers including the Polish ORP *Krakowiak*. Fire commenced at 05:10 hours and ended at 07:25 hours. The bombardment on all the British and Canadian beaches was 20 minutes longer than that on the American ones because half-tide, when the landings were scheduled, came later in the east.

HEAVY NAVAL GUNFIRE

General Bernard Montgomery, having fought with the Royal Warwickshire Regiment in World War I, was determined that air attacks and naval gunfire should be used to neutralize enemy positions and keep the cost in human lives as low as possible.

Fifteen minutes before H-Hour, Landing Craft (Rocket) opened fire on the beaches with ripples of 127mm (5in) rockets. 25pdr (87.6mm/3.45in) Sexton self-propelled guns in landing craft added their fire. Five minutes before H-Hour DD tanks were to be launched to swim ashore.

H-Hour was 07:30 hours but with a 15 knot (28km/h) wind whipping waves up to 1.2m (4ft) and strong tide it was decided that the DD tanks would be landed directly on the beach.

For the men, the 9000m (10,000yd) journey from the transports offshore by LCA to the beach was an agony of fear

and nausea. Though they had been issued hyoscine hydro-bromide anti-sea sickness tablets almost everyone filled the 'Bags, Vomit' and other available containers in the landing craft. Some landing craft foundered as they ploughed through the waves.

Ashore, among the men of German 726th Infantry Regiment, Grenadier Robert Vogt heard the shout: 'Enemy landing craft approaching!'

He said: 'I had a good view from the top of the cliffs and looked out over the ocean. What I saw scared the devil out of me. Even though the weather was so bad, we could see a huge number of ships. Ships as far as the eye could see, an entire fleet, and I thought, "Oh God, we're finished! We're done for now!"'

The first men to land were the Assault Engineers whose mission was to clear mines and obstacles. Seven minutes later, the assault battalions began to land. Almost as soon as they got on the beaches, the 1st Battalion Royal Hampshires started to take serious casualties. The commanding officer, his naval gunfire forward observers and men in his forward headquarters became casualties and shortly afterwards, his second-in-command was killed. With their radio links destroyed, the battalion could not contact the warships or

Above: A reassuring pat on the shoulder by a comrade as British soldiers prepare to exit from their landing craft. Men could hear small arms fire impacting on the hull and the thump of exploding shell and mortar fire in these final moments.

THE BREN GUN

The Bren light machine gun (LMG), initially built at the Royal Small Arms Factory at Enfield in north London, was based on the ZB 26, a LMG design from the Czechoslovakian small arms factory at Brno. The two names were combined to produce the name BrEn – Bren. The Bren gun was an air-cooled gas operated weapon that fired a 7.7mm (0.303in) round from a 30-round box magazine. It had a slow rate of fire – 500rpm – but was very accurate with sights set out to 1830m (2000yd). It was also light, weighing only 10kg (22lb) and was 115.5cm (45.5in) long. It was easy to strip and experienced gunners could change magazines or barrels in less than five seconds. Brens were also made in Australia, Canada and India during the course of the war.

aircraft. Despite this, the battalion closed with the defences of WN35 at Le Hamel, which included a 5cm (1.97in) KwK anti-tank gun as well as machine gun posts, and eventually cleared it by 16:00 hours.

THE ROYAL HAMPSHIRES IN ACTION

The Hampshires then swung westwards, clearing the radar station at St Côme de Fresné and by 21:00 hours had taken Arromanches. Their progress had been slow due to well-entrenched positions held by elements of the German 1st/915th and 2nd/916th of the 352nd Division and their inability to call down naval gunfire.

The 1st Dorsets landed further east, out of range of the position at Le Hamel and passing through WN40 near Les Roquettes pushed inland. They were followed by Flail tanks and AVRE that started to clear gaps through the minefields. No 47 Royal Marine Commando landed between the Dorsets and Hampshires at 08:25 hours. With the tide rising, three of the Commandos' landing craft foundered on underwater obstacles for the loss of 43 men. The 2nd Battalion The Dorsets landed at the same time as the Commandos.

To the east of this action, on King, the devastation from the naval bombardment was dramatic, but not all the

defences had been neutralized. The Green Howards landed at 07:30 hours on the open beaches between the Dorsets and the town of La Rivière. As the landing craft approached the shore, Company Sergeant Major (CSM) Stan Hollis of 'D' Company took a Bren gun from one of his soldiers, balanced it on the ramp of the LCI and opened fire on a German bunker close to the shore. It subsequently emerged that the bunker was a harmless shelter for a defunct tramline that had once served the beach. With seconds to go before the ramp went down, Hollis accidentally held the gun by its barrel and received a painful burn across his hand. He would joke afterwards: 'A self-inflicted wound, quite the most painful I had in the entire war, it took weeks to heal and the battle hadn't even started.'

D-DAY VICTORIA CROSS

Maj RJL Jackson of the Green Howards, who was a beach-master at King, remembered the beaches as quiet. Only when

Below: Distinguished by their green berets, Commandos give a confident thumbs up to a combat photographer after coming ashore on Gold. The selection and training of the Commandos ensured that they were an elite, a status of which they were justly proud.

his small party of radio operator and regimental policeman had advanced about 200m (220yd) and reached a fixed line, did the fighting start. 'They threw everything at us. The mortars took us first and I was hit badly in the leg. My radio operator and policeman were both killed outright.' Wounded and immobilized, he was only just saved from drowning as the tide washed over his legs.

Supported by AVREs, the Green Howards rapidly cleared the position at Hable de Heurtot and pushed on to the battered fortified battery complex at Mont Fleury. It was during these attacks that CSM Hollis won the Victoria Cross for bravery. He was the only man to receive this supreme decoration on D-Day.

His citation ended: 'Wherever fighting was heaviest CSM Hollis appeared, and in the course of a magnificent day's work he displayed the utmost gallantry, and on two separate occasions his courage and initiative prevented the enemy from holding up the advance at critical stages. It was largely through his heroism and resource that the Company's objectives were gained and casualties were not heavier, and by his own bravery he saved the lives of many of his men.'

Hollis recalled that earlier, as he directed the fire of the Bren gunners on the shore amongst the noise, dust and smoke of the battle, he spotted a line of seagulls sitting on the barbed wire only a short distance away. One Private Mullally saw them too and remarked with a typical soldier's understatement:

'No bloody wonder, Sergeant Major, there's no bloody room for them in the air.'

> It appeared that the main enemy fire was coming from a large... many storied house. I ordered the Churchill (AVRE) forward to demolish the house with the petard...
> Maximum covering fire was given by the Sherman tanks...
> The petard fired and something like a small flying dustbin hit the house just above the front door. It collapsed like a pack of cards, spilling the defenders with their machine guns, anti-tank weapons and an avalanche of bricks into the courtyard.
>
> *Major Peter Selerie*
> *Sherwood Rangers Yeomanry, British 8th Armoured Brigade*

Stan Hollis died in 1972. When his widow sold his VC at auction it fetched £32,000 ($50,000), a record at the time for this distinguished decoration.

The East Yorks were halted at La Rivière where German defences that housed machine guns and an 8.8cm (3.46in) anti-tank gun had survived. The German gun crew now began to pick off the AVREs. A single AVRE then worked its way round on a blind side of the gun crew and at a range of 100m (110yd) fired its heavy demolition gun, destroying the position. This permitted the East Yorks, who were sheltering under the sea wall, to move forward and clear the area. However, this took several hours, with fierce house-to-house fighting. The reserve battalion, the 7th Green Howards, which landed at 08:20 hours, bypassed La Rivière and pushed inland supported by tanks to capture the Meuvaines ridge.

The arrival of tanks of the Nottinghamshire Yeomanry, the 4th/7th Dragoon Guards as well as the Flail tanks of 22nd Westminster Dragoons later in the morning greatly increased Gen Graham's scope for a fast advance inland. The landing by the 4th/7th had gone largely according to plan, except that two tanks had been swamped when they went into submerged bomb craters on the

Left: A view of the Arromanches Mulberry Harbour from the clifftop above the town, The remains of this innovative solution to the logistic problems of amphibious warfare can be seen today, over half a century after the prefabricated harbour was put in position.

Above: The enormous size and strength of some of the positions of the Atlantic wall can be seen in this captured gun position. The embrasure is shielded from direct fire from the sea by a massive reinforced concrete wall, but the gun can cover the beaches and deliver interlocking fire.

beach. Three self-propelled field artillery regiments followed, providing close support and counter battery fire.

South of the village of Creully, in open country, the lead tanks of the 4th/7th were hit and caught fire. Some were victims of a German anti-tank gun, but tragically the pilot of an Allied Forward Observer Bombardment (FOB) aircraft had spotted the tanks, and assuming they were German, had called down fire from the Cruiser HMS *Orion*. A signal via the Army/Navy radio link rectified the error but the Cruiser's log for D-Day said: 'Enemy tanks destroyed – well done!'

On D-Day, there were 104 spotter planes to carry 39 FOB parties, composed of naval personnel with radio links to major warships. The British aircraft were under No 34 Tactical Reconnaissance Wing, RAF, 2nd Tactical Air Force and were made up of RN Seafire FIII and RAF Spitfire LVB based at Lee-on-Solent, Portsmouth.

GROUND STRAFING

On the ground, worse was to come for the tanks of the 4th/7th when a pilot of a roving USAAF Republic P-47

Thunderbolt, failing to see the yellow recognition panel on the deck behind the turret, made two strafing runs. Luckily, this time there were no casualties. The tank crews set off an orange smoke grenade and the pilot, waggling his wings, acknowledged his error and flew off to look for new targets.

By noon, men, weapons and stores were being landed at Gold beach. The coastal defenders still hung on at Le Hamel where machine guns continued to fire in enfilade on the beach. As mine and booby trap clearance operations progressed, unit assembly areas were delineated in areas south of the D514 coast road with the beach head expanding 10km (6 miles) inland.

The 56th Brigade Group landed and as planned, pushed off to the south-west to capture Bayeux. The 151st Brigade Group entered the line between the 56th and 69th Brigades to join the drive south-west.

During the afternoon, the most serious fighting happened when the 69th Brigade encountered two battalions of the German 352nd Division with anti-tank support in the area around Villiers le Sec and Bazenville. Bayeux could have been taken on D-Day but the commanding officers of the 56th and 151st Brigades feared that a German counter attack would be launched and reined in their troops.

By the end of the day, 25,000 troops had landed and Gold was secure for the loss of 413 men killed, wounded or missing.

CHAPTER NINE

JUNO BEACH

At Juno three brigades of the Canadian 3rd Infantry Division would land. They included men who had volunteered for service in 1939 and trained in Britain for nearly five years. For others this was a return to France, for a number of Canadians had fought and died in the Dieppe Raid in August 1942, and D-Day was to be their chance to get some 'pay back' for the losses two years earlier. Once ashore these 'Canucks' would achieve the deepest penetration inland of any of the Allied landings on D-Day.

ON THE ADVICE OF the *Kriegsmarine*, the stretch of coast between Courseulles and St Aubin that would become Juno beach, was not as heavily fortified as other areas of Normandy because the navy thought the offshore rocks would make any Allied landing too difficult. The staff of the naval headquarters of Admiral Hennecke at Cherbourg was convinced that a working port would be the priority objective for the Allies.

Despite this confidence, defences were constructed and the army requested that the navy mine the waters off the beach. Allied air superiority prevented them mining the approaches, so the 716th Division pioneers attempted an improvized minefield by positioning rock-filled crates containing explosive charges on the offshore rocks. It was a good idea in theory, but the tides and currents quickly wrecked the crates and dumped the remains on the foreshore at low tide.

The coastline was the responsibility of the 2nd/736th Grenadier Regiment, with its headquarters at Tailleville, and

Left: Laden with equipment, Allied soldiers wade ashore and man-handle a little Wellbike, a 2-stroke motorcycle. Originally designed for airborne forces, it had a maximum speed of 48.2km/h (30mph) and weighed 31.7kg (70lbs).

the 726th Regiment, which were both part of the 716th Infantry Division under General Richter. The division consisted of 180 officers, 1100 NCOs and 6500 soldiers. To bring it up to strength, it had 2000 *Osttruppen* in the 439th, 441st and 642nd Battalions. It was supported by the 5th, 6th and 7th Batteries of the 1716th Artillery Regiment commanded by Lieutenant Colonel Knupe. There were 16 heavy batteries, located either in casemates or gun pits on the coast, or in strongpoints inland at Reviers, Bény, Colomby-sur-Thaon as well as the 15cm (5.9in) *Graf Waldersee* battery at Plumetot. Most of the guns were horse-drawn and the division had nearly 1000 horses in June 1944, though there was a self-propelled gun battery commanded by Lt Scharf in Cresserons.

Above: Commando troops with lightweight bicycles and other equipment come ashore at Juno. They have made an almost 'dry' landing which was what every Commando hoped for – wading chest deep meant hours, if not days, of discomfort after the landing.

The 716th Division headquarters staff were comparatively elderly officers aged between 40 and 50. For offices and accommodation they had commandeered some of the more attractive villas in the suburbs of Caen. The *Divisionsgefechtsstand* (Division Command Post), was sited in a former limestone quarry. The main gallery of the command post had three side galleries protected by blast-proof doors covered by machine gun embrasures.

The headquarters contained the map room, General Richter's command post, signals facilities and the command post of the 1716th Artillery Regiment.

Behind the 716th Division was a more potent force, two units of the 21st Panzer Division. The 192nd

Left: A MG42 machine gunner of the Waffen-SS Division 'Hitler Jugend'. *Many of the recently-formed division were fanatical Nazis and former Hitler Youth members.*

Panzergrenadier Regiment with half-track vehicles had its headquarters at Mathieu with detachments at Biéville, Villons-les-Buissons, Buron and Cairon. There were also elements of the 200th Panzerjager Battalion with self-propelled anti-tank guns at Putot-en-Bessin, St Croix, Grand-Tonne and Cully. Its total strength was 16,000 men with 170 armoured vehicles.

On the shore there were four *Widerstandsnesten*, one on either side of the mouth of the River Seulles at Courseulles, one at Bernières and one at St Aubin. All were manned by men of the 441st Ost Battalion. The beach west of the Seulles was covered by a 7.5cm (2.95in) field gun, two 5cm (1.97in) Kwk guns in casemates, four similar guns in Tobruks, a Renault tank turret bunker and numerous machine gun and mortar positions. To the east of the river were two 7.5cm (2.95in) field guns and mortar and machine gun positions.

RADAR FORTRESS

At Basly-Douvres, there was a complex of *Luftwaffe* radars, designated *Distelfink*. These were protected by three anti-tank guns, three 5cm (1.97in) flak guns, a dozen flamethrowers and 20 machine guns. The garrison commanded by Lieutenant Igle consisted of 230 *Luftwaffe* ground troops and infantrymen and barbed wire fences. The camp, or *Luftwaffenstützpunkt*, had 30 buildings, two *Würzburg*, one *Freya* and one *Wassermann* radar as well as underground bunkers that covered an area of 12 hectares (30 acres). Three weeks before D-Day, the radar complex was destroyed by RAF attacks, but the buildings and defences were still intact and since they were on high ground, they represented a formidable defensive position.

CANADIANS IN ACTION

The troops assigned to land at Juno on D-Day and push inland were the Canadian 3rd Division under British-born Major General RFL Keller. They had been assigned to the invasion as far back as July 1943 and trained hard in Scotland and in the Portsmouth area, working with the 2nd Canadian Armoured Brigade under Brigadier Wyman with its DD tanks and the landing craft of the Royal Navy.

The leading formations for D-Day were the 6th Armoured Regiment (1st Hussars) with DD tanks. The Royal Winnipeg Rifles, The Regina Rifle Regiment, the 10th Armoured Regiment (Fort Garry Horse) with DD tanks, The Queen's Own Rifles of Canada and the North Shore (New Brunswick) Regiment.

On 26 May, the division was 'sealed' in its concentration area. The veteran correspondent Alan Moorehead wrote of

> The enemy are on top of my bunker. I have no means of resisting them and no communications with my men. What shall I do?
>
> *Signal from Colonel Krug commanding 736th Grenadier Regiment*
>
> I can give you no more orders: You must make your own decision now. Goodbye.
>
> *Reply from headquarters 716th Infantry Division 23:59 hours, 6 June*

this experience: 'Once the gate was closed you could no longer return to the normal world outside, not even to buy a packet of cigarettes at the shop on the corner of the street, nor have a haircut, nor telephone your friends. You were committed irrevocably to the landing, perhaps tomorrow, perhaps the day after; no-one knew for certain.'

Below: A diagram of the naval fire support that would be directed at a D-Day beach and position of the landing craft carrying troops and vehicles. On the flanks, ships like cruisers would engage coastal batteries and strong points. Observers in special craft corrected the fire.

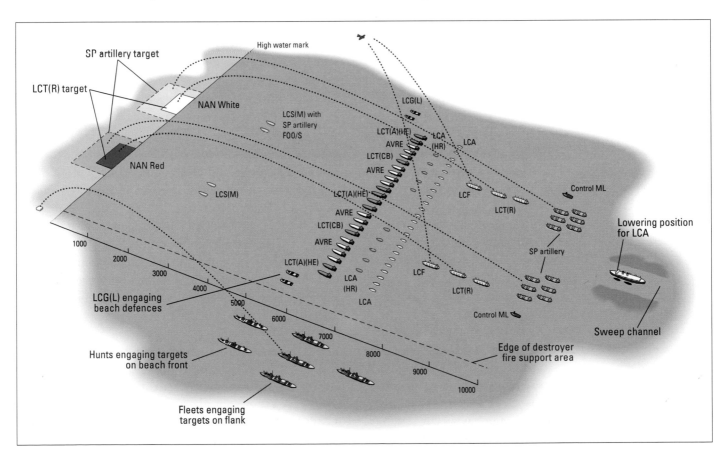

Kit was reduced to assault scales, quartermasters collected spare clothing and British troops packed their personal belongings into kitbags that were sent at no charge to their homes.

On 1 June, the 15,000 Canadians and 9000 British soldiers who made up the division began to board landing ships at Southampton.

For the landing, Juno had been divided into two beaches – 'Mike' to the west, and 'Nan' between Bernières and St Aubin to the east. Mike, the smaller beach, was subdivided into 'Green' and 'Red' and 'Nan' into 'Green', 'White' and 'Red'.

The 7th Canadian Brigade Group under Brig Foster would land on Mike and the 8th under Brig KG Blackader on Nan. Each brigade would have DD tanks in support. The 8th Brigade would be followed up by the 4th Special Service Brigade commanded by Brig Bernard 'Jumbo' Leicester RM. The brigade composed of No 41, 46, 47 and No 48 Royal Marine Commando would mop up and make contact with No 41 Royal Marine Commando, detached to the British 3rd Infantry Division to the east at Sword beach. Earlier in the war, Leicester had fallen out with many older Royal Marine officers when he pressed for the Corps to take on the new Commando role.

The follow up brigade, the 9th, would land either on Mike or Nan depending on the depth of the bridgehead. It would be tasked with occupying the high ground to the west of Caen near Carpiquet airfield.

The Canadians' initial objectives were the capture and clearance of the coastal villages and towns like Courseuilles, St Aubin and Bernières along Juno, and specific villages inland. They had three reporting lines inland, 'Yew', 'Elm' and 'Oak' that corresponded with the three phases of their D-Day plan. Oak was about 16km (10 miles) inland on the railway line just south of the N13 road from Caen to Bayeux.

ATTACK FROM SEA AND AIR

The beaches would receive the same treatment as the others of aerial attack by the RAF in the night followed by the USAAF in daylight. The naval bombardment force included the cruisers HMS *Belfast* and *Diadem* and 11 destroyers including the Free French FFS *Combattante* and Canadian HMCS *Algonquin* and *Sioux*.

At 08:05 hours the landing craft carrying the Canadians began to move towards the beaches. The two X-Craft midget submarine that had been on station surfaced and prepared to marshal the amphibious force. Among the variety of craft moving towards the beaches were the DD tanks.

Sergeant Leo Gariepy of 6th Armoured Regiment, driving his DD tank, remembered: 'A midget submarine appeared just

a few yards in front of me. His duty was to lead me to my primary target on the beach – a blockhouse sheltering a naval gun. High wind was forcing me to drift and the man in the submarine was trying to wave me back into line... As the water became shallower, the submarine stopped, its occupant stood up and wished me luck with his hands clasped over his head.'

The X-Craft had guided Gariepy to the shore 'as machine-gun bullets were ripping the water all around me and the occasional mortar fell among us'.

For a young Royal Marine coxswain on a LCA, the Royal Navy officer standing on the deck of the X-Craft appeared to be standing on the water. 'We had been told that RN officers walked on water, and here was visual proof.'

The original times set for the landings were 07:35 hours for Mike and 07:45 hours for Nan. However, rough seas forced a 30-minute delay, and on a rising tide, this would prove to be a fatal decision. The 7th Brigade lost eight DD tanks in the rough waves, but those that landed began to engage the surviving coastal positions. The 8th decided to land their tanks conventionally.

The rising tide and the waves drove some of the first waves of LCAs onto the mined obstacles on the foreshore. A Canadian naval officer reported:

'About three quarters of the troops had been disembarked from LCA 1150 when an explosion... blew in the port side... The port side of LCA 1059 was blown in by one of the mined obstructions after one third of the troops had been disembarked... two soldiers were killed. Another explosion holed LCA 1137 and stove in the starboard bow. All troops had been cleared from the craft without casualties... LCA 1138 was about to leave the beach when a wave lifted it on to an obstruction. The explosion which followed ripped the bottom out of the craft... An obstruction ripped the bottom out of LCA 1151. The crews transferred to an LCT and were eventually brought back to ship.'

LCAS LOST IN ACTION

In all, 20 LCAs were lost in one battalion landing and altogether 90 of 306 LCAs were lost or disabled in the morning.

Once the 7th Brigade was ashore, they became caught up in a hard fight for the defended village of Courseuilles. The greater part of the village on the east bank of the Seulles River had survived the bombardment. Though the Sherman tanks of the 6th Canadian Armoured Regiment gave supporting fire, the Regina Rifles had to fight from house to house. They were later supported up by AVREs and Centaurs or Mk VIII Cruiser (Centaur) (A27L) tanks, armed with a 95mm (3.74in) howitzer that were used by the Royal Marines

Above: Royal Engineers walk away as plastic explosive charges explode shattering Czech hedgehog anti-tank obstacles during a battlefield clearance operation after the landings. Other teams would be lifting mines and clearing barbed wire.

Armoured Support Group to give covering fire from LCTs during the D-Day landings. The Centaur AVRE team had cleared the area by the afternoon.

Meanwhile, the Winnepeg and part of the Canadian Scottish had cleared Vaux, Graye and St Croix. St Croix was held by 2nd Battalion 726th Grenadier Regiment commanded by Maj Lehmann. The major was killed and his adjutant defended the headquarter bunker with a few men until nightfall. A follow up company of the Regina Rifles bypassed Courseuilles and captured Reviers.

The defenders on the 8th Brigade front followed Rommel's dictum and waited until the Canadian troops were on the shore and within range. Six Shermans of the Canadian 10th Armoured Regiment were destroyed. When the Queen's Own Rifles and the North Shore Regiment raced to the sea wall and attacked St Aubin and Bernières, they found the villages heavily defended. At Bernières, a *Widerstandsnester* commanding the beach was only captured after naval gunfire support from an anti-aircraft ship that had almost grounded when it closed to the shore. The position had caused 50 percent casualties to the lead company of the Queen's Own. The Queen's Own

were, however, able to clear flanking positions and by 09:30 hours the village was secure.

It took a further hour to capture St Aubin and it was here that the Funnies proved invaluable, with DD tanks and AVREs blasting the German positions. One bunker that was silenced by a Centaur of the Royal Marine Armoured Support Regiment was found to contain 70 empty shell cases – a mute witness to the determination of the defenders.

CIVILIAN CASUALTIES

Among the casualties in St Aubin were Monsieur and Madame Serge Constant. He recalled the lethal impact of the bombardment. 'My wife was frightened and she left the house. There was a little alleyway and a garden at the end of it, and everybody went down into the garden. And we were all down there by the wall. And then suddenly, one of those – you know – torpedo rocket things exploded. Oh my God! My wife was wounded and two aunts were killed right by me.'

At the seaside village of Langrune, No 48 Royal Marine Commando stormed into a heavily fortified complex. Lateral roads were blocked, windows and doors of buildings had been bricked up and the defenders had dug underground tunnels to move under cover. The Commandos called for naval gunfire and a Centaur. When the tank had expended its ammunition another moved up but hit a mine. An anti-tank gun was then moved up and a Sherman

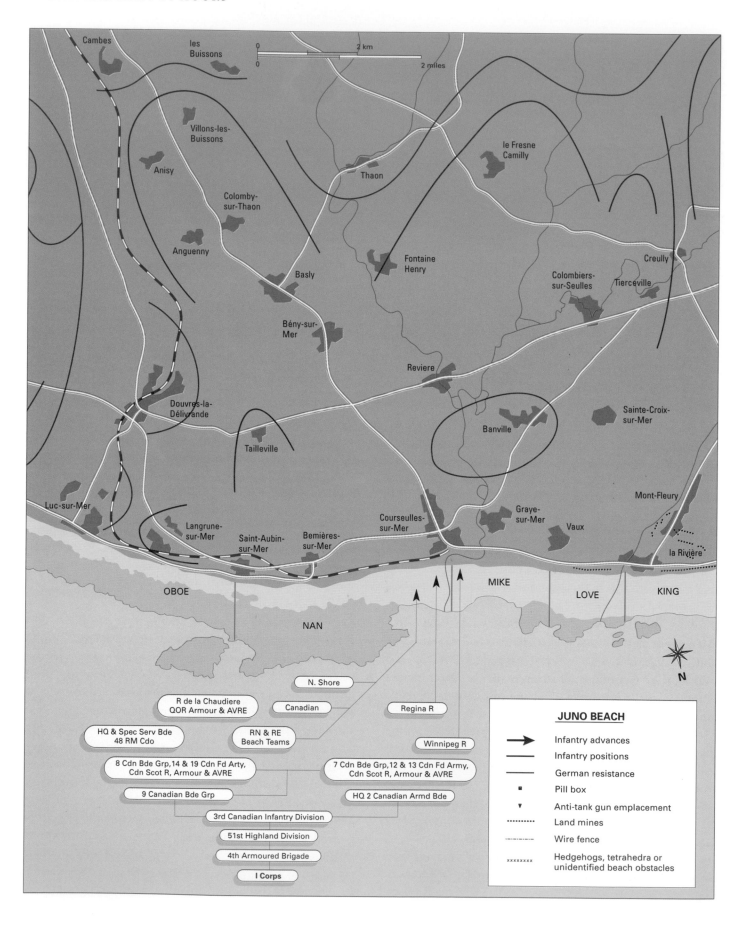

Cambes

les Buissons

Villons-les-Buissons

Anisy

Colomby-sur-Thaon

Anguenny

Basly

Thaon

le Fresne Camilly

Fontaine Henry

Creully

Colombiers-sur-Seulles

Tierceville

Bény-sur-Mer

Reviere

Douvres-la-Délivrande

Banville

Sainte-Croix-sur-Mer

Tailleville

Luc-sur-Mer

Langrune-sur-Mer

Saint-Aubin-sur-Mer

Bemières-sur-Mer

Courseulles-sur-Mer

Graye-sur-Mer

Vaux

Mont-Fleury

la Rivière

MIKE

LOVE

KING

OBOE

NAN

N

0   2 km
0   2 miles

N. Shore

R de la Chaudiere
QOR Armour & AVRE

Canadian

Regina R

HQ & Spec Serv Bde
48 RM Cdo

RN & RE
Beach Teams

Winnipeg R

8 Cdn Bde Grp,14 & 19 Cdn Fd Arty,
Cdn Scot R, Armour & AVRE

7 Cdn Bde Grp,12 & 13 Cdn Fd Army,
Cdn Scot R, Armour & AVRE

9 Canadian Bde Grp

HQ 2 Canadian Armd Bde

3rd Canadian Infantry Division

51st Highland Division

4th Armoured Brigade

I Corps

JUNO BEACH

→	Infantry advances
—	Infantry positions
—	German resistance
■	Pill box
▼	Anti-tank gun emplacement
·········	Land mines
─·─·─	Wire fence
xxxxxxxx	Hedgehogs, tetrahedra or unidentified beach obstacles

Above: The shattered remains of a timber roadblock provides cover for Canadian troops. The villages and small towns inshore from the beaches had been fortified and turned into strongpoints by the Germans over the previous year.

manoeuvring to give direct fire also hit a mine. Bitter hand-to-hand fighting followed as the Royal Marines fought from position to position and it was not until 7 June that 31 prisoners emerged from the shell-blasted and smoking wreckage of the town's buildings.

When the Regiment de la Chaudière reached Bény-sur-Mer, it was halted by heavy machine gun fire, backed by anti-tank guns sited on a spur. It was noon before the area was cleared. One bunker had been silenced by a Sapper armoured bulldozer driver filling the embrasures with sand and entombing the defenders.

Landings continued, but the coxswains of the landing craft had trouble with wrecks and obstacles and so the pace was slower than anticipated. As the tide rose, the beach became congested but assault engineers first opened two routes through the minefields along the shore before opening a

Left: Juno in the centre of the Anglo-Canadian beaches was ten kilometres (six miles) wide and had offshore reefs that screened the Love sector. Mike, however, was readily accessible through a central passage as was the Nan sector.

Our Support Craft was knocked out so we had no heavy weapons. The DD tanks had not come ashore. My platoon, approximately 36 strong, went through what we believe was enfilade fire from machine guns. The official battalion killed-in-action figures for 6 June 1944 numbered 63, 'B' Company 34. I don't have the figures for the platoon but I do know that only nine men moved inland, three of whom were walking wounded. Of the ten men in my section, seven were killed and two wounded. Of these ten men, six had been with the unit since June 1940. The one survivor, the latest replacement, had never done a 'landing' in training.

Lieutenant Corporal Ralph Jackson
Queen's Own Rifles of Canada, 3rd Infantry Division

Above: In the morning haze, troops move inland from Juno beach. The Allied planners had focused on the challenge of breaking through the Atlantic Wall, and they had not considered the grim fight that would face them in the Normandy countryside.

third. From 14:00 hours, the reserve brigade with four regiments of artillery and a third armoured regiment were then able to expand the bridgehead.

Maj Gen Keller left his HQ ship, HMS *Hilary*, at 11:45 hours and by 14:35 hours gave his first press conference in France in a small orchard outside Bernières. The press team had located the Hotel de Grave in Bernières and set up shop at 10:30 hours on D-Day. To the delight of the population on Juno, the Canadian troops, who looked like British 'Tommies', spoke French.

Keller's confident and rather flamboyant gesture did not reflect his competence as a general. General John Crocker, commanding I Corps, would say that Keller 'was not really fit temperamentally and perhaps physically (he is a man who has the appearance of having lived pretty well) for such a responsible command'. Montgomery concurred, saying that Keller 'was not good enough to command a Canadian division'. Keller was, however, popular with the Canadian troops and sacking him was politically unacceptable. The problem of his command was resolved on 8 August, when in error, bombers of the USAAF 8th Air Force attacked Keller's headquarters, nearly killing him, and obliging him to return wounded to the UK.

Away from the beaches on D-Day, Canadian armour and infantry advanced aggressively. The superb 7th Brigade crashed through a battalion of the German 726th Infantry Regiment and linked up with the British 50th Division at Creully. Shells were falling at random as their tanks stalked German anti-tank gun positions and reached the Caen–Arromanches road at Le Fresne-Camilly.

The 8th Brigade cleared the fortified villages of Tailleville, Basly and Colomby-sur-Thaon and at 18:30 hours, the 9th Brigade moved though them. The North Nova Scotia Highlanders and 27th Armoured Regiment (Sherbrooke Fusiliers), pushed forward through mortar and anti-tank gunfire to capture Villons-les Buissons and Anisy at last light. Tailleville, which had been the objective of 'C' Company North Shore Regiment, had been stubbornly defended by the German 736th Grenadier Regiment whose Command Post was in the village. It was not until 23:00 hours that the Canadians finally secured it.

At the end of the day at Bény the Canadian divisional commander discovered that the enemy 736th Grenadier Regiment still held a 4km (2.5 mile) front on the coast. There was a corridor to the coast dividing his troops from the British 3rd Division to the east.

Early in the morning of 6 June, a battle group of the 21st Panzer Division was advancing towards the coast along this corridor. A rifle company and six tanks of the 1st Battalion

192nd Panzer Grenadier Regiment did in fact reach the coast and reported this opening. However, the crews of the armoured vehicles then saw the huge air transport stream above them with its fighter escort. It was destined to reinforce the 6th Airborne Division in their DZ on the Orne. The men of the 21st Panzer Division assumed falsely that they would be dropped in the area and without back up the battle group withdrew fearing that the airbourne landings would cut them off.

Interrogated after the war, Lieutenant General Edgar Feuchtinger, an artilleryman commanding the 21st Panzer Division, recalled that the British and Canadian forces '…had made astonishing progress and had already occupied a strip of high ground about 10km (6 miles) from the sea. From here, the excellent anti-tank gunfire of the Allies knocked out 11 of my tanks before I had barely started… I now expected that some reinforcements would be forthcoming to help me hold my position, but nothing came. Another Allied parachute landing on both sides of the Orne, together with a sharp attack by English tanks, forced me to give up my hold on the coast.'

However, in the early hours of 6 June he was not available at his headquarters and his staff believed he was in Paris with his French mistress. Von Luck said of his CO: 'He was fond of all the good things of life, for which Paris was a natural attraction. Knowing that he had no combat experience or knowledge of tank warfare, Feuchtinger had to delegate most things, that is, leave the execution of orders to us experienced commanders.' It was a kind judgement on a man who though he had fought in World War I and France in 1940 and on the Leningrad Front in 1942, had progressed upwards through the army principally because of political connections within the Nazi Party.

Colonel Bodo Zimmermann of the German HQ OB West staff made a rather harsher assessment of Feuchtinger's performance on D-Day accusing him of running away. On Christmas Eve 1944, Feuchtinger's conduct caught up with him when an order arrived at the headquarters of the 21st Panzer Division, now fighting on the borders of the Reich, demanding that Feuchtinger explain his absence from his headquarters on 5 and 6 June. But once again the general was not at his headquarters and while his division fought in the bitter cold, he was at home with his family for Christmas. He was relieved of his command in January 1945 and condemned by a court martial in March. Using his Nazi Party connections he managed to avoid execution and was captured by the Americans at the end of the war.

Courage was not lacking among the technicians and *Luftwaffe* personnel at the radar complex at Basly-Douvres that was attacked at 07:00 hours on 7 June by the North Shore Regiment who had reached it at last light the day before. The Canadians met with strong opposition, which repulsed several attacks until 17 June, when a combat group of the 22nd Dragoons, No 41 Royal Marine Commando and 26th Assault Squadron RE attacked, supported by heavy artillery fire. The radar position had been held by men who were not front line soldiers for two weeks after D-Day. Futhermore, eight tanks had been damaged and four AVREs were written off in the final attack.

By the end of D-Day, the 3rd Canadian Division had secured its beach head but had not reached its inland objectives. However, 21,400 men, 3200 vehicles and 2130 tonnes (2100 tons) of stores had been landed. The division had suffered 946 casualties of whom 335 were killed.

Below: M4 Shermans manoeuvre past a signals truck. The crew of the lead tank have added track links to the glacis plate to improve protection and also ensure that there are spare links if the tracks are broken by an anti-tank mine. In reality the links did not provide much protection.

CHAPTER TEN

SWORD BEACH

On the extreme left of the Allied landings, the men of the British 3rd Infantry Division who went ashore at Sword had the important task of linking up with the airborne forces who had landed to the east of the River Orne. They were also faced by the 21st Panzer Division which, though it had some rather unusual armoured vehicles built from captured French tanks, was still a formidable force that could delay or even throw the British back into the sea.

THE DEFENCES ON THE COASTLINE between the village of St Aubin-sur-Mer and the mouth of the River Orne (that would be designated Sword beach) followed standard German practice. The beach had a slight curve that allowed defenders to site weapons in defilade with interlocking fields of fire. Some of the beach was rocky and in other areas was composed of soft mud – all this helped in the German coastal obstacle plan.

At the mouth of the Orne the Riva Bella defended area was 1.2km (0.75 miles) long and extended 200m (650ft) inland. Riva Bella, a modern seaside town, was laid out on a grid iron, with two roads running parallel down to the sea front. The defended *Widerstandsnesten*, WN18, was in two locations on the coast and contained 80 bunkers and had six 15cm (5.9in) K420(f) guns with a range of 21km (13 miles) in open concrete gun pits. There were also four

Left: Men of the 3rd Infantry Division wade ashore towards the sand dunes and flat beaches of Sword. The Germans had sited some excellent strong points covering the shore. The overcast conditions show how unsettled the weather was on 6 June.

*Above: Commandos, distinguished by their Bergen rucksacks and green
berets, disembark from a landing craft. The Commandos under Lord
Lovat, seen centre-left on his own in the water with his back towards the
camera, would push hard to reach the paras at Pegasus Bridge.*

7.62cm (3in) Russian field guns, seven 5cm (1.97in) KwK
guns of which three were in casemates, two flanking casemates, again with Russian 7.62cm (3in) field guns, two
Renault tank turrets, a 5cm (1.97in) and an 8.1cm (3.19in)
mortar, a 2cm (0.78in) flak gun, two armoured machine
gun turrets (Type R644) and a 15cm (5.9in) searchlight.
The command post for the defences was a four storey concrete tower topped by a 2cm (0.78in) flak gun. Within the
town, a concrete-lined V-shaped anti-tank ditch ran to the
left bank of the Orne Canal, dividing the sea front area
from the main town.

The Riva Bella position was manned by companies from
the 1st/736th Infantry Regiment and the 642nd Ost battalion
716th Static Infantry Division. Just before D-Day, the 1st
Battery of the 1260th Coastal Artillery Regiment was moved
inland to St Aubin d'Arquenay, the battery position for its
four 15.5cm (6.1in) guns position. WN12 was code-named
'Daimler'. It would have been in position to deliver indirect
fire on the beaches but a group composed of Sergeant Guy de
Montlaur, Petty Officer Joseph Nicot and Marcel Lefebre of
the Resistance had cut the telephone link from the OP.

MORRIS AND HILLMAN
In addition to the 7.5cm (2.95in) guns in casemates in
Ouistreham inland there were the 10cm (3.94in) emplacements WN16 and WN17 manned by the 1716th Artillery
Regiment between Colleville and Périers that were code-
named 'Morris' and 'Hillman', by Allied planners. To the east
of Hillman was the headquarters of the 736th Infantry
Regiment and to the south, on high ground, the headquarters of the 1716th Artillery Regiment.

To the west of WN18 at La Bréche was WN20, code-named 'Cod'. This position had a 7.5cm (2.95in) gun in a casemate, two 5cm (1.97in) guns, also in casemates, three 8.1cm (3.19in) mortars and a 3.7cm (1.45in) gun. Cod was actually 20 separate mutually supporting strong points. The depth positions would only be finally secured at 10:00 hours.

Finally, at Lion-sur-Mer, on the extreme right of Sword was WN21, code-named 'Trout' with two 5cm (1.97in) guns in casemates. The fish-type code names continued with 'Sole' (WN14), the headquarters of 1st/736th Infantry Regiment.

Sword beach, which would be the objective of the British 3rd Division under Major General TG Rennie was divided into 'Peter' and 'Queen'. The lead formations would be the 8th Infantry Brigade Group, 13/18th Royal Hussars in DD tanks, the 1st South Lancashire Regiment and 2nd East Yorkshire Regiment. The rocks close to the shore meant that they would attack on a narrow front the 'White' and 'Red' sectors of Queen.

Rennie had had a distinguished wartime career. He had been captured at St Valery in 1940 along with the 51st (Highland) Division but escaped within ten days. He

Below: A Sherman flail tank burns on the foreshore of Sword beach close to a track laying tank and a bulldozer. The specialist tanks known as 'Funnies' were invaluable for clearing the way through minefields, anti-tank ditches and other obstacles.

served in North Africa and commanded the Black Watch at El Alamein in 1942 where he won the DSO and subsequently fought in Sicily. Back in Britain, Rennie trained the 3rd Division hard for its D-Day role, but would be criticized for not emphasizing the need to quickly exploit unexpected opportunities.

FRENCH TANKS

The shore bombardment that would support the division would be delivered by an impressive force commanded by Rear Admiral Arthur Talbot. Two battleships, HMS *Warspite* and *Ramillies*, were on call as well as the monitor HMS *Roberts*, the cruisers HMS *Mauritius* (Flagship) *Arethusa*, *Frobisher* and *Danal* and the Polish ORP *Dragon*. Among the 13 destroyers was the Norwegian HMNS *Svenner*.

The bombardment force had several targets besides the heavy coastal batteries astride the Seine estuary. Their priority targets were the batteries at Villerville, Mount Canisy and Houlgate that would be engaged at 05:45 hours.

Aboard the *Ramillies*, Petty Officer Drake would only realize that they were on course for France and D-Day when the battleship put to sea on what he had thought was another exercise, and the Captain addressed the crew. The skipper's sonorous opening words were: 'The die is cast and we are committed to attack.'

Admiral Talbot recalled the poor response of the German defenders. 'The air was full of our bombers and fighters, and

of the noise and smoke of our bombardments. The enemy was obviously stunned by the sheer weight of support we were meting out.'

For the Allied planners, Sword was potentially the most vulnerable beach with 21st Panzer Division in and around Caen and the 12th *Waffen-SS-Panzer Division 'Hitler Jugend'* to the east. If they counter attacked when the Allies had limited numbers of tanks ashore they could drive the landing back into the sea. It was essential therefore to break through the coastal defences and gain a deep lodgement ashore.

WEAKENED OPPONENT

In fact, the 21st Panzer Division was not as formidable a force as had been feared. Much of the division was equipped with captured French vehicles from 1940 and obsolete weapons. Major Becker, who commanded the division's Panzerjäger Abteilung 200 anti-tank unit, was a reserve officer with family connections in the German armaments industry which he used to produce improvized vehicles for the division. Using the chassis of captured Hotchkiss and Lorraine tanks and armoured vehicles, they produced self-propelled anti-tank and artillery vehicles. These included the 7.5cm (2.95in) Pak 40 auf GW 39h(f), a self-propelled anti-tank gun on the French Hotchkiss H39 tank and the FH 18 auf GW Lorraine Schlepper, which mounted a 10.5cm (4.13in) howitzer.

Feuchtinger remembered that 'the tanks had gone rusty as they had been left out in the open for two years, they had to be dismantled and cleaned completely, and generally the parts of two or three tanks were required to build one new tank of as good as new quality'.

The vehicles looked top heavy with big open topped armoured boxes to protect the crew. Maj Hans von Luck commented: 'At first we laughed at the monstrous looking assault guns, but we soon came to know better.'

Of the ten Panzer and Panzer grenadier divisions in the west, it was the only one rated as unfit for service in Russia. The division had been reformed from the unit that had fought with distinction in North Africa but had been destroyed in May 1943. In July 1943 it was reformed in Normandy. The new formation was composed of:
• Panzer Aufklärung Abteilung 21
• Panzer Regiment 22 (two battalions)
• Panzergrenadier Regiment 125 (two battalions)
• Panzergrenadier Regiment 192 (two battalions)
• Panzer Artillerie Regiment 155 (three battalions)
• Panzerjäger Abteilung 200

• Nachrichten Abteilung 200
• Panzer Pioniere Bataillon 220

In addition there was the Divisional Headquarters, Divisional Headquarters *Abteilung* and divisional services. *Heeres Flak Abteilung 305* was added to the division later. Feuchtinger was dismissive about the quality of some of the men in his division. 'Another great difficulty in the training of the 21st, as in many other divisions, was that 15 percent of the replacements were so-called *Volksdeutchen* (German nationals from abroad), many of whom did not even have a proper control of the German language.'

The 12th *Waffen-SS-Panzer Division 'Hitler Jugend'* was a very different type of armoured formation. Recruited from volunteers in the leadership schools of Nazi youth movement and men from the veteran *Waffen-SS Division Leibstandarte 'Adolf Hitler'*, it was commanded by *Gruppenführer* Fritz Witt who in training, had placed the main emphasis on live firing field exercises.

Witt had joined the Nazi Party in 1931 and served with the *Waffen-SS* in Poland, France (where he won the Knight's Cross), the Balkans and the Eastern Front. When he was given command of 12th *Waffen-SS-Panzer Division 'Hitler Jugend'* he was only 35 and the second youngest divisional commander in the German armed forces.

'PANZER' MEYER

Witt's personal motto was 'Attack', and he committed his division on D-Day. He would be killed by shell fire on 14 June and his replacement Kurt 'Panzer' Meyer was a man made from the same mould.

The divisional strength of 20,540 men was slightly higher than the establishment but the formation had attracted large numbers of volunteers who were aged between 16 and 17. The young soldiers were aggressive and dedicated and in the weeks of June 1944 would be formidable and also cruel opponents. Many had been bombed out of their homes in Germany, had lost fathers and brothers in the war and witnessed the horrors of the massive RAF raids on German cities.

The division consisted of :
• SS Panzergrenadier Regiments 25 and 26 (three battalions)
• SS Panzer Aufklärung Abteilung 123
• SS Panzer Regiment 12 (three battalions)

Right: The forces landing at Sword beach had a tough fight to clear Ouistreham, which had been turned into a strong point covering the mouth of the Orne and Caen canal. Huge smoke screens hid the invasion fleet from the German coastal batteries to the east.

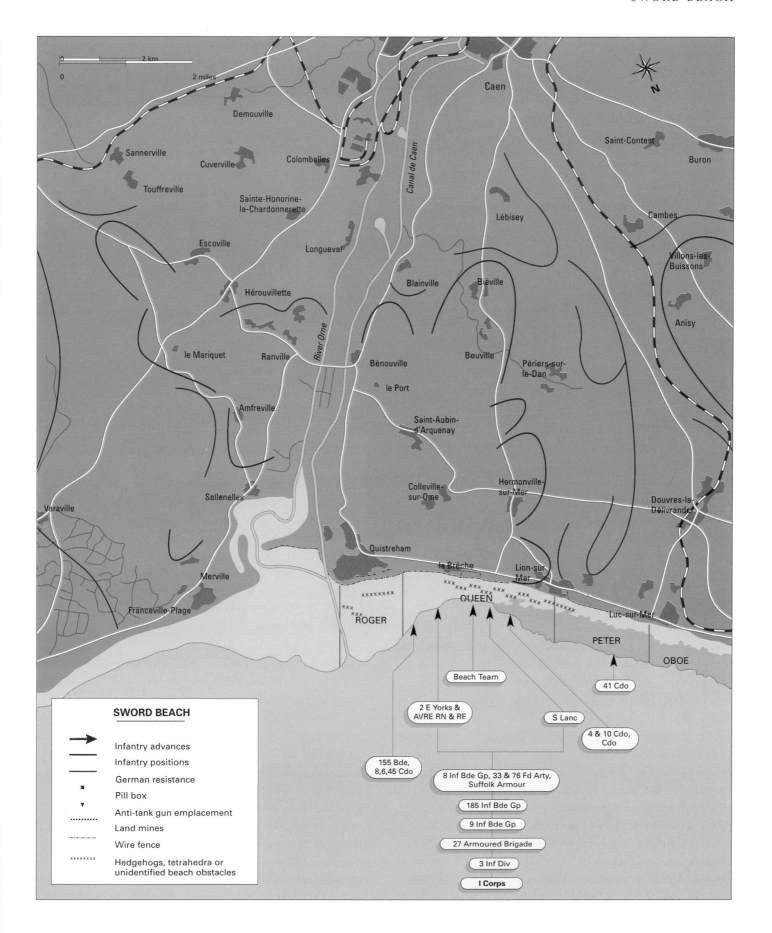

Caen

Saint-Contest

Demouville

Buron

Sannerville

Cuverville

Colombelles

Touffreville

Cambes

Sainte-Honorine-
la-Chardonnerette

Lébisey

Villons-les-
Buissons

Escoville

Longueval

Blainville

Biéville

Anisy

Hérouvillette

Beuville

le Mariquet

Ranville

Bénouville

Périers-sur-
le-Dan

River Orme

Canal de Caen

le Port

Amfreville

Saint-Aubin-
d'Arquenay

Colleville-
sur-Orne

Hermanville-
sur-Mer

Sallenelles

Douvres-la-
Délivrande

Varaville

Quistreham

la Brèche

Lion-sur-
Mer

Merville

ROGER

QUEEN

Luc-sur-Mer

Franceville-Plage

PETER

OBOE

Beach Team

41 Cdo

2 E Yorks &
AVRE RN & RE

S Lanc

4 & 10 Cdo,
Cdo

155 Bde,
8,6,45 Cdo

8 Inf Bde Gp, 33 & 76 Fd Arty,
Suffolk Armour

185 Inf Bde Gp

9 Inf Bde Gp

27 Armoured Brigade

3 Inf Div

I Corps

SWORD BEACH

→ Infantry advances

— Infantry positions

■ German resistance

▪ Pill box

▼ Anti-tank gun emplacement

•••••••• Land mines

—·—·— Wire fence

xxxxxxxx Hedgehogs, tetrahedra or
unidentified beach obstacles

0   2 km

0   2 miles

171

- SS Panzer Flak Abteilung 12
- SS Werfer Abteilung 12
- SS Panzerjäger Abteilung 12
- SS Panzer Nachrichten Abteilung 12
- SS Panzer Pioniere Bataillon 12
- Division HQ and Division HQ Abteilung

For the *Waffen-SS*, war was fought by the ruthless rules they applied on the Eastern Front. Small numbers of prisoners were sometimes shot because evacuating them to the rear would slow down operations and unarmed staff wearing the Red Cross in aid posts that were overrun in fighting might be shot in the blood lust of an attack. In the fighting in Normandy, some Allied troops would become as ruthless with captured SS soldiers.

About 130km (80 miles) inland was the superb Panzer Lehr Division, made up from demonstration units from tank training schools. Commanded by the veteran general, Fritz Bayerlein, it was equipped with PzKpfw V Panthers. The only drawback was that its personnel, though highly experienced, were mostly veterans of the Eastern Front and so had no experience of the huge weight of Allied firepower that could be brought to bear on even the smallest targets. Bayerlein, at 45, had had a career that included experience of combat in North Africa as well as the Eastern Front. The location of the

Above: A Sergeant smiles confidently at the photographer as troops form up on the beach ready to support the armour that is preparing to move off. The men have a canvas sleeve covering the bolt and working parts of their rifles to protect them from wet sand as they landed.

division reflected Field Marshal von Rundstedt's concept of a manoeuvre battle in which German armour would defeat the Allies once they were in France.

PANZER LEHR DIVISION

The Panzer Lehr Division consisted of two armoured infantry regiments, the 901st and 902nd Panzer Grenadier Lehr with an armoured regiment, the 130th Panzer Lehr Regiment. Within the 130th regiment the 2nd Battalion commanded by Maj Prince William von Schönberg-Waldenberg would fight hard outside Bayeux on 9 June delaying the British advance. The division also had its anti-tank, signals, engineer and reconnaissance units. In May 1944, it was at full strength and had 183 tanks, 58 anti-tank guns, some of which were self-propelled, and 53 artillery pieces. However, before it could play a part in the D-Day battle it would have to make its way along roads that had become the hunting ground for Allied ground attack aircraft. It would suffer grievously from the bombs, rockets and cannon fire of the ever present Jabos (fighter-bombers).

Faced with this opposition, the British 8th Brigade Group would have to move quickly along the Orne to relieve the Ox and Bucks Light Infantry holding Pegasus Bridge. No 4 Commando would clear east to Ouistréham Riva Bella, and No 41 Royal Marine Commando would clear west to link up with the Canadians at Langrune.

The follow up formation was the 185th Infantry Brigade Group, whose mission was to pass through 8th Brigade and 'seize Caen' or the high ground overlooking the city.

Force 'S' carrying the men destined for Sword beach was the only sea transport group to rendezvous to the east of the Solent. The men spent a wet night in the Channel swell. Then at 05:30 hours the leading infantry companies were lowered into their LCAs. Heading for the shore Maj CK 'Banger' King of the 2nd East Yorks read extracts from Shakespeare's *Henry V* to 'A' Company HQ over the Tannoy system.

Seventy-two 105mm (4.13in) self-propelled howitzers of the 3rd Division Artillery added the weight of their fire as their landing craft carried them towards Sword. In England, the self-propelled guns had been reversed into the LCTs with two guns forward and two back and in preparation for this unique fire mission, over 100 rounds of HE shells had been stacked ready. In the run in, the guns eventually fired some 6500 rounds.

Since landings had already begun at Utah and air attacks and airborne landings had alerted the Germans, Sword promised to be a tough fight. The first indications of this were when *S-Boote* from the 5th Flotilla based at Le Havre emerged through the smoke screen that had been laid by aircraft to cover the Allied fleet from the coastal guns at Le Havre. At 05:30 hours, the *S-Boote* fired a spread of 18 torpedoes at the huge target. Incredibly, only one hit. The *Svenner* was struck amidships and sank with a loss of one officer and 33 crewmen. Other torpedoes narrowly missed the HQ ship HMS *Largs* and battleships *Warspite* and *Ramilles*.

The *Svenner* was one of ten warships of the Royal Norwegian Navy in exile in action on D-Day. It also had three destroyers, three corvettes, three motor launches and one patrol vessel out in the Channel.

On the night of 6 June, all available German *S-Boote* were deployed, but the 5th Flotilla lost S 139 and S 140 to mines in the protective fields laid to cover the flanks of the D-Day beaches.

After 6 June, the *S-Boote* deployed almost every night, weather permitting, but faced by the massed firepower of the Allied fleet they enjoyed limited success. The reports of their actions were couched in dramatic language, which gave a false impression of their effectiveness.

The men of No 41 Royal Marine Commando had crossed the Channel in Landing Craft Infantry (Small) LCI (S) and it was a journey that would have tested the strongest stomach. It was not until they set off that they learned of their destination and objective.

ROUGH SEA

The sea was very rough with waves 2m (6.5ft) high and a 16 to 20 knot (30km/h/18.5mph – 37km/h/23mph) wind blowing. As a consequence the DD tanks were launched 5km (3 miles) from the shore not 8km (5 miles) as originally planned. The crews handled their ungainly tank 'craft' superbly and 21 out of 25 reached the shore, even though two had been rammed by a landing craft carrying the first wave of assault engineers.

Behind the DDs came the infantry of the 8th Brigade. Even though the beaches had been bombed and shelled, the defenders had taken cover and now emerged to deliver a brutal barrage of small arms and mortar fire. Maj AR Rouse of the South Lancashires recalled the final run in.

'During the last 100 yards (90m) of the run-in, everything seemed to happen at once. Out of the haze of smoke, the underwater obstacles loomed up. We had studied them on air photographs and knew exactly what to expect but somehow we had never realized the vertical height of them, and as we weaved in between iron rails and ramps and pickets with Teller mines on top, like gigantic mushrooms we seemed to be groping through a grotesque petrified forest. The noise was so continuous that it seemed like a siren.'

The commanding officer of the South Lancashires, Lieutenant Colonel Richard Burbury, landed carrying a flag in the battalion colours that he thought would give his troops a rallying point. Sadly this gesture from a bygone age made him conspicuous to a German machine gunner and Burbury was killed as he reached the beach wire. His second in command, Major Jack Stone, took over but without the battalion flag.

The East Yorkshire Regiment suffered 200 casualties in the first few minutes that it was ashore. The flail tanks and AVREs slowly cleared La Brèche. However, harassing fire did not stop until No 4 Commando had captured Ouistreham.

At 08:45 hours, the landing craft carrying No 41 RM Commando hit sand 180m (200yd) from the shore and came under intense mortar and machine gun fire. They were not on the correct beach but their CO, Lt Col TM Gray sent part

Although it seemed a long way from home, it was homely from the fact of being a battalion like the Warwicks... they were all local Birmingham lads, and in between the shells falling and the general noise of war you could hear a heated argument going on about the merits of Villa and Birmingham City football clubs in a couple of slit trenches just behind you, and it seemed then as if you weren't so far from home.

Private Geoff Peters
2nd Battalion Warwickshire Regiment
British 3rd Infantry Division

of the force east to link up with the South Staffordshire Regiment and part into Lion-sur-Mer. It was a tough fight, three supporting tanks were knocked out and between 16:00 hours and 18:00 hours naval gunfire support came from destroyers offshore.

As No 41 Commando, with a battalion of the Lincolnshires supported by the Royal Ulster Rifles, were about to put in a set piece attack, three Heinkel He 111 bombers roared in low and dropped sticks of bombs wounding Col Gray and his

Below: A clutter of soft skinned vehicles and specialist armour like an AVRE on the right crowd the beach. The rising tide reduced the space available as increasing numbers of troops and vehicles were landed during the day according to the strict timetable.

headquarters staff. Despite this, the attack went in and cleared Lion-sur-Mer, allowing the Commando to link up with No 46 Commando at Luc-sur-Mer.

At 09:30 hours, the Brigade's reserve battalion, the Suffolks, landed and moved off to clear Colleville and move on to Morris at 13:00 hours. Richard Harris, a young infantryman with the Suffolks, recalled the moment the landing craft reached the beach.

'Nearer and nearer we drew to the shore... Trembling, my rifle tightly clenched, I crouched awaiting the dreaded shout, "Ramps down!" We seemed to inch in, in between craft already beached, some of which were burning. The diesels went into reverse, the bows ground into the sand and pebbles and we came to a standstill. "Ramps down!" This was it, I was determined to present myself for the minimum

Oh, yes, I hit people. I personally saw people that I was firing at fall, on more than one occasion. I can say that without hesitation. Without bragging about being a good shot, a man only 100 or 150 yards (90 or 135m) away is an awful big target. And if it's an enemy soldier you don't just fire one shot, you fire a round, re-load and fire another, as quick as you can, another and another. Even when he has fallen, you still keep firing.

Private Dennis Bowen, aged 18
5th Battalion East Yorkshire Regiment

Above: Soldiers hunch behind an AVRE taking cover from machine gun fire as in the background an M10 tank destroyer known in British service as a 'Wolverine' swings its turret to engage a bunker. These open topped vehicles were later up-gunned with a British 17pdr.

time as a target at the top of the ramp and being one of the first to go I had a clear run.'

The assault on Hillman proved a harder task and was only achieved with artillery fire and direct support from the tanks of the Staffordshire Yeomanry. It was not until 20:15 hours that the position was secured.

To the east, the East Yorkshire Regiment and surviving tanks of the 13/18th Royal Hussars fought a hard battle behind Ouistreham and did not clear Daimler until 16:00 hours.

By 09:30 hours, the South Lancashire Regiment had cleared Hermanville and was moving towards the Périer ridge. This key feature was held by more determined troops, men of the 2nd/192nd Panzer Grenadier Regiment supported by 8.8cm (3.46in) guns of the 200th Panzerjager Battalion. They stopped the 8th Brigade advance that now awaited the arrival of the 195th Brigade.

At 08:20 hours, No 4 Commando landed from HMS *Princess Astrid* (which, like the assault ship that took them to France in August 1942 for Operation Cauldron, their successful part in the Dieppe raid, was a former Belgian Channel ferry) and HMS *Maid of Orleans* at Queen beach Red.

In their final run in Lt Murdoch McDougall, commanding 'F' Troop recalled that: 'Thirty-two pairs of eyes seemed to be fixed upon me. Panic seized me. My mouth was dry. God don't let me do anything idiotic. Please let me seem normal.' It was then that he saw Private McVeigh, a Bren gunner in the troop. His face green with sea sickness and fear, he muttered, 'for Chrissake get me ashore!' and the

Some of the local people came out into the street. I was handed a bottle by a middle-aged Frenchman and... found it to be a strong rawish spirit which I later discovered was distilled cider [Calvados]. We soon went through this village, and into open country until we came to the bridges. I can remember the bullets striking the ironwork... As I ran across one of the bridges I stopped near a dead British officer who had a Colt automatic .45 pistol attached to his neck with a lanyard. I broke the lanyard by putting my boots on it... and secured the pistol in an inner pocket of my BD [battle dress] blouse. This pistol came in very handy later on. This officer was one of the glider party that had landed during the night and did such good work capturing the bridges intact.

Tpr PH Pritchard
No 6 Commando, British 1st Special Service Brigade

young officer felt the relief of knowing that 'someone was in worse shape than myself'.

As they landed, they came under heavy fire suffering 40 casualties, among them the CO, the French speaking veteran of the Dieppe raid, Lt Col Robert Dawson, who suffered a leg and head wound.

ENTER THE LORD LOVAT

The Commando were part of the superb 1st Special Service (SS) Brigade commanded by Brigadier The Lord Lovat that was composed of No 3 Commando under Lt Col Peter Young, No 4 Commando under Dawson, No 6 Commando under Lt Col Derek Mills-Roberts and No 45 RM Commando under Lt Col NC Ries. No 41 RM Commando under Lt Col TM Gray was also part of the Brigade but had an independent role at Lion-sur-Mer.

The designation SS was soon dropped in part because it sounded like a German formation and also because in the US forces, the Special Services were a welfare organization for American troops. The SS Brigade became the Commando Brigade.

On D-Day, the SS Brigade HQ and No 6 Commando were piped ashore by Piper Bill Millin. 'I played *Highland Laddie*

towards the beach, which was very much under fire… I saw Lovat and the Brigade Major standing at the water's edge. Everyone else was lying down. So I joined them. He (Lovat) asked me to play. That sounded rather ridiculous to me to play the bagpipes and entertain people just like on Brighton sands in peacetime. Anyway… I started the pipes up and marched up and down. This Sergeant came running over and said: "Get down, you mad bastard. You're attracting attention to us." Anyway I continued marching up and down until we moved off the beach.'

Moving quickly across marshy ground and under enemy fire, the Commandos cleared two bunkers and reached the Caen Canal Bridge by 13:30 hours. As they approached, they broke out a large Union Flag and Millin played *Blue Bonnets over the Border* to ensure that the men of 'D' Company Ox and Bucks recognized them as friendly forces.

At the bridge they were met by Brig JHN Poett, the commander of the 5th Parachute Brigade which had

Below: With troops and vehicles ashore and through the crust of the Atlantic Wall, the priority was to push inland as fast as possible to expand the beachhead. Planners had set optimistic goals for the first day, and with each hour German resistance stiffened.

dropped during the night, who, with classic understatement, said: 'We are very pleased to see you.' He received a reply in a similar vein from the lead troop commander, who said: 'I am afraid we are a few minutes late sir.'

Millin then piped the group across Pegasus Bridge to cheers by the airborne forces and the crack of German sniper fire. Lovat, recalled Millin, 'was calmly walking, just as if he was strolling on his land, and he gestured to me to walk on'.

Within No 4 Commando were 171 French Commandos from No 1 and No 8 Troops of No 10 Inter Allied Commando under Captain Philippe Kieffer. They were the only French troops to land at D-Day and fought a bloody action in Ouistreham, clearing a sea front casino that had become a German sector headquarters.

Kieffer was able to call up a DD tank that arrived at 09:25 hours and opened fire on the casino before the Commandos went in. On their way to their objective, Keiffer's troops had encountered a local gendarme who gave them details of the German strengths and positions. When the fighting was over, he recalled hearing the amazed reaction of a small boy. 'Hey did you see that? They're great, the English; they thought of everything and they brought along guys who speak French as well as us!'

RISING TIDES

Back on the beach an onshore wind caused the tide to rise faster than had been anticipated. The foreshore shrank to 10m (33ft) and critically, the water covered the obstacles faster than the engineers could demolish them. This restricted the landing operations and delayed the follow up forces. Waiting for the beaches to clear, the 9th Brigade had to watch from its landing ships until mid-afternoon.

At 11:00 hours, the 185th Brigade had landed and moved forward. However, the tanks of the Staffordshire Yeomanry were not in place and it was not until around 12:00 hours that one-and-a-half squadrons of tanks had arrived. The assault went in on foot and the Périer ridge was captured at 14:25 hours after a fierce fight. Lt R Cadogan of the 27th Armoured Brigade recalled seeing survivors of the Staffordshire Yeomanry. 'They passed like zombies with burnt uniforms and staring eyes, oblivious to their surroundings. At the time I had never seen anyone badly shocked before and their appearance and burnt hands and faces frightened me when I thought of the days ahead.'

On the German side, Feuchtinger had finally received clear orders to attack the beach head. A battle group, built around 40 PzKpfw IV tanks, was ordered to attack. They

Above: Some of the first casualties are helped aboard a Royal Navy warship for evacuation back to England. Some soldiers were killed or wounded before they had even landed when their landing craft came under fire or hit submerged obstacles.

reached Périer ridge at around 16:00 hours and here suffered heavy losses, recorded by Feuchtinger. The Germans had bumped into a well-balanced force composed of the Kings Shropshire Light Infantry, tanks of the Staffordshire Yeomanry and M10 tank destroyers of the 41st Anti-Tank Battery RA. Despite their losses, the Germans pushed forward, finding a gap between the Canadians and the 3rd Division and reached the sea at Lion-sur-Mer.

This gap had been formed because of the delay in landing the 9th Brigade. When the brigade eventually began to land a German 8.1cm (3.19in) mortar barrage landed amongst the HQ, killing key officers including the CO, Brig Cunningham.

Back at Sword beach, Admiral Talbot had landed at 15:35 hours and found 24 landing craft stranded and much congestion on the beach. Nicknamed 'Noisy' by the sailors, he quickly ordered additional working parties ashore to clear exits from the beach.

By the end of the day, the 3rd Division was stalled 5km (3 miles) short of Caen, its D-Day objective. After brutal Allied air attacks, the town finally fell on 7 July. On the beaches, some 28,845 men had landed but for the loss of 107 casualties in the South Lancashire Regiment, 206 in the East Yorkshire Regiment while the KSLI suffered 113 casualties.

CHAPTER ELEVEN

THE PRICE

No battle is fought without casualties being suffered on one or both sides. D-Day was no exception, but only at Omaha had the worse fears of the Allied planners been realised. At Utah, the casualties were only about what would be expected on some of the tough live firing exercises that had been held in England before D-Day. In the days that followed 6 June 1944, the terse but tragic telegrams would arrive with news of death or loss for the relatives of the fallen.

EVERYONE INVOLVED IN THE NORMANDY operation knew that the landing craft that carried the soldiers to the beaches would also transport back the wounded, as well as German prisoners of war.

In the planning for D-Day, staff had estimated that the divisions that landed would suffer 15 percent casualties with their lead regiments taking 25 percent of this total. Of the casualties, 70 percent would be wounded and 30 per-cent killed, captured or missing. Of the wounded, some could be treated in the field and returned to action. Actual casualties, with some exceptions, like Omaha, fell below these expected rates.

In the hospitals of southern England, bed spaces had been cleared and nursing staff and auxiliaries – some only young girls – had been alerted. Older staff warned them that in the days and weeks that followed they would not only be very busy, but would see sights that would distress and horrify them.

Left: In the churned soil of the Pointe du Hoc, the smashed remains of a rifle and a GI helmet mark the temporary grave of a Ranger among the discarded ammunition boxes, rifle grenades and uprooted mines. Here lay just one of the many who died on 6 June 1944.

Above: On the evening of 6 June, servicemen and civilians in London follow the news of an invasion in the evening papers. Coverage by radio and print was thorough and – within the constraints of security and censorship – accurate and comprehensive.

The men who were about to land carried at least one first aid field dressing. This was an absorbent cotton pad attached to a length of bandage. It was sufficient to prevent bleeding from a gun shot or shrapnel wound. In addition, Sulphonamides ('sulfa' tablets and powder carried by every GI), which had already proved very effective in Sicily and Italy, were available. Before a field dressing was applied it was sprinkled into the wound to combat systemic septi-caemia. Men also carried a syrette of morphine, a highly effective painkiller.

Though there might not be time during the initial hours of the landing to recover or treat the wounded, once there were breaks in the fighting, antibiotic powder and fresh field dressings were applied. If a soldier had received morphine, the letter 'M' was written on his forehead to prevent him receiving further doses, which might be lethal. The newly developed drug, penicillin, was available to combat sepsis and it is estimated to have saved the lives of between 12 and 15 percent of casualties who otherwise would have died.

TREATING THE WOUNDED

Remarkably, malaria was among the 20 percent non-battle injuries suffered by the US Army in Normandy. Soldiers, who had landed in North Africa as part of the Torch operation, had contracted it. Now, triggered by bites from European mosquitoes, it reoccurred.

The landings and fighting took their psychological toll and the US Army admitted one combat stress sufferer for every 8.4 men who had been wounded in combat. The British estimated that nine days after D-Day, psychiatric

Right: A GI medic treats a wounded German NCO. On all sides there were moments of great humanity and also ghastly brutality. Once the news of a real or alleged atrocity began to circulate, it could be hard for men who wished to surrender to do so without being shot out of hand.

cases accounted for 13 percent of all casualties. They were treated by the Army Psychiatric Service at corps and army exhaustion centres prior to evacuation.

For the doctors and surgeons, although the casualties might be gravely injured, they were also men in the prime of life, fit and young and with a remarkable capacity for recovery.

However, war is never a clean and tidy business and the medical staff also knew that injuries would be neither antiseptic nor tidy. Sand, mud, clothing and oil would enter wounds – often under explosive pressure. Mines would rip off feet and legs, large pieces of shrapnel would cause massive injuries and multiple hits by automatic weapons would puncture vital organs.

As a rough figure, about 25 to 30 percent of casualties were caused by bullet wounds and the remainder were caused by mines, artillery and mortar fire. Some injuries would be unseen – blast from exploding shells and bombs would collapse lungs and internal organs.

Sometimes under the pressure of mass casualties, surgical staff would be forced to decide whether they could afford the time and effort necessary to save a gravely injured soldier's life. Sometimes they decided they could not.

The men of the 82nd and 101st Airborne knew that if they were wounded they would not automatically be evacuated. Initially the medical clearing companies and the 1st Army's auxiliary surgical group, who had landed by glider,

PRISONERS OF WAR

Between 6 and 18 June, the Allies lost 1700 men as prisoners. Most of these were either men from the airborne forces that had landed on the night of 6 June, or airmen who had been shot down. A quarter of these managed to escape while still near friendly forces.

In the same period, the Germans lost 6000 men. Of these, those officers or specialists who might possess valuable information were sent to the 'London Cage' but the bulk went to PoW camps in Edinburgh in Scotland and four camps in northern England at Catterick, Doncaster, Loughborough and the football stadium at Preston. Though overwhelming Allied firepower contributed to the German soldier's desire to surrender, the propaganda leaflets dropped or later fired into his lines were a major factor. The British Foreign Secretary, Anthony Eden, said in the House of Commons that 77 percent of prisoners reported that they read them.

On capture by British or Canadian forces, prisoners would be quizzed by a Regimental Intelligence Officer for battlefield intelligence – information that might be useful for operations in the next 12 to 24 hours. They would then be passed down the prisoner evacuation chain. Of greater intelligence value were captured maps and documents, particularly those taken from enemy headquarters.

For the Allies, the sight of prisoners was a sure indication that they were winning and also a chance to see their enemy safely at close range. To the young US officer, Lt Carrol, 'they looked like seasoned, rough men, 30 to 45 years old'.

Probably the two unluckiest PoWs on D-Day were the German soldier whose departure from Normandy on leave on 4 June had been delayed because he had contracted food poisoning. The other was a Royal Navy rating who, after his landing craft had been wrecked, moved inland with his army passengers, only to be snatched by a German fighting patrol.

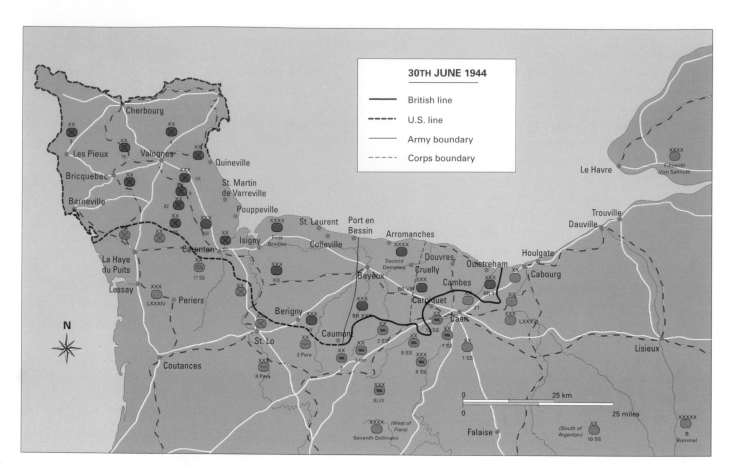

Above: By the end of June the Allies had captured the Cotentin Peninsula, but were still locked into hard fighting in the dense Normandy farmland. Thick hedges made ideal defensive positions for the Germans, who were still fighting hard.

Once we got to the Nissen hut where the Germans were being kept, we found... these people were just lying on top of their beds in an assortment of dirty clothes. None of them was particularly badly wounded, but they were filthy dirty, absolutely stinking dirty, very white, unhealthy, unwholesome looking people. They had the dirty pallor of tramps, a horrible, yellowy-grey unhealthy look. And nobody said anything. None spoke English to my knowledge, they just pointed. I sat somebody up – in those days you had feeding cups – and the smell was awful but by then it was too late to say you didn't like it. The main thing I remember was them staring, a sort of glazed staring... Some of them were only kids, they weren't really much older than me.

Naina Beaven, aged 16
Red Cross Nurse, Portsmouth

concentrated on stabilizing casualties. They would wait until the troops who had landed at Utah had linked up so the paratroopers could be evacuated by sea.

The US Navy was responsible for providing all medical care up to the high water mark on Utah and Omaha. The Army was responsible for loading patients onto landing craft. LSTs were modified to take 147 litters or stretchers and 100 were fitted out with operating facilities at the rear of the tank deck. Each LST had two doctors and 30 medical orderlies on loan from the Third Army.

The men who landed in the first waves came ashore with their company medics, followed shortly by their supporting Battalion Aid Stations. After about two hours, the Regimental Aid Stations landed with a Medical Collecting Company from the Divisional Medical Battalion, supporting each regiment. As the regimental beach heads were consolidated, a Medical Collecting Company from the Engineer Special Brigade supporting the landing began receiving patients from the Divisional Collecting Companies. This freed the Clearing Companies from the Divisional Medical Battalions to move inland and establish themselves away from the cluttered beaches.

To ensure that sufficient medical supplies were available in the initial landings, each of the first 200 LSTs had a special package of medical supplies that would be in high demand. These included litters, blankets, plasma and field dressings which were dumped on the beach, where the medics had easy access to them.

Like the Americans, the British had airborne medical units that landed in the early hours of D-Day. The 225th Parachute Field Ambulance (FA) landed at 01:00 hours and had their Main Dressing Station (MDS) operational by 03:00 hours. The 224th FA arrived a few hours later and finally the glider-borne 195th Air Landing FA, with three Jeeps and trailers, arrived in the second lift at 21:00 hours. In two weeks, the medical units of the 6th Airborne Division had suffered 128 casualties but had treated over 3000 casualties at MDSs.

For the men of the assault divisions that landed on the beaches, there was an integral medical organization of two

Below: USAAF fire fighters pour foam over a P-47 'Razorback'. This tough aircraft would eventually hold the record for tonnage of bombs dropped by a USAAF fighter-bomber – 104 million kg (113,963 tons) during World War II.

A chap was brought in with the top of his head blown off, brains spilling out into the stretcher. The Medical Orderly (MO) took one look at him. I said, 'Is there anything we can do?' He shrugged. So I gave him a lethal shot of morphine. When the MO came back, I told him. He said, 'Its OK, you did quite right. If he'd lived, he'd have been a vegetable for the rest of his days.' I am sure there were others like this. But we did not talk about it.

Private James Bramwell
9th Parachute Battalion, 6th Airborne Division

Field Dressing Stations (FDS), two Field Surgical Units (FSU) and one Field Transfusion Unit (FTU) in addition to surgical teams. Apart from one sector of the 50th Division's front at Le Hamel, FDSs were in operation 90 minutes after the first assault troops had landed.

The British, like the Americans, were keen to evacuate casualties to England where hospitals had been readied.

There were three categories, seven coastal or port hospitals with a total of 1200 beds which handled the most serious cases and 13 transit hospitals with 6550 beds which were similar in function to a Casualty Clearing Station (CCS). The heart of the system was the 97 home-base hospitals with a capacity of 50,000 beds of which 23,000 were available on D-Day. The existing military hospitals provided an extra 16,800 beds.

Modified LSTs fitted with racks for stretchers could transport 300 patients who were moved from the shore by DUKW. Nine days after D-Day, the Allies planned to evacuate a maximum of 900 patients a day by air to airfields on Salisbury Plain.

THE MEDICAL INFRASTRUCTURE

As the beachhead expanded, the normal medical infrastructure for a land campaign was established with Regimental Aid Posts, CCS and FDS. Four days after the landings, the first of seven general hospitals had been set up in Normandy.

The Germans also had a well-developed casualty evacuation system that had been tested in war. When a man had been wounded he was evacuated by company stretcher bearers to a casualty station and from there forwarded to a *Truppenverbandplatz (TVP)* (Battalion Field Dispensary) 3km (2 miles) behind the front line. Here, the battalion medical officer and his assistants gave low level treatment including pain relief and new dressings.

The casualty would then be moved to the bigger *Hauptverbandplatz (HVP)* (Main Dispensary). Here, six to ten kilometres (3.5 to 6 miles) from the front there was a staff of about 160 with three 'trains' – stretcher, dispensary and supply. The HVP could perform life-saving operations and had within its staff specialists like dentists.

The next level of care was the *Feldlazarett (FL)* (Field Hospital). With a staff of 76, it was equipped to perform complex surgery on difficult wounds like those to the abdomen. The FL was 15 to 20km (9 to 12.5 miles) from the front and was housed in solid buildings. It could handle 200 patients.

The end of the chain was the *Kriegslazarett* (Military Hospital) which for the Seventh Army was housed in the *École Militaire* in Paris, with 5000 beds. It had three surgeons, one internist, one hygienist, one neurologist and a pathologist. Some of these men would go into the field to assist with complex cases.

For those killed in action, there were some simple rites. One of their two identity disks, or as the Americans called them, 'dog tags', would be removed as evidence that they were dead, while the other remained with the body, so that it could be identified when it was reburied. The German soldiers had one disk that could be snapped in half, the top attached to the chain was buried with the soldier and the lower half was returned with all his personal possessions to his company commander. The US Army had two-on-two metal chains, the disc on the longer chain remained with the body, while that on the shorter chain was detached for a record. The British also had two, a red and blue fibre disk. On the disks were details that included the man's name, number, religion, blood group and date of birth, information that was also useful if he was an unconscious casualty.

When time allowed, the bodies of men killed in action were collected and personal items like rings, watches, cigarette cases or lighters placed in envelopes and identified, to be sent to the soldier's next of kin. The soldier's CO would send a personal letter to the widow or bereaved mother that might help to ease the pain of the official telegram reporting the man missing in action or dead.

On 6 June, in Southampton, 14-year-old Tom Hiett, a telegram boy with the Royal Mail recalled: 'At 11 o'clock I had the first death telegram to deliver. The lady came to the door and was horrified to see me standing there. I gave her the telegram, muttered, "No answer", and fled. It seemed I could hear crying all down the road and I thought, "Good God, how many more?"'

Wrapped in a blanket or ground sheet, the soldier would be buried and the location recorded. With the memory of the long lines of headstones in the military cemeteries of World War I, British soldiers knew that new headstones would appear in France. They would have the serviceman's name, rank, number, age, date of death and regimental or corps cap badge, as well as one or two personal lines from the family. Some, however, would only bear the words, 'A soldier known to God'.

BURIAL AT SEA

For the crews of warships the ceremony was as brief, with a burial at sea. Even the landing craft skippers who would be returning to England were under orders not to bring back their dead since this would impose an added burden on the logistic chain.

As D-Day drew to a close and the first dead were buried, casualties evacuated and the men dug in for an uncertain night, at 20:00 hours General de Gaulle broadcast to France on BBC Radio-Londres.

'The supreme battle is engaged: It is of course the Battle of France and the battle of the French people... France, sub-

Above: A convoy of ambulances makes its way to a hospital ship anchored at the Mulberry harbour at Arromanches. The confidence that there was a reliable and efficient casualty evacuation system was very important for the morale of front line soldiers.

merged over four years but not reduced and vanquished, still stands… Beyond the cloud of our blood and our tears, now appears the sun of our grandeur.'

In France, Marshal Pétain, who headed the collaborationist Vichy Government was more downbeat. 'The Anglo-Saxons have set on our soil. France is becoming a battlefield. Frenchmen do not attempt to commit any action which might bring terrible reprisals. Obey the orders of the government… The circumstances of the battle may induce the German Army to take special measures in the combat zone. I beg you to obey them.'

He feared that the landings would produce chaos and civil war and in the ensuing confusion the Communists would seize power. It was better to continue to collaborate than watch France go Communist.

In Britain, there was relief as the first radio reports told of successful landings. The first official news had come at 09:30 hours in Communiqué No 1 from Eisenhower's headquarters. It was terse and accurate. 'Under the command of General Eisenhower, Allied naval forces, supported by strong air forces, began landing Allied armies this morning on the

Sister was a young girl from London and she looked at us and said: 'When my boys come in, you girls might be the last thing these boys see on earth... I want a gentle smile, and when you bend over my boys have a nice look in your eyes and don't let your eyes reflect what you see.' One chap, who was very badly burned said to me: 'I'm quite good-looking really, you know, Nurse.' I said, 'Your eyes are not bad now, they're quite saucy.' So he said, 'You wouldn't like to give us a kiss, would you Nurse?' We weren't allowed, but I looked around and I bent down and kissed him on his horribly burned lips with the awful smell coming off his burns.

Mary Verrier
Hants 12th Detachment, VAD, Portsmouth

northern coast of France.' Around 01:00 hours on 7 June, Communiqué No 2 was equally understated, saying '...reports of operations so far show that our forces succeeded in their initial landings. Fighting continues.'

In London, on the evening of 6 June, the *Evening Standard* carried the bold headline 'Churchill Announces Successful Massed Air Landings Behind Enemy in France'. The following morning, the rest of the papers appeared, such as the Daily Telegraph with its measured headline: 'Allied Invasion Troops Several Miles into France' and provided the extra detail.

THE NEWS FROM BERLIN

In Berlin, the Reich Press Chief Dr Dietrich Dienstagmorgen announced the news in the hyperbole that had become familiar to German readers and listeners.

'This morning, on orders from Moscow, our enemies in the West have stepped forward to make their bloody sacrifice, held back for so long. The frequently heralded attack on the freedom of Europe by the Western friends of Bolshevism has begun. We will prepare a hot reception for them. Germany knows the significance of this hour.'

In a secret report on internal affairs, the German intelligence service, the *Sicherheitsdienst* (SD) noted on 8 June that:

Below: Liberated Italian former soldiers, who as German prisoners had been constructing coastal defences against the invasion, wait for US landing craft to evacuate them from Utah beach to England. They would later be repatriated to Italy.

Above: The stark and simple National Guard memorial at Omaha beach seen today, on the site of a former German gun position. The endless rows of headstones in the huge cemetery on the cliffs above the American beach convey a sense of the losses suffered on D-Day.

'...German people are universally experiencing the arrival of the invasion as a release from unbearable suspense and oppressive uncertainty. It is virtually the only topic of conversation. Everything else has receded completely into the background. The start of the invasion has

> You were just there and you did what you could, and when you came to a fellow dying, I'd tell him he was dying. You'd get a nod of the head from him. If he were a Roman Catholic, I'd anoint him. This was all done automatically, with a second for each, you see.
>
> *Captain RM Hicky*
> *Catholic Padre, North Shore Regiment, Canadian 3rd Division*

completely drowned out the news of our abandonment of Rome.'

In London at 21:00 hours on 6 June, King George VI broadcast from Buckingham Palace to his subjects in Britain and concluded:

'At this historic moment, surely not one of us is too busy, too young, or too old to play their part in a nationwide vigil of prayer as the great crusade sets forth.

If from every place of worship, from home and factory, from men and women of all ages and many races and occupations, our supplications rise, then, please God, both now and in a future not remote, the predictions of an ancient Psalm may be fulfilled: "The Lord will give strength unto his people: the Lord will give his people the blessing of peace."'

> Day and night there was some kind of shit flying at you. If it wasn't these machine guns it was tank guns, if it wasn't tank guns it was artillery, if it wasn't artillery it was some bugger in an aeroplane dropping bombs on you...
> I think what war teaches you is how fantastic human hate can be. Because it's clearly insane, really, this spectacle of men and machines trying to destroy one another. It's really quite hideously insane. And one wonders whether there is any future for an animal that can do this.
>
> *2nd Lieutenant David Holbrook aged 21*
> *East Yorkshire Yeomanry*

D-DAY ORDER OF BATTLE

ALLIED D-DAY ORBAT

21ST ARMY GROUP (Montgomery)

Second (British) Army (Dempsey)

Army Troops

79th Armoured Division
  30th Armoured Brigade
    22nd Dragoons
    1st Lothians and Border Horse
    2nd County of London Yeomanry
    (Westminster Dragoons)
    141st Regiment RAC
  1st Tank Brigade
    11th Battalion RTR
    42nd Battalion RTR
    49th Battalion RTR
  1st Assault Brigade RE
    5th Assault Regiment RE
    6th Assault Regiment RE
    42nd Assault Regiment RE
  79th Armoured Division Signals
  1st Canadian Armoured Personnel Carrier
  Regiment

GOLD

British XXX Corps (Bucknall)

50th (Northumbrian) Infantry Division
  69th Brigade
    5th Battalion The East Yorkshire Regiment
    6th Battalion The Green Howards
    7th Battalion The Green Howards
  151st Brigade
    6th Battalion The Durham Light Infantry
    8th Battalion The Durham Light Infantry
    9th Battalion The Durham Light Infantry
  231st Brigade
    2nd Battalion The Devonshire Regiment
    1st Battalion The Hampshire Regiment
    1st Battalion The Dorsetshire Regiment
Divisional Troops
  61st Reconnaissance Regiment RAC
  50th Divisional Engineers
  50th Divisional Signals
  74th, 90th and 124th Field Regiments RA
  102nd Anti-Tank Regiment RA
  25th Light Anti-aircraft Regiment RA
  2nd Battalion The Cheshire Regiment
  (Machine Gunners)

8th Armoured Brigade
  4th/7th Royal Dragoon Guards
  24th Lancers
  The Nottinghamshire Yeomanry

12th Battalion The King's Royal Rifle Corps
  (Motor)

56th Infantry Brigade
  2nd Battalion The South Wales Borderers
  2nd Battalion The Gloucestershire Regiment
  2nd Battalion The Essex Regiment

47 Royal Marine Commando (From 47th Special
  Service Brigade)

JUNO

British I Corps (Crocker)

3rd Canadian Infantry Division
  7th Canadian Infantry Brigade
    The Royal Winnipeg Rifles
    The Regina Rifle Regiment
    1st Battalion Canadian Scottish regiment
  8th Canadian Infantry Brigade
    The Queen's Own Rifles of Canada
    Le Régiment de la Chaudière
    The North Shore (New Brunswick)
  9th Canadian Infantry Brigade
    The Highland Light Infantry of Canada
    The Stormont, Dundas and Glengarry
    Highlanders
    The North Shore Nova Scotia Regiment
  Divisional Troops
    17th Duke of York's Canadian Hussars
    (reconnaissance regiment)
    3rd Canadian Divisional Engineers
    3rd Canadian Divisional Signals
    12th, 13th, and 14th Regiments, RCA
    3rd Anti-Tank Regiment, RCA
    4th Light AA Regiment, RCA
    The Cameron Highlanders of Ottawa
    (Machine Gunners)

2nd Canadian Armoured Brigade
  6th Armoured Regiment (1st Hussars)
  10th Armoured Regiment (The Fort Garry
  Horse)
  27th Armoured Regiment (The Sherbrooke
  Fusiliers Regiment)

48 Royal Marine Commando (From 47th Special
  Service Brigade)

SWORD

British I Corps (Crocker)
3rd (British) Division
  8th Brigade
    1st Battalion The Suffolk Regiment
    2nd Battalion The East Yorkshire Regiment
    1st Battalion The South Lancashire Rgt

  9th Brigade
    2nd Battalion The Lincolnshire Regiment
    1st Battalion The King's Own Scottish
    Borderers
    2nd Battalion The Royal Ulster Rifles
  185th Brigade
    2nd Battalion The Royal Warwickshire
    Regiment
    1st Battalion The Royal Norfolk Regiment
    2nd Battalion The King's Shropshire Light
    Infantry
  Divisional Troops
    3rd Reconnaissance Regiment RAC
    3rd Divisional Engineers
    3rd Divisional Signals
    7th, 33rd and 76th Field Regiments RA
    20th Anti-Tank Regiment RA
    92nd Light Anti-Aircraft Regiments RA
    2nd Battalion The Middlesex Regiment
    (Machine Gunners)

27th Armoured Brigade
  13/18th Royal Hussars
  1st East Riding Yeomanry
  The Staffordshire Yeomanry
1st Special Service Brigade
  3 Commando
  4 Commando
  6 Commando
  45 Royal Marine Commando

41 Royal Marine Commando (From 47th Special
  Service Brigade)

US First Army (Bradley)

UTAH

US VII Corps (Collins)

US 4th Infantry Division
  12th Regiment
  22nd Regiment
  8th Regiment
  359th Infantry Regiment (attached from 90th
  Division)

70th Tank Battlion

OMAHA

US V Corps (Gerow)

US 1st Infantry Division
  16th Infantry Regiment
  18th Infantry Regiment

US 29th Infantry Division
115th Infantry Regiment
116th Infantry Regiment
Divisional Troops
110th, 111th, 224th and 117th Field
Artillery Battalions
29th Signals Company
729th Ordnance Light Maintenance
Company
29th Quartermaster Company
29th Reconnaissance Troop
121st Engineer Combat Battalion
104th Medical Battalion
29th Counter Intelligence Corps
Detachment
29th Military Police Platoon
29th Infantry Division Band
29th Infantry Division Special Troops HQ

2nd Ranger Battalion
5th Ranger Battalion

AIRBORNE FORCES

British 6th Airborne Division
3rd Parachute Brigade
8th Parachute Battalion - (Royal
Warwickshire)
9th Parachute Battalion - (Essex Regiment)
1st Canadian Parachute Battalion
5th Parachute Brigade
7th Parachute Battalion - (Somerset Lt. Inf.)
12th Parachute Battalion - (Green
Howards)
13th Parachute Battalion - (S. Lancashire)
6th Airlanding Brigade
2nd Battalion Ox & Bucks Lt. Inf
1st Battalion Royal Ulster Rifles
12th Battalion Devonshire Regiment
Divisional Troops
22nd Independent Parachute Company,
(Pathfinders)
6th Airborne Armoured Reconnaissance
Regiment
53rd Airlanding Light Regiment, Royal
Artillery
2nd Forward Observation Unit (Airborne)
RA
3rd Airlanding Anti-tank Batteries, RA
4th Airlanding Anti-tank Batteries, RA
6th Airlanding Anti-Tank Batteries, RA
2nd Airlanding Light Anti-Aircraft Battery,
RA
6th Airborne Divisional Signals
3rd Parachute Squadron, RE
591st Parachute Squadron, RE
249th Field Company, RE
224th Parachute Field Ambulance, RAMC

225th Parachute Field Ambulance, RAMC
195th Airlanding Field Ambulance, RAMC
6th Airborne Provost Company
317th Field Security Section (Airborne)
Intelligence Corps
Glider Pilot Regiment

US 82nd Airborne Division
505th Parachute Infantry Regiment
507th Parachute Infantry Regiment
508th Parachute Infantry Regiment
325th Glider Infantry Regiment
Divisional Troops
376th Parachute Field Artillery Regiment
319th Glider Field Artillery Regiment
320th Glider Field Artillery Battalion
307th Airborne Engineer Battalion
307th Airborne Medical Company
82nd Airborne Military Police Platoon
82nd Airborne Signal Company
80th Airborne Antiaircraft Artillery Battalion
782nd Airborne Ordnance Maintenance
Company
407th Airborne Quartermaster Company

US 101st Airborne Division
501st Parachute Infantry Regiment
502nd Parachute Infantry Regiment
506th Parachute Infantry Regiment
327th Glider Infantry Regiment
401st Glider Infantry Regiment
Divisional troops
377th Parachute Field Artillery Battalion
321st Glider Field Artillery Regiment
907th Glider Field Artillery Regiment
326th Airborne Engineer Battalion
81st Airborne Antiaircraft Artillery Battalion
101st Airborne Signal Company
801st Airborne Ordnance Company
426th Airborne Quartermaster Company
326th Airborne Engineer Battalion
326th Airborne Medical Company
101st Counter Intelligence Corps
detachment
101st Airborne Division Military Police
Platoon

GERMAN D-DAY ORBAT

LXXXIV Corps (Marcks) (of 7th Army)

716th Infantry Division (static)

352nd Infantry Division
914th Grenadier Regiment

91st Luftlande Infantry Division

6th Parachute Regiment (attached to the 91st
Division)
1057th Grenadier Regiment
1058th Grenadier Regiment

709th Infantry Division (static)
919th Grenadier Regiment
729th Grenadier Regiment
739th Grenadier Regiment
649th Ost Battalion, attached
Sturm Battalion AOK 7 (attached to 709th
Division)

243rd Infantry Division (static)
920th Grenadier Regiment
921st Grenadier Regiment
922nd Grenadier Regiment

LXXXI Corps (Kuntzen) (of 15th Army)

711th Infantry Division (static)

Panzergruppe West or **Fifth Panzer** (von
Schweppenburg)

12th SS Panzer Division
SS-Panzer Regiment 12
SS-Panzergrenadier Regiment 25
SS-Panzergrenadier Regiment 26
SS-Panzeraufklärungsabteilung 12
SS-Panzerjägerabteilung 12
SS-Panzer Artillery Regiment 12
SS-Werferabteilung 12
SS-Flakabteilung 12
SS-Panzer Pioneer Battalion 12
SS-Panzernachrichtenabteilung 12
SS-Nachschubtruppen 12
SS-Instandsetzungsabteilung 12
SS-Wirtschaftsbataillon 12
SS-Sanitätsabteilung 12

21st Panzer Division
Panzer Regiment 22
Panzer Regiment
Panzergrenadier Regiment 125
Panzergrenadier Regiment 192
Panzer Artillerie Regiment 155
Panzer Aufklärung Abteilung 21
reconnaissance)
Panzer Jäger Abteilung 200 (anti-tank)
Panzer Pionier Battaillon 220 (engineers)

INDEX

Page number in *italic* indicate captions

Abwehr (German intelligence service) 42
air power 69–73
air reconnaissance 31–2, 36
aircraft
    Avro Lancaster 43, 69, 70, 97
    B-17 *34*, *70*
    B-24 Liberator 133
    B-26 Marauder *116*
    bombers 69–70
    C-47 Skytrain *68*, 71, *108*
    Consolidated Vultee Liberator 70
    Dakota 110
    Douglas Skytrain/Dakota 24
    fighters 71
    Flying Fortress *29*
    Focke Wulf Fw190 71
    gliders 71, 79, *96*, 97–8, *99*, 100, 103, 105
    Hawker Typhoon 71
    Heinkel He 111 174
    Heinkel He 177 71
    Junkers Ju 71
    Messerschmitt Bf 109 71
    P-47 'Razorback' *183*
Alderney 25
Allied air attacks *23*
Allied air strength 69
Allied Forward Observer Bombardment (FOB) 155
Allied landings, map *43*
anti-glider obstacles ('Rommel's Asparagus') 16
Anzio 8
Arromanches 74, 149, 153
    Mulberry harbour *154*
Assault Forces 60
Atlantic Wall 10–15, *11*, 23, 24–5, 32
    crew accommodation 18
    gun emplacements 18

'battle inoculation' exercise *27*
Bayerlein, Fritz 172
Bayeux 155
BBC Radio-Londres 33–4, *37*, 184
Bedell-Smith, General Walter 86, 89
Bénouville 104
Bernières 161, 164
'Bigot' code 33
'blitzkrieg' ('lightning war') 7
block-ships 74
'Bodyguard' deception plan 40–41
bombardment, map *58*
Bradley, General Omar *85*, 86, 134, 135, 139
    biography 84
briefings 43–4, 52
Britain
    position in 1941 8
    US troops in 27–9
British flank landings, map *98*
British units
    6th (Air Landing) Brigade *99*, 103, 105
    6th Airborne Armoured Reconnaissance
        Regiment 105
    211th Airborne Battery 105
    6th Airborne Division 38, 100, 102–3
    249th (Airborne) Field Company 100
    8th Armoured Brigade 62, 151
    79th Armoured Division 50

Eighth Army 8
2nd Battalion Oxfordshire and Buckinghamshire
    Light Infantry 78–9, *97*, 99–100, 105
9th Battalion Parachute Regiment 79, 103
1st Battalion Royal Hampshires 152–3
1st Battalion the Royal Ulster Regiment 105
8th Brigade Group 173
Commandos 52, *80*, 90, 102, 105, *153*, 161, *168*,
    173, 174, 175, 176–7
XXX Corps 38, 151
1st Dorsets 153
4th/7th Dragoon Guards 154–5
7th Green Howards 154
22nd Independent Parachute Company *93*, 103
185th Infantry Brigade 173
3rd Infantry Division 160, 167
50th Infantry Division 62, 164
7th, 12th and 13th (Lancashire) Battalions 103
50th Northumbrian Division 151
7th Parachute Battalion 101
8th Parachute Battalion 103
3rd Parachute Brigade 97, 102
5th Parachute Brigade 102, 176–7
Parachute Regiment 85
Royal Marines 160, 163
Special Air Services (SAS) 79–81, 95
    operations in France 82–3
7th (Yorkshire) Battalion 103
Bucknall, Lieutenant General 38, 151
bunkers 9, 10–11, *24*, 148
    camouflage 12–13
burial 184

Caen 177
Caen canal 78, 100
camouflage 12–13, *13*, 92
    German uniform 65
Canadian units 28, 38
    2nd Armoured Brigade 62
    6th Armoured Regiment 159, 160
    10th Armoured Regiment 159
    7th Brigade Group 160, 164
    8th Brigade Group 160, 164
    3rd Infantry Division 62, 157, 159
    1st Parachute Battalion 103, 105
    Queen's Own Rifles 159, 161
    Regiment de Levis *71*
casemates 147
casualties 179–86
    evacuation 183–4, *185*
    German evacuation system 184
    Glider Pilot Regiment 105
    Gold beach 155
    Juno beach 163
    Omaha beach 142
    Sword beach 176, 177
    Utah beach 113
Channel Islands 15, 24
    defences 24–5
Cherbourg *23*, 25
chronology of D-Day 19
Churchill, Winston 10, 38, 39, 44, 73
Clogstoun-Willmott, Captain Nigel 36–7, 61
coastal defences 10
collaborators 12
Collins, Lieutenant General 'Lightening Joe' 38
combat stress 180–81
Combined Operations Pilotage Parties (COPP)
    36–7

canoeists *38*
Cota, Brigadier General Norman 141, 142, 144
Cotentin Peninsula 25, 115, 116, *182*
Courseulles 160
covert operations 81
Crocker, General J T 38
'Czech Hedgehog' 11, *133*, 151, *161*

D-Day, chronology 19
dead, identity of 184
deception schemes 42–3, 95–6
decorations
    DSO 90, 169
    Knight's Cross 65, 106, 121
    Medal of Honor 120, 139, 144, 145
    Military Cross 85, 145
    Victoria Cross 154
defensive positions, Normandy *16*
Denmark 7
Devon *7*
Dieppe 10, 11, 15, 24, 48, 73
Dihm, Lieutenant General Friedrich 44
Dollman, General Friedrich 62, 65, 110, 111
    biography 106
'Donkey's Ears' (artillery binoculars) 136
'Dragon's Teeth' 11
Drop Zones (DZs) 17, 36, 79, 98, 102–3, 106

Eisenhower, General Dwight David 38, *39*, 69, *81*,
    85–6, 89, 108–9
    biography 83
El Alamein 8, 90
Enigma encryption machine 31, *32*, 33
'Eureka' conference 39
evacuation of casualties 183–5

Falley, Lieutenant General Wilhelm 106, 108, 110
Feuchtinger, Lieutenant General Edgar 165, 177
field defences 9
first aid supplies 180
flooding, as a defence 17, 116
Follow up forces 60
Fortress Europe 9
France
    defeat 7
    German troops in 9–10
    Resistance groups 10, 31, 33, 34, 36, 83
Free French 34, *37*
French troops 177
Freya radar system 25, 71
FUSAG (1st US Army Group) 41, 42

Gale, Major General 38, 102, 105
Gavin, Major General James 111, 112
Gerhardt, Major General Charles H. 134
German agents 43
German defences, map *62*
German High Command (OKW) 15
German units
    average age 116
    Afrika Korps 8
    91st Air Landing Division 106
    Sixth Army 8
    Seventh Army 62, 66
    Army Group B 15
    1260th Artillery Regiment 125, 149
    1261st Artillery Regiment 124
    1716th Artillery Regiment 149, 168
    LXXXIV Corps 15, 25

91st Division 65
243rd Division 65
2nd Grenadier Regiment 157–8
736th Grenadier Regiment 157–8, 164
919th Grenadier Regiment 121
'Hitler Jugend' *158*, 170, 172
1st Infantry Division 168
346th Infantry Divisions 103
352nd Infantry Division 65, 116
709th Infantry Division 65, 116
711th Infantry Division 103, 104
716th Infantry Division 65, 104, 158
736th Infantry Division 168
726th Infantry Regiment 152
Naval Group Command West 55
Ost Battalions 65, 66, 116–17, 158, 168
First Panzer Army 9
21st Panzer Division 65, 104, 158, 164–5, 170
125th Panzer Grenadier Regiment 104
Panzer Lehr Division 172–3
6th Parachute Regiment 65, 112, 123
716th Static Infantry Division 125, 168
Gerow, Lieutenant General Leonard 'Gee' 38
Goebbels, Dr Joseph 40
Gold beach 38, 59, 60, 62, 147–55
    air attacks on 151
    casualties 155
    defences 147–9
    landings 151-5
    map *151*
    mines 149, 151
    resistance 149–51
'Golden city' 124
Gonneville 98
'Gooseberries' (block ships) 74
Greece 7–8
Guderian, Heinz *32*
gun positions 77–8

Harris, Air Chief Marshal Sir Arthur 69
Hitler, Adolf, D-day timetable 113
Hobart, Major General Sir Percy 49
Hollis, Stan 154
Horrocks, Lieutenant General Brian 151
hospitals 184
Howard, Major 100, 101, 102, 103, 105
Huebner, Major General Clarence R. 134, 145

Inter-Services Topographical Unit 36
Italy 8

Jahnke, Lieutenant Arthur 121, 123
Japan, assault on Pearl Harbor 8
'jedburgh' teams 81
Johnson, Lieutenant Colonel 113
Juno beach 38, 59, 60, 62, 157–165
    aerial attack 160
    casualties 163, 165
    civilian casualties 161
    defences 157, 158–9
    landings 160–64
    map *163*
    mines 160, 161
    naval bombardment 160

Keller, Major General 159, 164
Kieffer, Captain Philippe 177
Kraiss, Major General Dietrich 65, 97

Kriegsmarine 17, 32, 55–6, 147, 157
la Barquette 113
La Mare Fontaine 149
land forces 62–9
landing craft 59, 62, *78*, 160
    tank landing craft (LCT) 61
Landing Craft Infantry (LCI) *90*
Landing Craft Infantry (small) 173
landing craft obstacles 16
Landing Craft, Vehicle and Personnel (LCVP)
    (Higgins Boats) 116, *117*
'leaf' propaganda leaflets 39–40
Lee, General Bill 112–13
Leicester, Brigadier Bernard 160
Leigh-Mallory, Air Chief Marshal Sir Trafford *81*, 86, 100, 108, 109
Les Longues *147*
Lovat, Lord 176, 177
Luftwaffe 25, 29, 66, 71–3

malaria 180
Maquis 34
media coverage 52, *180*, 185–6
medical infrastructure 184
medical staff 181–3, 186
Merville 79, 97, 98–9
Meyer, Kurt 170
MI6 34
mine warfare 17, 23, 119
minesweepers 61–2
Monte Cassino 8
Montgomery, Field Marshal Sir Bernard Law 38, 44, *81*, 86, 89, 151
    biography 90
Morgan, Lieutenant General Frederick 33, 38
Mountbatten 73
Mulberry Harbours *67*, 73–4, *73*
    Arromanches *154*
Mussolini, Benito 8

National Guard memorial, Omaha beach *187*
naval fire support *159*
Normandy
    beaches 38
    defensive positions *16*
    map of beaches 21–2
    position on 30th June 1944 *182*
Norway 7, 42

observation post *147*
Oelze, Colonel 25
Office of Strategic Services (OSS) 34, 81
Ohmsen, Walter 124, 125
Omaha beach 18, 38, 50, 57, 60, 77, 129–45
    casualties 142, *144*, 145
    cross section *134*
    defences 130–31
    depth positions 131
    landing diagram *143*
    landings 133–40
    map *130*
    minefields 131
    National Guard memorial *187*
    pre-landing bombardment 132–3
    radio communications 144–5
Operation
    Barbarossa 8
    Bulbasket 84
    Cooney 83
    Dingson/Grog 83

Dynamo 56
Fortitude North 42
Fortitude South 40, 41, 104
Glimmer 43
Green 36
Houndsworth 85
Jubillee 73
Neptune 38
Overlord 39, 43, 51
Pluto 74
Pointblank 69
'Quicksilver' 41
Samwest 84–5
Sea Lion 9
Taxable 43
Titanic 95–7
Tortoise 36
Organization Todt 9, 12, 70
Orne bridge 101
Orne River 78, 100, 167
Ostarbeiter 12

parachutes 101
Pas de Calais 15
Patton, General George 41, *44*
Pearl Harbor 8
Pegasus Bridge *98*, 100–101, *103*, 104, 113
Picture Post 103
Pierced Steel Planks (PSPs) 51
Pintail bombs 96
plastic explosives 36
Pluto (Pipe Line Under Ocean) 74
Pointe du Hoc *77*–8, 125, 127, *179*
    map *126*
Poitiers–Tours railway 84
Poland 7, 9
prefabricated harbours 73–4
prisoners of war 181
propaganda 39–40
psychiatric cases 180–81

radar systems 25, 71, 158–9
radios, S-Phone 82
railways 70
    and the French Resistance 36
Ramsay, Admiral Sir Bertram *81*, 86
    biography 56
Reichert, Major General Josef 104
Rennie, Major General T.G. 169
rescue at sea 60
Resistance groups, France 10, 31, 33, 34, 36, 83
Reviers 161
Richter, Lieutenant General Wilhelm 104, 158
Ridgway, Major General Matthew B. 38, 106
Riva Bella 167, 168
rocket firing landing ships 47
Rommel, Field Marshal Erwin 50, 57, 93
    biography 15
Roosevelt, Brigadier General Theodore Jr. 115, 119, 120
Roseveare, Major 105
Royal Naval Volunteer Reserve (RNVR) 60
Rudder, Lieutenant Colonel James 125, 127
Rundstedt, Field Marshal Karl Rudolf Gerd von 15, 24, 34
    biography 18

S-Bootes 56, 173
St Aubin 16
St Nazaire 10

seapower 55–62
'Second Front' 9, 38, 89
security precautions 33
Sextant conference 39
SHAEF 89
ships
	KVS *Admiral Scheer* 55
	HMS *Ajax* 59, 148, 151
	HMCS *Algonquin* 160
	USS *Ancon* 60, 132, 145
	HMS *Arethusa* 59, 99, 169
	HMS *Argonaut* 59, 151
	USS *Arkansas* 58, 125, 132, 148
	USS *Augusta* 57
	HMS *Bachaquero* 61
	USS *Bayfield* 60
	HMS *Belfast* 57, 58, 59, 149, 160
	HMS *Black Prince* 58
	HMS *Bulolo* 60, 148, *149*
	USS *Chase* 93
	FFS *Combattante* 59, 160
	USS *Corry* 125
	HMS *Danal* 59, 169
	HMS *Diadem* 59, 160
	ORP *Dragon* 59, 169
	HMS *Emerald* 59, 151
	HMS *Enterprise* 58
	HMS *Erebus* 57, 58
	HNMS *Flores* 59, 151
	HMS *Frobisher* 59, 169
	FFS *Georges* 58
	FFS *Georges Leygues* 132, 148
	HMS *Glasgow* 58, 132
	HMS *Hawkins* 58
	HMS *Hilary* 60, 164
	HMS *Holmes* 55
	ORP *Krakowiak* 59, 151
	HMS *Largs* 60, 173
	HMS *Maid of Orleans* 175
	USS *Maloy* 60
	HMS *Mauritius* 59, 169
	HMS *Misoa* 61
	FFS *Montcalm* 58, 132
	USS *Nelson* 56
	USS *Nevada* 58, 125
	HMS *Obedient* 56
	HMS *Orion* 59, 149, 151, 155
	HMS *Princess Astrid* 175
	USS *Quincy* 58, 113
	HMS *Ramillies* 57, 59, 169, 173
	HMS *Roberts* 57, 59
	HMS *Rodney* 25
	HSS *Satterlee* 126
	HMS *Scylla* 57, 58
	HMCS *Sioux* 160
	HNMS *Soemba* 58
	HNMS *Svenner* 59, 169
	HMS *Talybont* 126
	HMS *Tasajera* 61
	USS *Texas* 57, 58, 78, 125, 132
	USS *Tuscaloosa* 58
	HMS *Warspite* 57, 59, 169, 173
	see also landing craft
Sicily 8
Signal magazine 15, 66
Soviet Union, non-aggression treaty 8
Special Operations Executive (SOE) 34, 81, 84, 85
Stalingrad 8
Ste Mère Eglise 111–12

supply drops *34*
Sword beach 38, 50, 59, 60, 77, 167–77
	casualties 176, 177, *177*
	defences 167–9
	landings 173–7
	map *170*
	naval bombardment 169–70

Talbot, Rear Admiral Arthur 169, 177
tanks
	Bobbin 48
	Centaur 160–61
	Churchill 48, 154
	'Crabs' 49
	Duplex Drive (DD) Sherman tanks 48, 49–50, 116
	Flail tanks 153
	'Funnies' 48–50, *169*
	Hotchkiss 170
	Lorraine 170
	Panther 68
	PzKpfw IV 68–9
	Sherman *58*, 67–8, *86*, 120, 154, *165*
	Tetrach Light Tank (A17) 105
	Tiger 68, 68–9
Taylor, Major General Maxwell 106, 108, 112, 113
Tedder, Air Chief Marshal Sir Arthur *81*, 86, 89
	biography 93
Tennant, Rear Admiral William 74
'Tiger' convoy 56
Tonkin, Captain John 84, 95
training *47*, 51–4
training exercise *7*
Transportation Plan 69, 86, 93
'Trident' conference 39

U-boats 32, 55
Ultra 32, 36, 43
US
	armaments industry 29
	black soldiers 28–9
	entry into war 38
	Office of Strategic Services (OSS) 81
	troops in Britain 27–9
US Coast Guard (USCG) 60
US units
	equipment *86*
	8th Air force 29
	82nd Airborne Division 38, 65, 95, 106, 111
	101st Airborne Division 38, 65, 95, 106, 108–9, 112, 113
	V Corps 38, 125, 139
	VII Corps 38
	4th Division 125
	1st Infantry Division 52, 62, 134, *141*
	4th Infantry Division 52, 56, 62, 116
	29th Infantry Division 134–6
	116th Infantry Division 138
	Parachute Infantry Regiments 106, 113
	paratroopers *89*, *92*, *107*, *112*
	2nd Ranger Battalion 78
	Rangers 125–7, 141
	8th Regiment 116
	12th Regiment 116
	22nd Regiment 116
	Regimental Combat Teams 134, 144
Utah beach 38, 60, 62, 77, 106, 115–27
	airborne assault, map *110*
	counter attack on 110–11
	defences 125

	landing 117–20
	map of landing *119*
	plan 116–20

Van Fleet, Colonel James A 115
vehicles
	'Amphijeeps' *25*
	ARKs (Armoured Ramp Carriers) 49, *50*
	Armoured Vehicle Royal Engineers (AVRE) 48, *49*, 154, 160
	BARV (Beach Armoured Recovery Vehicle) 49
	bicycles 51
	DUKW amphibious trucks 50, *51*, 78, *92*
	Goliath remote controlled demolition vehicle 122
	half-track *32*
	Jeeps 29, *74*
	tracked vehicles *65*
Ver-sur-Mer 149
Very lights 96
Vian, Rear Admiral Sir Phillip 57
Vierville 130, 139, 141, 142, 145

weapons
	7.5 cm (2.95in) Feldkanone 38 6136
	15cm (5.9in) guns 124
	15cm (5.9in) K 18 gun *8*
	40.6cm (16in) guns 9
	105 mle 1913 Schneider gun 6136
	anti-aircraft guns *65*
	anti-tank guns *60*, 67
	assault guns 69
	Banglore torpedo 97
	'Bazooka' 106, *123*, 145
	Besa machine gun 48
	Bren Light Machine Gun *34*, 152
	C/36 guns 147
	Churchill Crocodile flame-thrower 48
	Defence Flamethrower 23
	flak guns 124
	German 66–7
		on Utah beach 121–2
	grenades *148*
	Kar 98K rifle *131*
	Landing Craft (Rocket) 151
	M1 'Garand' rifle 62, 66
	M1A1 Carbine 106
	M42 'Spandau' 137
	machine guns 69
	naval guns 59
	Nebelwerfer 66
	Oerlion guns 59
	Pack Howitzer M1A1 113
	plastic explosives 36
	self-propelled howitzers 173
	Sexton self-propelled guns 151
	Skoda K52 guns 124
	V-1 rockets 40, *42*, 70
	see also mine warfare
weather conditions 89
weather forecasts 79
Widerstandsnester (Resistance nests) 116, 117, 129, 130–31, 137, 149, 151, 158, 167, 169
Witt, Fritz 170
World War I 57
Wurzburg radar system 25
Wurzburg-Riese radar station 149

X-craft (miniature submarines) 36, 37, 60–62, 160

Yugoslavia *7*